AN INTRODUCTION TO POETRY AND CRITICISM

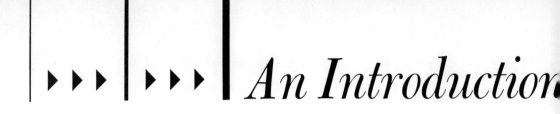

# An Introduction

## EMIL HURTIK
## ROBERT YARBER

SAN DIEGO MESA COLLEGE

# to Poetry and Criticism

XEROX COLLEGE PUBLISHING

LEXINGTON, MASSACHUSETTS | TORONTO

# PREFACE

Poetry has been with man as long as language itself. Poetry is the most personal type of communication; it reaches into the thoughts, emotions, beliefs, and the very being of man. It is from the matrix of poetry that our language developed into the versatile tool that it is today. Poetry is bounded by physical action on the one side and pure thought on the other. Only the senses themselves have a more direct entry into the emotions.

What is the best way to introduce poetry? We believe that building upon the knowledge and experience that the student has already is a good beginning. From there we can go to the subtleties and ambiguities of language until the edge of the sublime is touched. Some of the poems in this anthology are here because they are familiar. Others are included in an attempt to stretch the awareness into uncharted byways of thought and emotion. An introduction should include all types and modes; we have included the old and the new, the easy and the esoteric, the facile and the complex.

The introductions to the sections are an attempt to give a unity to that arbitrary division so that the student has the experience of organizing his knowledge into understandable units. Items not mentioned in the unit introductions are usually explained in the glossary.

The introduction to criticism is meant to be just that, an introduction. We have included in this section the major questions and approaches that are of pragmatic value to someone who will be expected to write about poetry in an organized fashion. The critical essays may serve several purposes: they may be used as sample essays that the student may try to emulate in his own exposition; they illustrate some of the principles of criticism as that art is practiced in analyzing poetry; and they amplify some of the elementary concepts· presented in the introductions.

Finally, we have tried to make the experience of poetry relevant to the college student without being trite or patronizing. We have tried to walk that narrow road between pedantry on the one side and trivial contemporaneity on the other.

We thank our wives, Barbara and Mary, for their aid and comfort in this endeavor.

EMIL HURTIK
ROBERT YARBER

v

# ACKNOWLEDGMENTS

A. R. Ammons, "Terrain" from *Expressions of Sea Level* by A. R. Ammons. Originally published in the *Hudson Review*. Copyright © 1960 by A. R. Ammons. Reprinted by permission of the Ohio State University Press.

W. H. Auden, "In Memory of W. B. Yeats," "Law Like Love," "Lay Your Sleeping Head, My Love," "Musée des Beaux Arts," and "The Unknown Citizen" from *Collected Shorter Poems 1927–1957*. Copyright 1940 and renewed 1968 by W. H. Auden. Reprinted by permission of Random House, Inc. and Faber and Faber Ltd.

Philip Booth, "Maine" from *The Islanders* by Philip Booth. Copyright © 1960 by Philip Booth. All Rights Reserved. Reprinted by permission of The Viking Press, Inc.

Robert Bridges, "London Snow" from *The Poetical Works of Robert Bridges*. Reprinted by permission of the Clarendon Press, Oxford.

John Ciardi, "Divorced, Husband Demolishes House" from *In the Stoneworks* by John Ciardi. Copyright 1961 by Rutgers, The State University. Reprinted by permission of the author.

Gregory Corso, "But I do not need kindness" from *Gasoline* by Gregory Corso. Copyright © 1958 by Gregory Corso. Reprinted by permission of City Lights Books. "Marriage" from *The Happy Birthday of Death* by Gregory Corso. Copyright © 1960 by New Directions Publishing Corporation. Reprinted by permission of New Directions Publishing Corporation.

Herbert R. Coursen, Jr., "The Ghost of Christmas Past: Stopping by Woods on a Snowy Evening" from *College English*, December 1962. Reprinted by permission of the author.

Hart Crane, "Chaplinesque" and "The Bridge: To Brooklyn Bridge" from *Complete Poems and Selected Letters and Prose of Hart Crane*. Copyright 1933, 1958, 1966 by Liveright Publishing Corp. Reprinted by permission of Liveright, Publishers, New York.

Robert Creeley, "The Name" (Copyright © 1961, Robert Creeley) is reprinted with the permission of Charles Scribner's Sons from *For Love* by Robert Creeley.

David Daiches, "The Poetry of Dylan Thomas" from *College English*, November 1960, pp. 123–128. Reprinted by permission of the National Council of Teachers of English and the author.

James Dickey, "A Dog Sleeping on My Feet" (first published in *Poetry*) and "In a Tree House at Night" (first published in *The New Yorker*) from *Drowning with Others* by James Dickey. Copyright © 1961, 1962 by James Dickey. Reprinted by permission of Wesleyan University Press.

Emily Dickinson, "Because I Could Not Stop for Death," "I Like to See It Lap the Miles," "'Hope' is the Thing with Feathers," "These are the Days when Birds Come Back," "My Life Closed Twice Before Its Close," There's a Certain Slant of Light," and "I Heard a Fly Buzz when I Died" reprinted by permission of the publishers and the Trustees of Amherst College from Thomas H. Johnson, editor, *The Poems of Emily Dickinson*, Cambridge, Mass.: The Belknap Press of Harvard University, Copyright, 1951, 1955, by the President and Fellows of Harvard College. "My Life Had Stood a Loaded Gun" from *The Complete Poems of Emily Dickinson*, edited by Thomas H. Johnson. Copyright 1929, © 1957 by Mary L. Hampson. Reprinted by permission of Little, Brown and Company.

Richard Eberhart, "The Groundhog" from *Collected Poems 1930–1960* by Richard Eberhart. © 1960 by Richard Eberhart. Reprinted by permission of Oxford University Press, Inc. and Chatto and Windus Ltd.

T. S. Eliot, "The Love Song of J. Alfred Prufrock," "Preludes," and "Sweeney among the Nightingales" from *Collected Poems 1909–1962* by T. S. Eliot. Copyright, 1936, by Harcourt Brace Jovanovich, Inc.; Copyright © 1963, 1964 by T. S. Eliot. Reprinted by permission of Harcourt Brace Jovanovich, Inc. and Faber and Faber Ltd.

William Empson, "Ignorance of Death" from *Collected Poems* by William Empson. Copyright, 1949, by William Empson. Reprinted by permission of Harcourt Brace Jovanovich, Inc. and Chatto and Windus Ltd.

Paul Engle, "Beasts" and "Fossil" from *Word of Love* by Paul Engle. Copyright 1950 by Paul Engle. Reprinted by permission of Random House, Inc.

Virginia Faulkner, "More Frosting on the Woods" from *College English*, April 1963, pp. 560–561. Reprinted by permission of the National Council of Teachers of English and the author.

Kenneth Fearing, "Dirge" from *New and Selected Poems* by Kenneth Fearing. Copyright © 1956 by Kenneth Fearing. Reprinted by permission of Indiana University Press.

L. Ferlinghetti, "Loud prayer" from *Beatitude Anthology*. Copyright © 1960 by City Lights Books. Reprinted by permission of City Lights Books.

Robert Frost, "Birches," "Fire and Ice," "Mending Wall," "The Road Not Taken," "Stopping by Woods on a Snowy Evening," "The Pasture," and "The Gift Outright" from *The Poetry of*

*Robert Frost* edited by Edward Connery Lathem. Copyright 1916, 1923, 1930, 1939, © 1967, 1969 by Holt, Rinehart and Winston, Inc. Copyright 1942, 1944, 1951, © 1958 by Robert Frost. Copyright © 1967, 1970 by Lesley Frost Ballantine. Reprinted by permission of Holt, Rinehart and Winston, Inc.

GEORGE GARRETT, "In the Hospital" is reprinted with the permission of Charles Scribner's Sons from The Reverend Ghost: Poems by George Garrett. Copyright © 1956, 1957 George Garrett. (*Poets of Today IV*).

ALLEN GINSBERG, "America" and "A Supermarket in California" from *Howl and Other Poems* by Allen Ginsberg. Copyright © 1956, 1959 by Allen Ginsberg. "Poem Rocket" from *Kaddish and Other Poems* by Allen Ginsberg. Copyright © 1961 by Allen Ginsberg. Reprinted by permission of City Lights Books.

THOM GUNN, "Innocence" from *My Sad Captains* by Thom Gunn. Copyright © 1961 by Thom Gunn. Reprinted by permission of The University of Chicago Press and Faber and Faber Ltd.

THOMAS HARDY, "Ah, Are You Digging on My Grave" and "The Darkling Thrush" from *Collected Poems of Thomas Hardy*, Copyright 1925 by The Macmillan Company. "Snow in the Suburbs" from *Collected Poems of Thomas Hardy*, Copyright 1925 by the Macmillan Company, renewed 1953 by Lloyds Bank, Ltd. Reprinted by permission of The Macmillan Company, the Hardy Estate, Macmillan London & Basingstoke, and the Macmillan Company of Canada, Limited.

JOAN HARTWIG, "The Principle of Measure in 'To His Coy Mistress'" from *College English*, May 1964, pp. 572–575. Reprinted by permission of the National Council of Teachers of English and the author.

A. E. HOUSMAN, "Loveliest of Trees," "'Terence, this is stupid stuff,'" "To an Athlete Dying Young," "When I was One-and-Twenty," "With rue my heart is laden" from "A Shropshire Lad," authorised edition from *The Collected Poems of A. E. Housman*, Copyright 1939, 1940, © 1959 by Holt, Rinehart and Winston, Inc., Copyright © 1967, 1968 by Robert E. Symons. And "The Laws of God, the Laws of Men" from *The Collected Poems of A. E. Housman*, Copyright 1922 by Holt, Rinehart and Winston, Inc., Copyright 1950 by Barclays Bank Ltd. Reprinted by permission of Holt, Rinehart and Winston, Inc., The Society of Authors as the literary representative of the Estate of A. E. Housman, and Jonathan Cape Ltd., publishers of A. E. Housman's *Collected Poems*.

LANGSTON HUGHES, "Dream Deferred" from *The Panther and the Lash* by Langston Hughes. Copyright 1951 by Langston Hughes. Reprinted by permission of Alfred A. Knopf, Inc. "I, Too" from *Selected Poems* by Langston Hughes. Copyright 1924 by Alfred A. Knopf, Inc., and renewed 1952 by Langston Hughes. Reprinted by permission of the publisher.

TED HUGHES, "Hawk Roosting" from *Lupercal* by Ted Hughes. Copyright © 1959 by Ted Hughes. Reprinted by permission of Harper and Row, Publishers, Inc. and Faber and Faber Ltd.

RANDALL JARRELL, "The Death of the Ball Turret Gunner" from *The Complete Poems* by Randall Jarrell. Copyright 1945, 1969 by Mrs. Randall Jarrell. Reprinted by permission of Farrar, Straus and Giroux, Inc.

ROBINSON JEFFERS, "Hurt Hawks" from *The Selected Poetry of Robinson Jeffers*, Copyright 1925 and renewed 1953 by Robinson Jeffers. Reprinted by permission of Random House, Inc.

LEROI JONES, "The Clearing" from *Preface to a Twenty Volume Suicide Note* by LeRoi Jones. Copyright © 1960 by Totem Press, Corinth Books. Reprinted by permission of Corinth Books.

PHILIP LARKIN, "Church Going" from *The Less Deceived* by Philip Larkin, Copyright © 1955, 1970 by The Marvell Press. Reprinted by permission of The Marvell Press, Hessle, Yorkshire, England.

D. H. LAWRENCE, "Piano" from *The Complete Poems of D. H. Lawrence*, Vol. I, edited by Vivian de Sola Pinto and F. Warren Roberts, Copyright 1920 by B. W. Huebsch, Inc., renewed 1948 by Frieda Lawrence. And "Snake" from *The Complete Poems of D. H. Lawrence*, Vol. I, edited by Vivian de Sola Pinto and F. Warren Roberts, Copyright 1923, renewed 1951 by Frieda Lawrence. Reprinted by permission of The Viking Press, Inc.

CECIL DAY LEWIS, "Let us now praise famous men" from "The Magnetic Mountain" taken from *Collected Poems 1954*. Reprinted by permission of Jonathan Cape Ltd., and the Hogarth Press.

AMY LOWELL, "Patterns" from *The Complete Works of Amy Lowell*, Copyright 1955, by Houghton Mifflin Company. Reprinted by permission of the publisher, Houghton Mifflin Company.

ROBERT LOWELL, "Mr. Edwards and the Spider" from *Lord Weary's Castle* by Robert Lowell, Copyright 1944, 1946 by Robert Lowell. Reprinted by permission of Harcourt Brace Jovanovich, Inc. "Skunk Hour" from *Life Studies* by Robert Lowell, Copyright © 1958 by Robert Lowell. Reprinted by permission of Farrar, Straus and Giroux, Inc.

HUGH MACDIARMID, "Reflections in a Slum" from *Collected Poems* by Hugh MacDiarmid, © 1948, 1962, Christopher Murray Grieve. Reprinted with permission of The Macmillan Company.

ROD MCKUEN, "How Can We Be Sure of Anything" from *Listen to the Warm* by Rod McKuen. Reprinted by permission of Random House, Inc.

ARCHIBALD MACLEISH, "Ars Poetica" from *Collected Poems 1917–1952* by Archibald MacLeish, Copyright 1952 by Archibald MacLeish. Reprinted by permission of the publisher, Houghton

Mifflin Company. "Dover Beach—A Note to that Poem" from *Public Speech* by Archibald Mac-Leish, Copyright 1936, © 1964 by Archibald MacLeish. Reprinted by permission of Holt, Rinehart and Winston, Inc.

PETER L. McNAMARA, "The Multi-Faceted Blackbird and Wallace Steven's Poetic Vision" from *College English*, March 1964, pp. 446–448. Reprinted by permission of the National Council of Teachers of English and the author.

LOUIS MACNEICE, from "Autumn Journal" from *Collected Poems of Louis MacNeice*, edited by E. R. Dodds, Copyright © 1966 by The Estate of Louis MacNeice. Reprinted by permission of Oxford University Press, Inc. and Faber and Faber Ltd.

EDNA ST. VINCENT MILLAY, from "Epitaph for the Race of Man" and "What Lips My Lips Have Kissed" from *Collected Poems* by Edna St. Vincent Millay, Harper and Row, publishers; Copyright 1923, 1934, 1951, 1962 by Edna St. Vincent Millay and Norma Millay Ellis. Reprinted by permission of Norma Millay Ellis.

MARIANNE MOORE, "Poetry" and "Silence" from *Collected Poems* by Marianne Moore, Copyright 1935 by Marianne Moore, renewed 1963 by Marianne Moore and T. S. Eliot. Reprinted with permission of The Macmillan Company.

WILFRED OWEN, "Anthem for Doomed Youth" and "The Next War" from *Collected Poems* by Wilfred Owen, Copyright 1946, © 1963 by Chatto and Windus, Ltd. Reprinted by permission of New Directions Publishing Corporation and Chatto and Windus, Ltd.

JOHN E. PARISH, "No. 14 of Donne's Holy Sonnets" from *College English*, January 1963, pp. 299-302. Reprinted by permission of the National Council of Teachers of English and the author.

DOROTHY PARKER, "A Fairly Sad Tale" and "Second Love," Copyright 1928, renewed 1956 by Dorothy Parker, and "Fighting Words," Copyright 1926, renewed 1954 by Dorothy Parker, reprinted from *The Portable Dorothy Parker* by Dorothy Parker with the permission of The Viking Press, Inc.

SYLVIA PLATH, "Daddy" and "Fever 103°" from *Ariel* by Sylvia Plath, Copyright © 1963 by Ted Hughes. Reprinted by permission of Harper and Row, Publishers, Inc., and Owen Hughes.

EZRA POUND, "In a Station of the Metro" and "Salutation" from *Personae*, Copyright 1926 by Ezra Pound. Reprinted by permission of New Directions Publishing Corporation.

JOHN CROWE RANSOM, "Bells for John Whiteside's Daughter" from *Selected Poems* by John Crowe Ransom, Copyright 1924 by Alfred A. Knopf, Inc. Reprinted by permission of the publisher.

HENRY REED, "Naming of Parts" from *A Map of Verona and Other Poems*, Copyright 1947 by Henry Reed. Reprinted by permission of Harcourt Brace Jovanovich, Inc. and Jonathan Cape Ltd

JACK E. REESE, "Sound and Sense: The Teaching of Prosody" from *College English*, February 1966, pp. 368–373. Reprinted by permission of the National Council of Teachers of English and the author.

EDWIN ARLINGTON ROBINSON, "Richard Cory" from *The Children of the Night* (1897) and "Miniver Cheevy" (Copyright 1907 Charles Scribner's Sons; renewal copyright 1935) from *The Town Down the River* by Edwin Arlington Robinson are reprinted by permission of Charles Scribner's Sons.

THEODORE ROETHKE, "Dolor," Copyright 1943 by Modern Poetry Association, Inc., and "The Waking," Copyright 1953 by Theodore Roethke; both from *The Collected Poems of Theodore Roethke*. Reprinted by permission of Doubleday and Company, Inc.

EDWARD H. ROSENBERRY, "Toward Notes for 'Stopping by Woods' Some Classical Analogs" from *College English*, April 1963, pp. 526–528. Reprinted by permission of the National Council of Teachers of English and the author.

CARL SANDBURG, "Chicago" and "Fog" from *Chicago Poems* by Carl Sandburg, Copyright 1916 by Holt, Rinehart and Winston, Inc., Copyright 1944 by Carl Sandburg. Reprinted by permission of Holt, Rinehart and Winston, Inc.

DELMORE SCHWARTZ, "In the Naked Bed, in Plato's Cave" and "The Heavy Bear Who Goes with Me" from *Selected Poems: Summer Knowledge* by Delmore Schwartz, Copyright 1938 by New Directions. Reprinted by permission of New Directions Publishing Corporation.

ANNE SEXTON, "Some Foreign Letters" from *To Bedlam and Part Way Back* by Anne Sexton, Copyright © 1960 by Anne Sexton. Reprinted by permission of the publisher, Houghton Mifflin Company.

KARL SHAPIRO, "Auto Wreck" from *Selected Poems* by Karl Shapiro, Copyright 1942 by Karl Shapiro. And Sections 14, 67, 77 "from *The Bourgeois Poet*" by Karl Shapiro, Copyright © 1962, 1963, 1964 by Karl Shapiro. Reprinted by permission of Random House, Inc.

W. D. SNODGRASS, "Returned to Frisco 1946" from *Heart's Needle* by W. D. Snodgrass, Copyright © 1957 by W. D. Snodgrass. Reprinted by permission of Alfred A. Knopf, Inc.

STEPHEN SPENDER, "I Think Continually of Those" and "What I Expected" from *Selected Poems* by Stephen Spender, Copyright 1934 and renewed 1962 by Stephen Spender. Reprinted by permission of Random House, Inc. and Faber and Faber Ltd.

DANIEL STEMPEL, "A Reading of 'The Windhover'" from *College English*, January 1962, pp. 305-307. Reprinted by permission of the National Council of Teachers of English and the author.

# CONTENTS

## INTRODUCTION TO CRITICISM

# INTRODUCTION
## *to Poetry*

Poetry is a literary genre in which ideas, experiences, perceptions, and truths are expressed in a unique and powerful way. It is a synthesis, a strictly unified combination of a number of diverse elements, which, though they can be individually analyzed, must finally be considered not as separate and distinct entities but as integral parts of the poem as a whole. Though this unity and cohesion are necessary in all literary forms, they are especially vital to poetry, for a poem's conciseness, its singleness of focus, its tightness of structure demand interdependence and harmony; everything must contribute to the central theme and impact. Thus, an inseparable blend of form and content, of technique and subject, is essential. A poem's meaning evolves from and is implicit in its combination of structure, language, rhythmic and metrical patterns, tone, mood, sound, and symbolism. While one or more of these elements may dominate, depending on the type and purpose of the poem, all must be interrelated and ultimately subordinate to the work as a whole.

Poetry differs from prose in several ways, some of which are generally obvious, others subtle. Outward form, of course, is a primary point of difference; the poet is concerned not only with finding and arranging the words which will best express his meaning, but also with structuring and organizing these words so that they define, enhance, and even qualify meaning. The choice, sound, and order of words, while significant in prose, are ultimately of secondary importance; their value lie almost solely in their function of expressing ideas. In poetry, these considerations tend to be more vital; words, in a sense, not only reveal meaning but create it. In this respect, then, a poem is a total work of art; it carries abstract meaning but is also meaningful in itself, in its sound, even in its appearance.

Another distinguishing factor is poetry's concentration on communicating a particular perception or experience. Like the short story, the poem usually does not cover a wide range of subjects and viewpoints but reveals one individual's thoughts about an aspect of the human experience. Long narrative epics or ballads may represent exceptions in some cases, but most poetry is limited and specific in focus. This characteristic is related to another of poetry's qualities; its impact, which, at least initially, often tends toward the emotional. Poetry's emphasis on particularization of the abstract, on demonstration rather than explanation, on specific examples and images, its frequent use of a personal, subjective tone, its stress on beauty and originality of language, all of these factors contribute to a power and immediacy of expression. The reader first of all gains a sense of the poem, a feeling of what it suggests or represents; then, he experiences an immediate, subjective reaction.

While prose can in some sense be analyzed even as it is being read, poetry demands an initial grasp of the whole, an overall view such as one gives a painting or sculpture. The reader then must draw on his own associations, his imagination, his subconscious, in response to the images and implications of the poem. Finally, he must consider the poem from a somewhat more objective and analytical viewpoint: he must examine the various possible levels and shades of meaning and determine the role of each element in relation to the central idea. Only in this way can he achieve a full awareness of the poem's significance and value.

Poetry is classified in a number of different ways; by form, by subject, by treatment of theme, by point of view, and by method of expression. Three very general categories of types of poetry are the narrative, the lyric, and the dramatic. Narrative poetry relates events or incidents, frequently from a first person point of view; thus, many narrative poems are simply stories told in verse. Traditional examples are the epic, a series of adventures usually centered around one main character who represents a particular culture or national group, the ballad, similar to the epic though less extensive, both in length and scope, the mock, or satirical, epic, a light treatment of this usually serious form, and various types of historical and romantic stories written in verse.

Lyric poetry usually stresses the purely subjective, emotions, reflection, and attitudes; traditional examples here are the ode, an expression of deep emotion toward a particular theme or object, the elegy, a lament and praise for the dead, the sonnet, in which form and content work as a single unit to express an emotion or idea, certain types of ballads stressing the emotional or mental aspects of adventure, and the idyll, a description of a pleasant style or aspect of life. Didactic poetry, which strives to make clear a specific moral or lesson, and satirical poetry, which points out some human or societal deficiency or failing with irony and subtlety,

are also frequently included in this category. Dramatic poetry is usually presented as a monologue similar to a speech in an actual drama; both narrative and lyric poems can be dramatic as well.

These categories, basically arbitrary, frequently blending and overlapping, provide nothing more than a rough guide. This is especially true with respect to contemporary poetry, much of which defies orderly and rigid classification by either type or form. General categories of form are continuous, or an uninterrupted flow of lines; stanzaic, in which the poem is divided into sections, each of which usually contains the same number of lines and the same metrical pattern and rime scheme; the whole or fixed form, which never varies in number and arrangement of lines (of which the sonnet is the best example); blank verse, unrimed but containing a regular metrical pattern; free verse, irregular in both rime and metre; and poetry in prose.

Poetry is not a static literary form; though its basic purpose, the communication of experience and perception, has not changed, its modes of expression are constantly evolving and adapting to new conditions and circumstances. Structure, form, language, and tone are modified to correspond with new conceptions of reality, with new attitudes toward communication of ideas. Some traditional poetical conventions are eliminated or replaced, others are revitalized and applied in new ways. This adaptability enables poetry to retain its position of power, but, perhaps, an even more significant source of this power is poetry's essential timelessness. A good poem, regardless of its historical era, appeals to and affects the emotions, imagination, and intellect of its readers; the harmony, unity, and balance inherent in such a poem shape the readers' various levels of response and implicitly reveal the central purpose. Individual consideration of theme and idea, metrics, figurative language, imagery, tone, and symbolism may give further insight into the nature of poetry, particularly into the way in which each of these elements reflects and contributes to the poem's totality of meaning.

# PARAPHRASE: IDEA, THEME, SUBJECT

In order to understand and appreciate a poem fully, the reader must examine it at various levels and approach it from a number of angles. His main concern, of course, is to grasp and evaluate the poem's theme or idea; but, in order to reach this understanding, he must first consider all of the poem's other aspects. The theme, and the poet's attitude toward it, are inevitably connected with and revealed through the poem's style, tone, language, form, metric patterns, imagery, and symbolism. These elements not only reveal and clarify the theme but also develop and shape it to some extent. These elements work together to produce a certain idea; they can, of course, be abstracted and considered individually, but they must finally be seen in context with each other, as parts of a whole. For poetry demands a unity and cohesion of parts even greater than that which is necessary in other literary genres, such as short stories.

What the poet is saying is in a very real sense inseparable from how he says it. Content and form can be evaluated individually, and their relationship may differ greatly from poem to poem; ideas may be ordered and arranged in order to fit a specific form, such as the sonnet, or the form may be developed out of the expression of ideas. In any case, content and form are so intertwined and mutually dependent that, in the final consideration of the poem they create, they are indistinguishable; one cannot have any real existence without the other.

Analysis and interpretation of the theme and meaning which evolve from the poem's various elements involve consideration of the poem at two levels: literal and figurative. Literal interpretation involves the poem's facts, its obvious, surface meaning. At this stage, a paraphrase, a prose summary of the poem, is often helpful. By concentrating on the essentials needed for a prose translation (the speaker, situation, setting, conflict, action, and so forth), the reader sorts facts and asks questions which lead to analysis on a deeper level. In examining the poem's literal level, one should consider diction, the selection and use of words, syntax, the arrangement of words, their grammatical and sense relationships, and, finally, denotation, the words' literal meanings or dictionary definitions. This type of literal analysis may serve to clarify the poem's basic facts and explicit ideas and may provide a basis for further examination. It is often really difficult to separate the literal from the figurative level, as most poems are a combination of both: their meaning is derived from the interaction of the two. Furthermore, there are many poems which are obviously symbolic, even on the first, most primary level; literal paraphrasing is obviously not applicable in this case. Nevertheless, when some distinction between the two levels of poetry is discovered, as it can be in most poems, it may serve as a useful aid to interpretation.

The figurative or symbolic level or levels (many poems contain a number of possible symbolic meanings) of interpretation involve consideration of symbols, connotation, and tone. At this level, the reader attempts to discover not only what the poet is saying, but what he really means and what the implications of this are. Symbols, which give the poem its richness, depth, and complexity, can be discovered by determining *how* a word or phrase is used, what it actually means, and what it suggests or implies. Such involve connotation, the inferences and implications of words, phrases, and images. At this level, the reader must be concerned with mental associations, with the meaning of words in a number of contexts. Connotation directly involves the reader, his mental images, reactions, experiences, emotions, imagination, intellect, perception, and memory. It is a mixture, a balance, of general, universal conceptions and personal interpretation. Thus, the reader must consider the possible meanings of words and phrases, the relationships between these meanings, the context in which the meanings appear, and the associations with other words and ideas which they inspire.

Tone is another important aspect of symbolic interpretation: irony, a statement or appearance contrary to real meanings, ambiguity, double meanings or uncertainty, ambivalence, conflicting and contradictory attitudes toward the same objects, hyperbole, exaggeration or overstatement, and understatement are all elements of tone which play an important role on the figurative level. The manner in which an idea is expressed not only modifies that idea but sheds light on the poet's attitude toward his subject, on his intentions and purpose.

There are, then, several means of determining and examining the poem's theme; a paraphrase on the literal level may yield a variety of interpretations, each of which may be valid in one particular context. Once the reader has a clear idea of the overall theme, he can, by observing and analyzing the interaction between the literal and figurative, the outer and inner, the explicit and implicit aspects, gain insight into the poet's ultimate purpose and meaning. Consciousness of the tensions, conflicts, and contradictions between the poem's various levels and perspectives is essential for full understanding and appreciation; equally important to the reader is evaluation of his particular reactions and impressions. As most poetry tends to be fairly subjective, as the poet usually attempts to appeal to and influence the reader's emotions and imagination, personal response is a valid consideration.

Analysis on the first level, then, yields the poem's general theme or idea; the meanings, implications, and attitudes behind this chosen theme evolve from analysis on the figurative level. Some poems, of course, are almost entirely explicit and obvious, while others are completely symbolic; naturally, different approaches are necessary. But, as a general rule, all poems of literary value exist primarily on the figurative and symbolic level, and, in most of these poems, there is a vital relationship between the exterior and interior, the surface and the depths. Hence, the method of analysis outlined above is generally applicable.

When the reader discovers what the poem is about, when he develops some conception of the nature of the theme, the way in which it is presented, and its significance, he has accomplished a great deal, but he has not yet reached his goal of full comprehension and appreciation of the poem. A restatement of the poet's idea, a prose explication, cannot communicate the totality of the poet's expression. The paraphrase, a concise abstraction of idea and meaning, must finally be considered not as an entity in itself, but must be seen in relation to the unified work of art. It is not enough to explain a painting, it must be seen, experienced; the same is true of a poem. Theme, the vital directing force, must be given extensive consideration, but should be treated as ultimately subordinate to the poem it shapes.

*(anonymous)*

# THE TWA CORBIES

As I was walking all alane,
I heard twa corbies making a mane;
The tane unto the t'other say,
"Where sall we gang and dine to-day?"

"In behint yon auld fail dyke,
I wot there lies a new slain knight;
And naebody kens that he lies there,
But his hawk, his hound, and lady fair.

"His hound is to the hunting gane,
His hawk to fetch the wild-fowl hame,    10
His lady's ta'en another mate,
So we may mak' our dinner sweet.

"Ye'll sit on his white hause-bane,
And I'll pike out his bonny blue e'en;
Wi' ae lock o' his gowden hair
We'll theek our nest when it grows bare.

"Mony a ane for him makes mane,
But nane sall ken where he is gane;
O'er his white banes, when they are bare,
The wind sal blow for evermair."    20

---

*(anonymous ca. 16-17 century?)*

# BONNY BARBARA ALLAN

It was in and about the Martinmas time,
    When the green leaves were a falling,
That Sir John Graeme, in the West Country,
    Fell in love with Barbara Allan.

He sent his man down through the town,
    To the place where she was dwelling;
"O haste and come to my master dear,
    Gin ye be Barbara Allan."

O hooly, hooly rose she up,
    To the place where he was lying,    10
And when she drew the curtain by,
    "Young man, I think you're dying."

"O it's I'm sick, and very, very sick,
    And 'tis a' for Barbara Allan."
"O the better for me ye's never be,
    Tho your heart's blood were a spilling.

"O dinna ye mind, young man," said she,
    "When ye was in the tavern a drinking,
That ye made the healths gae round and round,
    And slighted Barbara Allan?"    20

He turned his face unto the wall,
    And death was with him dealing:
"Adieu, adieu, my dear friends all,
    And be kind to Barbara Allan."

And slowly, slowly raise she up,
    And slowly, slowly left him,
And sighing said she could not stay,
    Since death of life had reft him.

PARAPHRASE: IDEA, THEME, SUBJECT    5

She had not gane a mile but twa,
    When she heard the dead-bell ringing;
And every jow that the dead-bell geid,
    It cry'd "Woe to Barbara Allan!"

"O mother, mother, make my bed!
    O make it soft and narrow!
Since my love died for me today,
    I'll die for him tomorrow."

▶ *Edmund Spenser (ca. 1552-1599)*

# ONE DAY I WROTE HER NAME

One day I wrote her name upon the strand,
But came the waves and washed it away;
Again I wrote it with a second hand,
But came the tide, and made my pains his prey.
"Vain man," said she, "that dost in vain essay
A mortal thing so to immortalize,
For I myself shall like to this decay,
And eke my name be wiped out likewise."
"Not so (quoth I) let baser things devise
To die in dust, but you shall live by fame;
My verse your virtues rare shall eternize,
And in the heavens write your glorious name,
Where whenas death shall all the world subdue,
Our love shall live, and later life renew."

▶ *Christopher Marlowe (1564-1593)*

# THE PASSIONATE SHEPHERD TO HIS LOVE

Come live with me and be my love,
And we will all the pleasures prove
That hills and valleys, dales and fields,
And all the craggy mountains yields.

There we will sit upon the rocks
Seeing the shepherds feed their flocks,
By shallow rivers, to whose falls
Melodious birds sing madrigals.

And I will make thee beds of roses
With a thousand fragrant posies,
A cap of flowers and a kirtle

Embroidered all with leaves of myrtle.

A gown made of the finest wool
Which from our pretty lambs we pull;
Fair linèd slippers for the cold,
With buckles of the purest gold;

A belt of straw and ivy buds,
With coral clasps and amber studs;
And if these pleasures may thee move,
Come live with me and be my love.                    20

The shepherd swains shall dance and sing
For thy delight each May-morning;
If these delights thy mind may move,
Then live with me and be my love.


▶ *Sir Walter Raleigh (ca. 1552-1618)*

# THE NYMPH'S REPLY TO THE SHEPHERD

If all the world and love were young,
And truth in every shepherd's tongue,
These pretty pleasures might me move,
To live with thee, and be thy love.

Time drives the flocks from field to fold,
When rivers rage, and rocks grow cold,
And Philomel becometh dumb,
The rest complains of cares to come.

The flowers do fade, and wanton fields,
To wayward winter reckoning yields,                  10
A honey tongue, a heart of gall,
Is fancy's spring, but sorrow's fall.

Thy gowns, thy shoes, thy beds of roses,
Thy cap, thy kirtle, and thy posies,
Soon break, soon wither, soon forgotten:
In folly ripe, in reason rotten.

Thy belt of straw and ivy buds,
Thy coral clasps and amber studs,
All these in me no means can move,
To come to thee, and be thy love.                    20

But could youth last, and love still breed,
Had joys no date, nor age no need,
Then these delights my mind might move,
To live with thee and be thy love.

► *William Shakespeare (1564-1616)*

## SONNET 18

Shall I compare thee to a summer's day?
Thou art more lovely and more temperate.
Rough winds do shake the darling buds of May,
And summer's lease hath all too short a date.
Sometime too hot the eye of heaven shines,
And often is his gold complexion dimmed;
And every fair from fair sometime declines,
By chance or nature's changing course untrimmed;
But thy eternal summer shall not fade
Nor lose possession of that fair thou owest,　　　　　10
Nor shall Death brag thou wand'rest in his shade
When in eternal lines to time thou growest.
　　So long as men can breathe or eyes can see,
　　So long lives this, and this gives life to thee.


► *Ben Jonson (1572-1637)*

## ON MY FIRST SON

Farewell, thou child of my right hand, and joy;
　　My sin was too much hope of thee, lov'd boy,
Seven years thou wert lent to me, and I thee pay,
　　Exacted by thy fate, on the just day.
O, could I lose all father, now. For why
　　Will man lament the state he should envy?
To have so soon scap'd world's, and flesh's rage,
　　And, if no other misery, yet age?
Rest in soft peace, and, ask'd, say here doth lie
　　Ben Jonson his best piece of *poetry*.　　　　　10
For whose sake, henceforth, all his vows be such,
　　As what he loves may never like too much.


► *John Donne (1572-1631)*

## THE BAIT

Come live with me, and be my love,
And we will some new pleasures prove,
Of golden sands, and crystal brooks,
With silken lines, and silver hooks.

There will the river whispering run,
Warmed by thy eyes more than the sun.

And there th' enamoured fish will stay,
Begging themselves they may betray.

When thou wilt swim in that live bath,
Each fish, which every channel hath,　　　　　10
Will amorously to thee swim,
Gladder to catch thee, than thou him.

If thou, to be so seen, beest loath,
By sun or moon, thou dark'nest both;
And if myself have leave to see,
I need not their light, having thee.

Let others freeze with angling reeds,
And cut their legs with shells and weeds,
Or treacherously poor fish beset
With strangling snare, or windowy net.                    20

Let coarse bold hands from slimy nest
The bedded fish in banks out-wrest,

Or curious traitors, sleave-silk flies,
Bewitch poor fishes' wandering eyes.

For thee, thou need'st no such deceit,
For thou thyself art thine own bait;
That fish that is not catched thereby,
Alas, is wiser far than I.

## HOLY SONNET X

Death, be not proud, though some have callèd thee
Mighty and dreadful, for thou art not so;
For those whom thou think'st thou dost overthrow
Die not, poor Death; nor yet canst thou kill me.
From rest and sleep, which but thy pictures be,
Much pleasure; then from thee much more must flow;
And soonest our best men with thee do go—
Rest of their bones and souls' delivery!
Thou'rt slave to fate, chance, kings, and desperate men,
And dost with poison, war, and sickness dwell;                    10
And poppy or charms can make us sleep as well
And better than thy stroke. Why swell'st thou then?
One short sleep past, we wake eternally,
And Death shall be no more: Death, thou shalt die.

▶ *Robert Herrick (1591-1674)*

## TO THE VIRGINS,
## TO MAKE MUCH OF TIME

Gather ye rose-buds while ye may,
    Old time is still a-flying:
And this same flower that smiles today,
    Tomorrow will be dying.

The glorious lamp of heaven, the sun,
    The higher he's a-getting,
The sooner will his race be run,
    And nearer he's to setting.

That age is best which is the first,
    When youth and blood are warmer;                    10
But being spent, the worse, and worst
    Times, still succeed the former.

Then be not coy, but use your time;
    And while ye may, go marry:
For having lost but once your prime,
    You may for ever tarry.

▶ *Andrew Marvell (1621-1678)*

# TO HIS COY MISTRESS

Had we but world enough, and time,
This coyness, lady, were no crime.
We would sit down, and think which way
To walk, and pass our long love's day.
Thou by the Indian Ganges' side
Should'st rubies find: I by the tide
Of Humber would complain. I would
Love you ten years before the Flood,
And you should, if you please, refuse
Till the conversion of the Jews.                          10
My vegetable love should grow
Vaster than empires, and more slow.
An hundred years should go to praise
Thine eyes, and on thy forehead gaze:
Two hundred to adore each breast:
But thirty thousand to the rest;
An age at least to every part,
And the last age should show your heart.
For, lady, you deserve this state,
Nor would I love at lower rate.                           20
    But at my back I always hear
Time's wingèd chariot hurrying near:
And yonder all before us lie
Deserts of vast eternity.
Thy beauty shall no more be found;
Nor, in thy marble vault, shall sound
My echoing song: then worms shall try
That long-preserved virginity,
And your quaint honor turn to dust,
And into ashes all my lust.                               30
The grave's a fine and private place,
But none, I think, do there embrace.
    Now, therefore, while the youthful hue
Sits on thy skin like morning dew,
And while thy willing soul transpires
At every pore with instant fires,
Now let us sport us while we may;
And now, like amorous birds of prey,
Rather at once our Time devour,
Than languish in his slow-chapt power.                    40
Let us roll all our strength and all
Our sweetness up into one ball.
And tear our pleasures with rough strife
Through the iron gates of life.
Thus, though we cannot make our sun
Stand still, yet we will make him run.

▶ *Robert Burns (1759-1796)*

## AFTON WATER

Flow gently, sweet Afton, among the green braes,
Flow gently, I'll sing thee a song in thy praise;
My Mary's asleep by the murmuring stream,
Flow gently, sweet Afton, disturb not her dream.

Thou stock dove whose echo resounds through the glen,
Ye wild whistling blackbirds in yon thorny den,
Thou green-crested lapwing thy screaming forbear,
I charge you disturb not my slumbering fair.

How lofty, sweet Afton, thy neighbouring hills,
Far marked with the courses of clear, winding rills;          10
There daily I wander as noon rises high,
My flocks and my Mary's sweet cot in my eye.

How pleasant thy banks and green valleys below,
Where wild in the woodlands the primroses blow;
There oft as mild evening weeps over the lea,
The sweet-scented birk shades my Mary and me.

Thy crystal stream, Afton, how lovely it glides,
And winds by the cot where my Mary resides;
How wanton thy waters her snowy feet lave,
As gathering sweet flowerets she stems thy clear wave.        20

Flow gently, sweet Afton, among thy green braes,
Flow gently, sweet river, the theme of my lays;
My Mary's asleep by thy murmuring stream,
Flow gently, sweet Afton, disturb not her dream.

▶ *Percy Bysshe Shelley (1792-1822)*

## DEATH

### I

Death is here and death is there,
Death is busy everywhere,
All around, within, beneath,
Above is death—and we are death.

### II

Death has set his mark and seal
On all we are and all we feel,
On all we know and all we fear,
. . . . . . . . . . . . . . . . . . . . . . . .

### III

First our pleasures die—and then
Our hopes, and then our fears—and when
These are dead, the debt is due,          10
Dust claims dust—and we die too.

### IV

All things that we love and cherish,
Like ourselves, must fade and perish;
Such is our rude mortal lot—
Love itself would, did they not.

▶ *John Keats (1795-1821)*

# ODE ON A GRECIAN URN

### I

Thou still unravished bride of quietness,
   Thou foster-child of silence and slow time,
Sylvan historian, who canst thus express
   A flowery tale more sweetly than our rhyme:
What leaf-fringed legend haunts about thy shape
   Of deities or mortals, or of both,
     In Tempe or the dales of Arcady?
What men or gods are these? What maidens loth?
What mad pursuit? What struggle to escape?
     What pipes and timbrels? What wild ecstasy?     10

### II

Heard melodies are sweet, but those unheard
   Are sweeter; therefore, ye soft pipes, play on;
Not to the sensual ear, but, more endeared,
   Pipe to the spirit ditties of no tone:
Fair youth, beneath the trees, thou canst not leave
   Thy song, nor ever can those trees be bare;
     Bold Lover, never, never canst thou kiss,
Though winning near the goal—yet, do not grieve;
   She cannot fade, though thou hast not thy bliss,
     For ever wilt thou love, and she be fair!     20

### III

Ah, happy, happy boughs! that cannot shed
   Your leaves, nor ever bid the Spring adieu;
And, happy melodist, unwearièd,
   For ever piping songs for ever new;
More happy love! more happy, happy love!
   For ever warm and still to be enjoyed,
     For ever panting, and for ever young;
All breathing human passion far above,
   That leaves a heart high-sorrowful and cloyed,
     A burning forehead, and a parching tongue.     30

### IV

Who are these coming to the sacrifice?
   To what green altar, O mysterious priest,
Lead'st thou that heifer lowing at the skies,
   And all her silken flanks with garlands drest?
What little town by river or sea shore,
   Or mountain built with peaceful citadel,
     Is emptied of this folk, this pious morn?
And, little town, thy streets for evermore
   Will silent be; and not a soul to tell
     Why thou art desolate, can e'er return.     40

V

O Attic shape! Fair attitude! with brede
   Of marble men and maidens overwrought,
With forest branches and the trodden weed;
   Thou, silent form, dost tease us out of thought
As doth eternity: Cold Pastoral!
   When old age shall this generation waste,
      Thou shalt remain, in midst of other woe
   Than ours, a friend to man, to whom thou say'st,
   "Beauty is truth, truth beauty,—that is all
      Ye know on earth, and all ye need to know."

## WHEN I HAVE FEARS THAT I MAY CEASE TO BE

When I have fears that I may cease to be
Before my pen has gleaned my teeming brain,
Before high-piled books, in charactery,
Hold like rich garners the full-ripened grain;
When I behold, upon the night's starred face,
Huge cloudy symbols of a high romance,
And think that I may never live to trace
Their shadows, with the magic hand of chance;
And when I feel, fair creature of an hour,
That I shall never look upon thee more,         10
Never have relish in the faery power
Of unreflecting love;—then on the shore
Of the wide world I stand alone, and think
Till love and fame to nothingness do sink.

▶ *William Cullen Bryant (1794-1878)*

## THANATOPSIS

   To him who in the love of Nature holds
Communion with her visible forms, she speaks
A various language; for his gayer hours
She has a voice of gladness, and a smile
And eloquence of beauty, and she glides
Into his darker musings, with a mild
And healing sympathy, that steals away
Their sharpness, ere he is aware. When thoughts
Of the last bitter hour come like a blight
Over thy spirit, and sad images         10
Of the stern agony, and shroud, and pall,
And breathless darkness, and the narrow house,
Make thee to shudder, and grow sick at heart;—
Go forth, under the open sky, and list
To Nature's teachings, while from all around—

Earth and her waters, and the depths of air—
Comes a still voice—Yet a few days, and thee
The all-beholding sun shall see no more
In all his course; nor yet in the cold ground,
Where thy pale form was laid, with many tears,          20
Nor in the embrace of ocean, shall exist
Thy image. Earth, that nourished thee, shall claim
Thy growth, to be resolved to earth again,
And, lost each human trace, surrendering up
Thine individual being, shalt thou go
To mix for ever with the elements,
To be a brother to the insensible rock
And to the sluggish clod, which the rude swain
Turns with his share, and treads upon. The oak
Shall send his roots abroad, and pierce thy mould.     30

    Yet not to thine eternal resting-place
Shall thou retire alone, nor couldst thou wish
Couch more magnificent. Thou shalt lie down
With patriarchs of the infant world—with kings,
The powerful of the earth—the wise, the good,
Fair forms, and hoary seers of ages past,
All in one mighty sepulchre. The hills
Rock-ribbed and ancient as the sun—the vales
Stretching in pensive quietness between;
The venerable woods—rivers that move                    40
In majesty, and the complaining brooks
That make the meadows green; and, poured round all,
Old Ocean's gray and melancholy waste,—
Are but the solemn decorations all
Of the great tomb of man. The golden sun,
The planets, all the infinite host of heaven,
Are shining on the sad abodes of death,
Through the still lapse of ages. All that tread
The globe are but a handful to the tribes
That slumber in its bosom.—Take the wings               50
Of morning, pierce the Barcan wilderness,
Or lose thyself in the continuous woods
Where rolls the Oregon, and hears no sound,
Save his own dashings—yet the dead are there:
And millions in those solitudes, since first
The flight of years began, have laid them down
In their last sleep—the dead reign there alone.
So shalt thou rest, and what if thou withdraw
In silence from the living and no friend
Take note of thy departure? All that breathe            60
Will share thy destiny. The gay will laugh
When thou art gone, the solemn brood of care
Plod on, and each one as before will chase
His favorite phantom; yet all these shall leave
Their mirth and their employments, and shall come

And make their bed with thee. As the long train
Of ages glides away, the sons of men,
The youth in life's fresh spring, and he who goes
In the full strength of years, matron and maid,
The speechless babe, and the gray-headed man—                    70
Shall one by one be gathered to thy side,
By those, who in their turn shall follow them.

    So live, that when thy summons comes to join
The innumerable caravan, which moves
To that mysterious realm, where each shall take
His chamber in the silent halls of death,
Thou go not, like the quarry-slave at night,
Scourged to his dungeon, but, sustained and soothed
By an unfaltering trust, approach thy grave,
Like one who wraps the drapery of his couch                       80
About him, and lies down to pleasant dreams.


▶ *Elizabeth Barrett Browning (1806-1861)*

# SONNET 43

How do I love thee? Let me count the ways.
I love thee to the depth and breadth and height
My soul can reach, when feeling out of sight
For the ends of Being and ideal Grace.
I love thee to the level of everyday's
Most quiet need, by sun and candle light.
I love thee freely, as men strive for Right;
I love thee purely, as they turn from Praise.
I love thee with the passion put to use
In my old griefs, and with my childhood's faith.                  10
I love thee with a love I seemed to lose
With my lost saints—I love thee with the breath,
Smiles, tears, of all my life!—and, if God choose,
I shall but love thee better after death.


▶ *Robert Browning (1812-1889)*

# MY LAST DUCHESS

*Ferrara*

That's my last Duchess painted on the wall,
Looking as if she were alive. I call
That piece a wonder, now; Frà Pandolf's hands
Worked busily a day, and there she stands.
Will't please you sit and look at her? I said
"Frà Pandolf" by design, for never read

Strangers like you that pictured countenance,
The depth and passion of its earnest glance,
But to myself they turned (since none puts by
The curtain I have drawn for you, but I)                               10
And seemed as they would ask me, if they durst,
How such a glance came there; so, not the first
Are you to turn and ask thus. Sir, 'twas not
Her husband's presence only, called that spot
Of joy into the Duchess' cheek; perhaps
Frà Pandolf chanced to say "Her mantle laps
Over my Lady's wrist too much," or, "Paint
Must never hope to reproduce the faint
Half-flush that dies along her throat." Such stuff
Was courtesy, she thought, and cause enough                            20
For calling up that spot of joy. She had
A heart—how shall I say?—too soon made glad,
Too easily impressed; she liked whate'er
She looked on, and her looks went everywhere.
Sir, 'twas all one! My favor at her breast,
The dropping of the daylight in the west,
The bough of cherries some officious fool
Broke in the orchard for her, the white mule
She rode with round the terrace—all and each
Would draw from her alike the approving speech,                        30
Or blush, at least. She thanked men—good! but thanked
Somehow—I know not how—as if she ranked
My gift of a nine-hundred-years-old name
With anybody's gift. Who'd stoop to blame
This sort of trifling? Even had you skill
In speech—(which I have not)—to make your will
Quite clear to such an one, and say, "Just this
Or that in you disgusts me; here you miss,
Or there exceed the mark"—and if she let
Herself be lessoned so, nor plainly set                                40
Her wits to yours, forsooth, and made excuse,
—E'en then would be some stooping; and I choose
Never to stoop. Oh, Sir, she smiled, no doubt,
Whene'er I passed her; but who passed without
Much the same smile? This grew; I gave commands;
Then all smiles stopped together. There she stands
As if alive. Will't please you rise? We'll meet
The company below, then. I repeat,
The Count your master's known munificence
Is ample warrant that no just pretence                                 50
Of mine for dowry will be disallowed;
Though his fair daughter's self, as I avowed
At starting, is my object. Nay, we'll go
Together down, Sir. Notice Neptune, though,
Taming a sea-horse, thought a rarity,
Which Claus of Innsbruck cast in bronze for me!

# PROSPICE

Fear death?—to feel the fog in my throat,
   The mist in my face,
When the snows begin, and the blasts denote
   I am nearing the place,
The power of the night, the press of the storm,
   The post of the foe;
Where he stands, the Arch Fear in a visible form,
   Yet the strong man must go:
For the journey is done and the summit attained,
   And the barriers fall,                                    10
Though a battle's to fight ere the guerdon be gained,
   The reward of it all.
I was ever a fighter, so—one fight more,
   The best and the last!
I would hate that death bandaged my eyes, and forbore,
   And bade me creep past.
No! let me taste the whole of it, fare like my peers,
   The heroes of old,
Bear the brunt, in a minute pay glad life's arrears
   Of pain, darkness, and cold.                             20
For sudden the worst turns the best to the brave,
   The black minute's at end,
And the elements' rage, the fiend-voices that rave,
   Shall dwindle, shall blend,
Shall change, shall become first a peace out of pain,
   Then a light, then thy breast,
O thou soul of my soul! I shall clasp thee again,
   And with God be the rest!

▶ *Matthew Arnold (1822-1888)*

# DOVER BEACH

The sea is calm to-night.
The tide is full, the moon lies fair
Upon the straits;—on the French coast the light
Gleams and is gone; the cliffs of England stand,
Glimmering and vast, out in the tranquil bay.

Come to the window, sweet is the night air!
Only, from the long line of spray
Where the sea meets the moon-blanch'd land,
Listen! you hear the grating roar
Of pebbles which the waves draw back, and fling,      10
At their return, up the high strand,
Begin, and cease, and then again begin,
With tremulous cadence slow, and bring
The eternal note of sadness in.

Sophocles long ago
Heard it on the Ægean, and it brought
Into his mind the turbid ebb and flow
Of human misery; we
Find also in the sound a thought,
Hearing it by this distant northern sea.          20

The Sea of Faith
Was once, too, at the full, and round earth's shore
Lay like the folds of a bright girdle furl'd.
But now I only hear
Its melancholy, long, withdrawing roar,
Retreating, to the breath
Of the night-wind, down the vast edges drear
And naked shingles of the world.
Ah, love, let us be true
To one another! for the world, which seems          30
To lie before us like a land of dreams,
So various, so beautiful, so new,
Hath really neither joy, nor love, nor light,
Nor certitude, nor peace, nor help for pain;
And we are here as on a darkling plain
Swept with confused alarms of struggle and flight,
Where ignorant armies clash by night.


▶  *George Meredith (1828-1909)*

## YOUTH IN AGE

Once I was part of the music I heard
  On the boughs or sweet between earth and sky;
  For joy of the beating of wings on high
My heart shot into the breast of the bird.

I hear it now and I see it fly,
  And a life in wrinkles again is stirred;
  My heart shoots into the breast of the bird,
As it will for sheer love till the last long sigh.

► *Emily Dickinson (1830-1886)*

## THESE ARE THE DAYS
## WHEN BIRDS COME BACK

These are the days when Birds come back—
A very few—a Bird or two—
To take a backward look.

These are the days when skies resume
The old—old sophistries of June—
A blue and gold mistake.

Oh fraud that cannot cheat the Bee—
Almost thy plausibility
Induces my belief.

Till ranks of seeds their witness bear—          10
And softly thro' the altered air
Hurries a timid leaf.

Oh Sacrament of summer days,
Oh Last Communion in the Haze—
Permit a child to join.

Thy sacred emblems to partake—
Thy consecrated bread to take
And thine immortal wine!


## THERE'S A CERTAIN SLANT
## OF LIGHT

There's a certain slant of light,
On winter afternoons,
That oppresses, like the weight
Of cathedral tunes.

Heavenly hurt it gives us;
We can find no scar,
But internal difference
Where the meanings are.

None may teach it anything,
'Tis the seal, despair,—                          10
An imperial affliction
Sent us of the air.

When it comes, the landscape listens,
Shadows hold their breath;
When it goes, 'tis like the distance
On the look of death.

► *A. E. Housman (1859-1936)*

## THE LAWS OF GOD,
## THE LAWS OF MAN

The laws of God, the laws of man,
He may keep that will and can;
Not I: let God and man decree
Laws for themselves and not for me;
And if my ways are not as theirs
Let them mind their own affairs.
Their deeds I judge and much condemn,
Yet when did I make laws for them?
Please yourselves, say I, and they
Need only look the other way.                     10
But no, they will not; they must still
Wrest their neighbour to their will,
And make me dance as they desire
With jail and gallows and hell-fire.
And how am I to face the odds
Of man's bedevilment and God's?
I, a stranger and afraid
In a world I never made.
They will be master, right or wrong;
Though both are foolish, both are strong.         20
And since, my soul, we cannot fly
To Saturn nor to Mercury,
Keep we must, if keep we can,
These foreign laws of God and man.

▶ *Amy Lowell (1874-1925)*

# PATTERNS

I walk down the garden paths,
And all the daffodils
Are blowing, and the bright blue squills.
I walk down the patterned garden paths
In my stiff, brocaded gown.
With my powdered hair and jewelled fan,
I too am a rare
Pattern. As I wander down
The garden paths.

My dress is richly figured,                            10
And the train
Makes a pink and silver stain
On the gravel, and the thrift
Of the borders.
Just a plate of current fashion,
Tripping by in high-heeled, ribboned shoes.
Not a softness anywhere about me,
Only whalebone and brocade.
And I sink on a seat in the shade
Of a lime tree. For my passion                         20
Wars against the stiff brocade.
The daffodils and squills
Flutter in the breeze
As they please.
And I weep;
For the lime tree is in blossom
And one small flower has dropped upon my bosom.

And the plashing of waterdrops
In the marble fountain
Comes down the garden paths.                           30
The dripping never stops.
Underneath my stiffened gown
Is the softness of a woman bathing in a marble basin,
A basin in the midst of hedges grown
So thick, she cannot see her lover hiding,
But she guesses he is near,
And the sliding of the water
Seems the stroking of a dear
Hand upon her.
What is summer in a fine brocaded gown!                40
I should like to see it lying in a heap upon the ground.
All the pink and silver crumpled up on the ground.

I would be the pink and silver as I ran along the paths,
And he would stumble after,

Bewildered by my laughter.
I should see the sun flashing from his sword-hilt and the buckles on
    his shoes.
I would choose
To lead him in a maze along the patterned paths,
A bright and laughing maze for my heavy-booted lover.
Till he caught me in the shade,                                    50
And the buttons of his waistcoat bruised my body as he clasped me,
Aching, melting, unafraid.
With the shadows of the leaves and the sundrops,
And the plopping of the waterdrops,
All about us in the open afternoon—
I am very like to swoon
With the weight of this brocade,
For the sun sifts through the shade.

Underneath the fallen blossom
In my bosom,                                                      60
Is a letter I have hid.
It was brought to me this morning by a rider from the Duke.
"Madam, we regret to inform you that Lord Hartwell
Died in action Thursday se'nnight."
As I read it in the white, morning sunlight,
The letters squirmed like snakes.
"Any answer, Madam," said my footman.
"No," I told him.
"See that the messenger takes some refreshment.
No, no answer."                                                   70
And I walked into the garden,
Up and down the patterned paths,
In my stiff, correct brocade.
The blue and yellow flowers stood up proudly in the sun,
Each one.
I stood upright too,
Held rigid to the pattern
By the stiffness of my gown.
Up and down I walked,
Up and down.                                                      80

In a month he would have been my husband.
In a month, here, underneath this lime,
We would have broke the pattern;
He for me, and I for him,
He as Colonel, I as Lady,
On this shady seat.
He had a whim
That sunlight carried blessing.
And I answered, "It shall be as you have said."
Now he is dead.                                                   90

In summer and in winter I shall walk

Up and down
The patterned garden paths
In my stiff, brocaded gown.
The squills and daffodils
Will give place to pillared roses, and to asters, and to snow.
I shall go
Up and down,
In my gown.
Gorgeously arrayed,                                                       100
Boned and stayed.
And the softness of my body will be guarded from embrace
By each button, hook, and lace.
For the man who should loose me is dead,
Fighting with the Duke in Flanders,
In a pattern called a war.
Christ! What are patterns for?

▶ *Robert Frost (1874-1963)*

# BIRCHES

When I see birches bend to left and right
Across the lines of straighter darker trees,
I like to think some boy's been swinging them.
But swinging doesn't bend them down to stay
As ice-storms do. Often you must have seen them
Loaded with ice a sunny winter morning
After a rain. They click upon themselves
As the breeze rises, and turn many-colored
As the stir cracks and crazes their enamel.
Soon the sun's warmth makes them shed crystal shells        10
Shattering and avalanching on the snow-crust—
Such heaps of broken glass to sweep away
You'd think the inner dome of heaven had fallen.
They are dragged to the withered bracken by the load,
And they seem not to break; though once they are bowed
So low for long, they never right themselves:
You may see their trunks arching in the woods
Years afterwards, trailing their leaves on the ground
Like girls on hands and knees that throw their hair
Before them over their heads to dry in the sun.            20
But I was going to say when Truth broke in
With all her matter-of-fact about the ice-storm
I should prefer to have some boy bend them
As he went out and in to fetch the cows—
Some boy too far from town to learn baseball,
Whose only play was what he found himself,
Summer or winter, and could play alone.

One by one he subdued his father's trees
By riding them down over and over again
Until he took the stiffness out of them,                                    30
And not one but hung limp, not one was left
For him to conquer. He learned all there was
To learn about not launching out too soon
And so not carrying the tree away
Clear to the ground. He always kept his poise
To the top branches, climbing carefully
With the same pains you use to fill a cup
Up to the brim, and even above the brim.
Then he flung outward, feet first, with a swish,
Kicking his way down through the air to the ground.                         40
So was I once myself a swinger of birches.
And so I dream of going back to be.
It's when I'm weary of considerations,
And life is too much like a pathless wood
Where your face burns and tickles with the cobwebs
Broken across it, and one eye is weeping
From a twig's having lashed across it open.
I'd like to get away from earth awhile
And then come back to it and begin over.
May no fate willfully misunderstand me                                      50
And half grant what I wish and snatch me away
Not to return. Earth's the right place for love:
I don't know where it's likely to go better.
I'd like to go by climbing a birch tree,
And climb black branches up a snow-white trunk
*Toward* heaven, till the tree could bear no more,
But dipped its top and set me down again.
That would be good both going and coming back.
One could do worse than be a swinger of birches.

# MENDING WALL

Something there is that doesn't love a wall,
That sends the frozen ground swell under it,
And spills the upper boulders in the sun;
And makes gaps even two can pass abreast.
The work of hunters is another thing:
I have come after them and made repair
Where they have left not one stone on a stone,
But they would have the rabbit out of hiding,
To please yelping dogs. The gaps I mean,
No one has seen them made or heard them made,                               10
But at spring mending time we find them there.
I let my neighbor know beyond the hill;
And on a day we meet to walk the line
And set the wall between us once again.

We keep the wall between us as we go.
To each the boulders that have fallen to each.
And some are loaves and some so nearly balls
We have to use a spell to make them balance:
"Stay where you are till our backs are turned!"
We wear our fingers rough with handling them.     20
Oh, just another kind of outdoor game,
One on a side. It comes to little more:
There where it is we do not need the wall:
He is all pine and I am apple orchard.
My apple trees will never get across
And eat the cones under his pines, I tell him.
He only says, "Good fences make good neighbors."
Spring is the mischief in me, and I wonder
If I could put a notion in his head:
"*Why* do they make good neighbors? Isn't it     30
Where there are cows? But here there are no cows.
Before I built a wall I'd ask to know
What I was walling in or walling out,
And to whom I was like to give offense.
Something there is that doesn't love a wall,
That wants it down." I could say "Elves" to him.
But it's not elves exactly, and I'd rather
He said it for himself. I see him there
Bringing a stone grasped firmly by the top
In each hand, like an old stone savage armed.     40
He moves in darkness as it seems to me,
Not of woods only and the shade of trees.
He will not go behind his father's saying,
And he likes having thought of it so well
He says again, "Good fences make good neighbors."

# THE GIFT OUTRIGHT

The land was ours before we were the land's.
She was our land more than a hundred years
Before we were her people. She was ours
In Massachusetts, in Virginia,
But we were England's, still colonials,
Possessing what we still were unpossessed by,
Possessed by what we now no more possessed.
Something we were withholding made us weak
Until we found out that it was ourselves
We were witholding from our land of living,     10
And forthwith found salvation in surrender.
Such as we were we gave ourselves outright
(The deed of gift was many deeds of wars)
To the land vaguely realizing westward,
But still unstoried, artless, unenhanced,
Such as she was, such as she would become.

*William Carlos Williams (1883-1963)*

# TRACT

I will teach you my townspeople
how to perform a funeral
for you have it over a troop
of artists—
unless one should scour the world—
you have the ground sense necessary.

See! the hearse leads.
I begin with a design for a hearse.
For Christ's sake not black—
nor white either—and not polished!          10
Let it be weathered—like a farm wagon—
with gilt wheels (this could be
applied fresh at small expense)
or no wheels at all:
a rough dray to drag over the ground.

Knock the glass out!
My God—glass, my townspeople!
For what purpose? It it for the dead
to look out or for us to see
how well he is housed or to see          20
the flowers or the lack of them—
or what?
To keep the rain and snow from him?
He will have a heavier rain soon:
pebbles and dirt and what not.
Let there be no glass—
and no upholstery, phew!
and no little brass rollers
and small easy wheels on the bottom—
my townspeople what are you thinking of?          30
A rough plain hearse then
with gilt wheels and no top at all.
On this the coffin lies
by its own weight.

          No wreaths please—
especially no hot-house flowers.
Some common memento is better,
something he prized and is known by:
his old clothes—a few books perhaps—
God knows what! You realize          40
how we are about these things
my townspeople—
something will be found—anything
even flowers if he had come to that.
So much for the hearse.

For heaven's sake though see to the driver!
Take off the silk hat! In fact
that's no place at all for him—
up there unceremoniously
dragging our friend out to his own dignity!
Bring him down—bring him down!
Low and inconspicuous! I'd not have him ride
on the wagon at all—damn him—
the undertaker's understrapper!
Let him hold the reins
and walk at the side
and inconspicuously too!

Then briefly as to yourselves:
Walk behind—as they do in France,
seventh class, or if you ride
Hell take curtains! Go with some show
of inconvenience; sit openly—
to the weather as to grief.
Or do you think you can shut grief in?
What—from us? We who have perhaps
nothing to lose? Share with us
share with us—it will be money
in your pockets.

     Go now
I think you are ready.

▶ *Robinson Jeffers (1887-1962)*

# HURT HAWKS

## I

The broken pillar of the wing jags from the clotted shoulder,
The wing trails like a banner in defeat,
No more to use the sky forever but live with famine
And pain a few days: cat nor coyote
Will shorten the week of waiting for death, there is game without
  talons.

He stands under the oak-bush and waits
The lame feet of salvation; at night he remembers freedom
And flies in a dream, the dawns ruin it.
He is strong and pain is worse to the strong, incapacity is worse.
The curs of the day come and torment him
At distance, no one but death the redeemer will humble that head,
The intrepid readiness, the terrible eyes.
The wild God of the world is sometimes merciful to those
That ask mercy, not often to the arrogant.

You do not know him, you communal people, or you have forgotten
    him;
Intemperate and savage, the hawk remembers him;
Beautiful and wild, the hawks, and men that are dying, remember him.

## II

I'd sooner, except the penalties, kill a man than a hawk; but the great
    redtail
Had nothing left but unable misery
From the bone too shattered for mending, the wing that trailed under
    his talons when he moved.                                      20
We had fed him six weeks, I gave him freedom,
He wandered over the foreland hill and returned in the evening,
    asking for death,
Not like a beggar, still eyed with the old
Implacable arrogance. I gave him the lead gift in the twilight.
    What fell was relaxed,
Owl-downy, soft feminine feathers; but what
Soared: the fierce rush: the night-herons by the flooded river cried
    fear at its rising
Before it was quite unsheathed from reality.

▶ *Marianne Moore (1887-        )*

# SILENCE

My father used to say,
"Superior people never make long visits,
have to be shown Longfellow's grave
or the glass flowers at Harvard.
Self-reliant like the cat—
that takes its prey to privacy,
the mouse's limp tail hanging like a shoelace from its mouth—
they sometimes enjoy solitude,
and can be robbed of speech
by speech which has delighted them.                               10
The deepest feeling always shows itself in silence;
not in silence, but restraint."
Nor was he insincere in saying, "Make my house your inn."
Inns are not residences.

# POETRY

I, too, dislike it: there are things that are important beyond all this fiddle.
    Reading it, however, with a perfect contempt for it, one discovers in
    it after all, a place for the genuine.
        Hands that can grasp, eyes

that can dilate, hair that can rise
    if it must, these things are important not because a

high-sounding interpretation can be put upon them but because they are
    useful. When they become so derivative as to become unintelligible,
    the same thing may be said for all of us, that we
        do not admire what                      10
      we cannot understand: the bat
        holding on upside down or in quest of something to

eat, elephants pushing, a wild horse taking a roll, a tireless wolf under
    a tree, the immovable critic twitching his skin like a horse that feels a flea,
        the base-
    ball fan, the statistician—
      nor is it valid
        to discriminate against "business documents and

school-books"; all these phenomena are important. One must make a
           distinction
    however: when dragged into prominence by half poets, the result is not
        poetry,
    nor till the poets among us can be               20
      "literalists of
      the imagination"—above
        insolence and triviality and can present

for inspection, "imaginary gardens with real toads in them," shall we have
    it. In the meantime, if you demand on the one hand,
    the raw material of poetry in
      all its rawness and
      that which is on the other hand
        genuine, you are interested in poetry.


▶ *T. S. Eliot (1888-1965)*

# THE LOVE SONG OF J. ALFRED PRUFROCK

*S'io credesse che mia risposta fosse*
*A persona che mai tornasse al mondo,*
*Questa fiamma staria senza piu scosse.*
*Ma perciocche giammai di questo fondo*
*Non torno vivo alcun, s'i'odo il vero,*
*Senza tema d'infamia ti rispondo.**

Let us go then, you and I,
When the evening is spread out against the sky
Like a patient etherised upon a table;

---

* Dante, *Inferno*, XXVII, ll. 61-66: "If I thought that my answer were directed to anyone who
could ever return to the world, this flame would quiver no longer; but because, as I hear, no one
ever returns alive from this depth, I reply to you without fear of infamy."

Let us go, through certain half-deserted streets,
The muttering retreats
Of restless nights in one-night cheap hotels
And sawdust restaurants with oyster-shells:

Streets that follow like a tedious argument
Of insidious intent
To lead you to an overwhelming question . . .                     10
Oh, do not ask, "What is it?"
Let us go and make our visit.

In the room the women come and go
Talking of Michelangelo.

The yellow fog that rubs its back upon the window-panes,
The yellow smoke that rubs its muzzle on the window-panes,
Licked its tongue into the corners of the evening.
Lingered upon the pools that stand in drains,
Let fall upon its back the soot that falls from chimneys,
Slipped by the terrace, made a sudden leap.                       20
And seeing that it was a soft October night,
Curled once about the house, and fell asleep.

And indeed there will be time
For the yellow smoke that slides along the street,
Rubbing its back upon the window-panes;
There will be time, there will be time
To prepare a face to meet the faces that you meet;
There will be time to murder and create,
And time for all the works and days of hands
That lift and drop a question on your plate;                      30
Time for you and time for me,
And time yet for a hundred indecisions,
And for a hundred visions and revisions,
Before the taking of a toast and tea.

In the room the women come and go
Talking of Michelangelo.

And indeed there will be time
To wonder, "Do I dare?" and, "Do I dare?"
Time to turn back and descend the stair,
With a bald spot in the middle of my hair—                       40
[They will say: "How his hair is growing thin!"]
My morning coat, my collar mounting firmly to the chin,
My necktie rich and modest, but asserted by a simple pin—
[They will say: "But how his arms and legs are thin!"]

Do I dare
Disturb the universe?
In a minute there is time
For decisions and revisions which a minute will reverse.

For I have known them all already, known them all:
Have known the evenings, mornings, afternoons,                    50
I have measured out my life with coffee spoons;
I know the voices dying with a dying fall
Beneath the music from a farther room.
   So how should I presume?

And I have known the eyes already, known them all—
The eyes that fix you in a formulated phrase,
And when I am formulated, sprawling on a pin,
When I am pinned and wriggling on the wall,
Then how should I begin
To spit out all the butt-ends of my days and ways?                60
   And how should I presume?

And I have known the arms already, known them all—
Arms that are braceleted and white and bare
(But in the lamplight, downed with light brown hair!)
Is it perfume from a dress
That makes me so digress?
Arms that lie along a table, or wrap about a shawl.
   And should I then presume?
   And how should I begin?
. . . . . . . . . . . . . . . . . . . . .

Shall I say, I have gone at dusk through narrow streets            70
And watched the smoke that rises from the pipes
Of lonely men in shirt-sleeves, leaning out of windows? . . .

I should have been a pair of ragged claws
Scuttling across the floors of silent seas.
. . . . . . . . . . . . . . . . . . . . . . . . . . . . .

And the afternoon, the evening, sleeps so peacefully!
Smoothed by long fingers,
Asleep . . . tired . . . or it malingers,
Stretched on the floor, here beside you and me.
Should I, after tea and cakes and ices,
Have the strength to force the moment to its crisis?              80
But though I have wept and fasted, wept and prayed,
Though I have seen my head (grown slightly bald) brought in upon a platter,
I am no prophet—and here's no great matter;
I have seen the moment of my greatness flicker,
And I have seen the eternal Footman hold my coat, and snicker,
And in short, I was afraid.

And would it have been worth it, after all,
After the cups, the marmalade, the tea,
Among the porcelain, among some talk of you and me,
Would it have been worth while,                                   90
To have bitten off the matter with a smile,
To have squeezed the universe into a ball
To roll it toward some overwhelming question,

To say: "I am Lazarus, come from the dead,
Come back to tell you all, I shall tell you all"—
If one, settling a pillow by her head,
    Should say: "That is not what I meant at all;
    That is not it, at all."
And would it have been worth it, after all,
Would it have been worth while,                                   100
After the sunsets and the dooryards and the sprinkled streets,
After the novels, after the teacups, after the skirts that trail along the floor—
And this, and so much more?—
It is impossible to say just what I mean!
But as if a magic lantern threw the nerves in patterns on a screen:
Would it have been worth while
If one, settling a pillow or throwing off a shawl,
And turning toward the window, should say:
    "That is not it at all,
    That is not what I meant, at all."                           110
. . . . . . . . . . . . . . . . . . . . . . . . . . . . . .
No! I am not Prince Hamlet, nor was meant to be;
Am an attendant lord, one that will do
To swell a progress, start a scene or two,
Advise the prince; no doubt, an easy tool,
Deferential, glad to be of use,
Politic, cautious, and meticulous;
Full of high sentence, but a bit obtuse;
At times, indeed, almost ridiculous—
Almost, at times, the Fool.

I grow old . . . I grow old . . .                                 120
I shall wear the bottoms of my trousers rolled.

Shall I part my hair behind? Do I dare to eat a peach?
I shall wear white flannel trousers, and walk upon the beach.
I have heard the mermaids singing, each to each.

I do not think that they will sing to me.

I have seen them riding seaward on the waves
Combing the white hair of the waves blown back
When the wind blows the water white and black.

We have lingered in the chambers of the sea
By sea-girls wreathed with seaweed red and brown                 130
Till human voices wake us, and we drown.

## ARS POETICA

    A poem should be palpable and mute
    As a globed fruit,
    Dumb
    As old medallions to the thumb,
    Silent as the sleeve-worn stone
    Of casement ledges where the moss has grown—
    A poem should be wordless
    As the flight of birds.

    A poem should be motionless in time
    As the moon climbs,             10
    Leaving, as the moon releases
    Twig by twig the night-entangled trees,
    Leaving, as the moon behind the winter leaves,
    Memory by memory the mind—
    A poem should be motionless in time
    As the moon climbs.

    A poem should be equal to:
    Not true.
    For all the history of grief
    An empty doorway and a maple leaf.        20
    For love
    The leaning grasses and two lights above the sea—
    A poem should not mean
    But be.

▶ *Edna St. Vincent Millay (1892-1950)*

## WHAT LIPS MY LIPS HAVE KISSED

    What lips my lips have kissed, and where, and why,
    I have forgotten, and what arms have lain
    Under my head till morning; but the rain
    Is full of ghosts tonight, that tap and sigh
    Upon the glass and listen for reply,
    And in my heart there stirs a quiet pain
    For unremembered lads that not again
    Will turn to me at midnight with a cry.
    Thus in the winter stands the lonely tree,
    Nor knows what birds have vanished one by one,      10
    Yet knows its boughs more silent than before;
    I cannot say what loves have come and gone,
    I only know that summer sang in me
    A little while, that in me sings no more.

## *from* EPITAPH FOR THE RACE OF MAN

Here lies, and none to mourn him but the sea,
That falls incessant on the empty shore,
Most various Man, cut down to spring no more;
Before his prime, even in his infancy
Cut down, and all the clamour that was he,
Silenced; and all the riveted pride he wore,
A rusted iron column whose tall core
The rains have tunnelled like an aspen tree.
Man, doughty Man, what power has brought you low,
That heaven itself in arms could not persuade          10
To lay aside the lever and the spade
And be as dust among the dusts that blow?
Whence, whence the broadside? whose the heavy blade? . . .
Strive not to speak, poor scattered mouth; I know.


▶  *Langston Hughes (1902-1967)*

# I, TOO, SING AMERICA

I, too, sing America.

I am the darker brother.
They send me to eat in the kitchen
When company comes,
But I laugh,
And eat well,
And grow strong.

Tomorrow,
I'll sit at the table
When company comes.          10
Nobody'll dare
Say to me,
"Eat in the kitchen,"
Then.

Besides,
They'll see how beautiful I am
And be ashamed—

I, too, am America.


▶  *William Empson (1906-    )*

# IGNORANCE OF DEATH

Then there is this civilising love of death, by which
Even music and painting tell you what else to love.
Buddhists and Christians contrive to agree about death

Making death their ideal basis for different ideals.
The communists however disapprove of death
Except when practical. The people who dig up

Corpses and rape them are I understand not reported.
The Freudians regard the death-wish as fundamental,
Though 'the clamour of life' proceeds from its rival 'Eros.'

Whether you are to admire a given case for making less clamour          10
Is not their story. Liberal hopefulness
Regards death as a mere border to an improving picture.

Because we have neither hereditary nor direct knowledge of death
It is the trigger of the literary man's biggest gun
And we are happy to equate it to any conceived calm.

Heaven me, when a man is ready to die about something
Other than himself, and is in fact ready because of that,
Not because of himself, that is something clear about himself.

Otherwise I feel very blank upon this topic,
And think that though important, and proper for anyone to bring up,     20
It is one that most people should be prepared to be blank upon.

▶ *W. H. Auden (1907-     )*

## LAW LIKE LOVE

Law, say the gardeners, is the sun,
Law is the one
All gardeners obey
Tomorrow, yesterday, today.

Law is the wisdom of the old
The impotent grandfathers shrilly scold;
The grandchildren put out a treble tongue,
Law is the senses of the young.

Law, says the priest with a priestly look,
Expounding to an unpriestly people,     10
Law is the words in my priestly book,
Law is my pulpit and my steeple.

Law, says the judge as he looks down his nose,
Speaking clearly and most severely,
Law is as I've told you before,
Law is as you know I suppose,
Law is but let me explain it once more,
Law is The Law.

Yet law-abiding scholars write;
Law is neither wrong nor right,     20
Law is only crimes
Punished by places and by times,
Law is the clothes men wear
Anytime, anywhere,
Law is Good-morning and Good-night.

Others say, Law is our Fate;
Others say, Law is our State;
Others say, others say

Law is no more
Law has gone away.     30

And always the loud angry crowd
Very angry and very loud
Law is We,
And always the soft idiot softly Me.

If we, dear, know we know no more
Than they about the law,
If I no more than you
Know what we should and should not do
Except that all agree
Gladly or miserably     40
That the law is
And that all know this,
If therefore thinking it absurd
To identify Law with some other word,
Unlike so many men
I cannot say Law is again,
No more than they can we suppress
The universal wish to guess

Or slip out of our own position
Into an unconcerned condition.     50
Although I can at least confine
Your vanity and mine
To stating timidly
A timid similarity,
We shall boast anyway:
Like love I say.

Like love we don't know where or why
Like love we can't compel or fly
Like love we often weep
Like love we seldom keep.     60

## MUSÉE DES BEAUX ARTS

About suffering they were never wrong,
The Old Masters: how well they understood
Its human position; how it takes place

While someone else is eating or opening a window or just
     walking dully along;
How, when the aged are reverently, passionately waiting
For the miraculous birth, there always must be
Children who did not specially want it to happen, skating
On a pond at the edge of the wood:
They never forgot
That even the dreadful martyrdom must run its course         10
Anyhow in a corner, some untidy spot
Where the dogs go on with their doggy life and the
     torturer's horse
Scratches its innocent behind on a tree.

In Brueghel's *Icarus,* for instance: how everything turns away
Quite leisurely from the disaster; the ploughman may
Have heard the splash, the forsaken cry,
But for him it was not an important failure; the sun shone
As it had to on the white legs disappearing into the green
Water; and the expensive delicate ship that must have seen
Something amazing, a boy falling out of the sky,         20
Had somewhere to get to and sailed calmly on.


▶ *Paul Engle (1908-     )*

# BEASTS

PART I

That was a shocking day
When we watched, lying prone,
The two trout sidle under
The underwater stone:

When we saw there beyond
The hedge of hardy thorn
The sexual touch of summer
Luring the lifted corn:

When down the slope the two
Running red fox dared         10
Daylight in their need,
Poised, aloof and paired:

When cardinals from green
Willows, with red cries,

Scarlet scream of bird,
Plunged in our pool of eyes:

For we, merely woman
And man, did not believe
Living things could love
Wholly, and not grieve:         20

For love had always been
A nimble animal
That could lure innocence
Or lewd on its belly crawl:

By snarl, by sensual cry,
Love lived, but in a cage,
Barred by my own tight pride
And your rehearsed pure rage:

Pride, pride that would not let
Self give up utterly,         30
Rage, rage that self would give
Itself up utterly:

They leapt at us like fire
And burned us with our blame,
Defied us with delight,
And shamed our human shame.

## FOSSIL

We walked in that green field
Between the golden bell
Of Sunday morning and
The golden clover smell.

Beneath resisting grass,
Being too tired to climb,
We found in rotten rock
The fossil lost in time,

Stood staring till I found 10
Power and sense to shove
Inside my coat dead stone
And your live hand of love.

There we were beaten with
Bronze minutes from the bell
That battered our delight
And bronzed the clover smell.

One hour rock, clover watched
Our deliberate climb
Into eternity
Loudly tongued with time. 20

Out of green water came
The shell that we could shove
Into the glittering light
That was our wave of love

In which I felt your pulse
Beating, red rung bell,
And heard the quiet boom
Of the red clover smell,

And felt along my hand
That shell whose silent climb 30
From dark seas into light
Shrieked the cruel cry of time

Accusing us of pride
That we in hope could shove
Up from its salty depth
The muscle of our love.

Stroke by brazen stroke
We answered that pure bell,

As red bloom by red bloom
Clover clanged its smell. 40

We learned from that dead life,
Shell of old shell: we climb
The living earth to learn
That as we fall through time,

Geologist of joy,
Defining day, will shove,
Layer on layered hour,
Our lapidary love.

▶ *Stephen Spender (1909-    )*

## WHAT I EXPECTED

What I expected was
Thunder, fighting,
Long struggles with men
And climbing.
After continual straining
I should grow strong;
Then the rocks would shake
And I should rest long.

What I had not foreseen
Was the gradual day 10
Weakening the will
Leaking the brightness away,
The lack of good to touch
The fading of body and soul
Like smoke before wind
Corrupt, unsubstantial.

The wearing of Time,
And the watching of cripples pass
With limbs shaped like questions
In their odd twist, 20
The pulverous grief
Melting the bones with pity,
The sick falling from earth—
These, I could not foresee.

For I had expected always
Some brightness to hold in trust,
Some final innocence
To save from dust;
That, hanging solid,
Would dangle through all 30
Like the created poem
Or the dazzling crystal.

# I THINK CONTINUALLY OF THOSE

I think continually of those who were truly great.
Who, from the womb, remembered the soul's history
Through corridors of light where the hours are suns,
Endless and singing. Whose lovely ambition
Was that their lips, still touched with fire,
Should tell of the spirit clothed from head to foot in song.
And who hoarded from the spring branches
The desires falling across their bodies like blossoms.

What is precious is never to forget
The essential delight of the blood drawn from ageless springs          10
Breaking through rocks in worlds before our earth.
Never to deny its pleasure in the morning simple light
Nor its grave evening demand for love.
Never to allow gradually the traffic to smother
With noise and fog the flowering of the spirit.

Near the snow, near the sun, in the highest fields,
See how these names are fêted by the waving grass
And by the streamers of white cloud
And whispers of wind in the listening sky.
The names of those who in their lives fought for life,                  20
Who wore at their hearts the fire's centre.
Born of the sun, they travelled a short while toward the sun
And left the vivid air signed with their honour.

▶ *Karl Shapiro (1913-      )*

## *from* THE BOURGEOIS POET

### 14

The password of the twentieth century: Communications (as if we had to invent them). Animals and cannibals have communications; birds and bees and even a few human creatures, called artists (generally held to be insane). But the bulk of humanity had to invent Communications. The Romans had the best roads in the world, but had nothing to communicate over them except other [10] Romans. Americans have conquered world-time and world-space and chat with the four corners of the earth at breakfast and have nothing to communicate except other Americans. The Russians communicate other Russians to the moon. The entire solar system is in the hands of cartoonists.

I am sitting in the kitchen in Nebraska and watching a shrouded woman amble down [20] the market in Karachi. She is going to get her morning smallpox shot. It's cold and mental love they want: It's the mystic sexuality of Communications. Money was love. Power was love. Communications now are love. Sex-object of the telephone, let's kiss. The girl hugs the hi-fi speaker to her belly: it pours into her openings like gravy. In the spring, Hitler arises. This is the time of tramp- [30] ling. My japanned birds in the radio-active snow are calling.

A man appears at the corner of the street; I prepare myself for hospitality. Man or angel, welcome! But I am afraid and double-lock the door. On the occasion of the death of a political party, I send an epitaph by Western Union. I didn't go to the funeral of poetry. I stayed home and watched it on television. Moon in the bottom of the Steuben glass, sun nesting in New Mexican deserts—the primitive Christian communicated with a dirty big toe. He drew a fish in the dust.

### 67

As you say (not without sadness), poets don't see, they feel. And that's why people who have turned to feelers seem like poets. Why children seem poetic. Why when the sap rises in the adolescent heart the young write poetry. Why great catastrophes are stated in verse. Why lunatics are named for the moon. Yet poetry isn't feeling with hands. A poem is not a kiss. Poems are what ideas feel like. Ideas on Sunday thoughts on vacation.

Poets don't see, they feel. They are conductors of the senses of men, as teachers and preachers are the insulators. The poets go up and feel the insulators. Now and again they feel the wrong thing and are thrown through a wall by a million-volt shock. All insulation makes the poet anxious: clothes, strait jackets, iambic five. He pulls at the seams like a boy whose trousers are cutting him in half. Poets think along the electric currents. The words are constantly not making sense when he reads. He flunks economics, logic, history. Then he describes what it feels like to flunk economics, logic, history. After that he feels better.

People say: it is sad to see a grown man feeling his way, sad to see a man so naked, desireless of any defenses. The people walk back into their boxes and triple-lock the doors. When their children begin to read poetry the parents watch them from the corner of their eye.

It's only a phase, they aver. Parents like the word "aver" though they don't use it.

### 77

Why am I happy writing this textbook? What sublime idiocy! What a waste of time! A textbook on prosody at that. Yet when I sit down to comb the business out, when I address the easel of this task, I burn with an even flame, I'm cooking with gas. There are some things so dull they hypnotize like the pendulum of a clock; so clockwork and quotidian they make the flesh delirious like fresh water. X-ray the poem, give it a thorough physical, a clean bill of health. We can see everything but the flow of blood. What Latin and Greek nomenclature! But this is order, order made to order. This is system to plot and plan. This is definition, edges clean as razors. Simplification, boldface, indented. I know there is no such thing as a textbook. I know that all textbooks are sold the second the course is over. I know that a book sold is a dead book. And I dream, like others, of writing a textbook that is not a textbook, a book that not even a student would part with, a book that makes even prosody breathe. So, when the sun shines with the nine o'clock brightness and the coffee swims in my throat and the smoke floats over the page like the smoke of a ship's funnel, then I romanticize. I make a muse of prosody, old hag. She's just a registered nurse, I know, I know, but I have her sashay, grind and bump, register Alcaics, Sapphics, choriambs (my predilection). She's trained all right. She's second nature herself. She knows her job, I mine. We'll work it out: it may be poetry. Blueprints are blue. They have their dreams.

*Dylan Thomas (1914-1953)*

# FERN HILL

Now as I was young and easy under the apple boughs
About the lilting house and happy as the grass was green,
   The night above the dingle starry,
    Time let me hail and climb
   Golden in the heydays of his eyes,
And honored among wagons I was prince of the apple towns
And once below a time I lordly had the trees and leaves
    Trail with daisies and barley
   Down the rivers of the windfall light.

And as I was green and carefree, famous among the barns    10
About the happy yard and singing as the farm was home,
   In the sun that is young once only,
    Time let me play and be
   Golden in the mercy of his means,
And green and golden I was huntsman and herdsman, the calves
Sang to my horn, the foxes on the hills barked clear and cold,
    And the sabbath rang slowly
   In the pebbles of the holy streams.

All the sun long it was running, it was lovely, the hay
Fields high as the house, the tunes from the chimneys, it was air    20
   And playing, lovely and watery
    And fire green as grass.
   And nightly under the simple stars
As I rode to sleep the owls were bearing the farm away,
All the moon long I heard, blessed among stables, the night-jars
   Flying with the ricks, and the horses
    Flashing into the dark.

And then to awake, and the farm, like a wanderer white
With the dew, come back, the cock on his shoulder: it was all
   Shining, it was Adam and maiden,    30
    The sky gathered again
   And the sun grew round that very day.
So it must have been after the birth of the simple light
In the first, spinning place, the spellbound horses walking warm
   Out of the whinnying green stable
    On to the fields of praise.

And honored among foxes and pheasants by the gay house
Under the new made clouds and happy as the heart was long,
   In the sun born over and over,
    I ran my heedless ways,    40
   My wishes raced through the house high hay
And nothing I cared, at my sky blue trades, that time allows
In all his tuneful turning so few and such morning songs
   Before the children green and golden
    Follow him out of grace.

Nothing I cared, in the lamb white days, that time would take me
Up to the swallow thronged loft by the shadow of my hand,
   In the moon that is always rising,
     Nor that riding to sleep
  I should hear him fly with the high fields         50
And wake to the farm forever fled from the childless land.
Oh as I was young and easy in the mercy of his means,
   Time held me green and dying
  Though I sang in my chains like the sea.


# AND DEATH SHALL HAVE NO DOMINION

And death shall have no dominion.
Dead men naked they shall be one
With the man in the wind and the west moon;
When their bones are picked clean and the clean bones gone,
They shall have stars at elbow and foot;
Though they go mad they shall be sane,
Though they sink through the sea they shall rise again;
Though lovers be lost love shall not;
And death shall have no dominion.

And death shall have no dominion.         10
Under the windings of the sea
They lying long shall not die windily;
Twisting on racks when sinews give way,
Strapped to a wheel, yet they shall not break;
Faith in their hands shall snap in two,
And the unicorn evils run them through;
Split all ends up they shan't crack;
And death shall have no dominion.

And death shall have no dominion.
No more may gulls cry at their ears         20
Or waves break loud on the seashores;
Where blew a flower may a flower no more
Lift its head to the blows of the rain;
Though they be mad and dead as nails,
Heads of the characters hammer through daisies;
Break in the sun till the sun breaks down,
And death shall have no dominion.

▶ *Randall Jarrell (1914-1965)*

# THE DEATH OF THE BALL TURRET GUNNER

From my mother's sleep I fell into the State,
And I hunched in its belly till my wet fur froze.
Six miles from earth, loosed from its dream of life,
I woke to black flak and the nightmare fighters.
When I died they washed me out of the turret with a hose.


▶ *Robert Lowell (1917-      )*

# MR. EDWARDS AND THE SPIDER

I saw the spiders marching through the air,
   Swimming from tree to tree that mildewed day
     In latter August when the hay
     Came creaking to the barn. But where
       The wind is westerly,
   Where gnarled November makes the spiders fly
   Into the apparitions of the sky,
   They purpose nothing but their ease and die
Urgently beating east to sunrise and the sea;

   What are we in the hands of the great God?           10
   It was in vain you set up thorn and briar
     In battle array against the fire
     And treason cracking in your blood;
       For the wild thorns grow tame
   And will do nothing to oppose the flame;
   Your lacerations tell the losing game
   You play against a sickness past your cure.
How will the hands be strong? How will the heart endure?

   A very little thing, a little worm,
   Or hourglass-blazoned spider, it is said,          20
     Can kill a tiger. Will the dead
     Hold up his mirror and affirm
       To the four winds the smell
   And flash of his authority? It's well
   If God who holds you to the pit of hell,
   Much as one holds a spider, will destroy,
Baffle and dissipate your soul. As a small boy

   On Windsor Marsh, I saw the spider die
   When thrown into the bowels of fierce fire:
     There's no long struggle, no desire          30
     To get up on its feet and fly—
       It stretches out its feet
   And dies. This is the sinner's last retreat;

Yes, and no strength exerted on the heat
Then sinews the abolished will, when sick
And full of burning, it will whistle on a brick.

But who can plumb the sinking of that soul?
Josiah Hawley, picture yourself cast
   Into a brick-kiln where the blast
    Fans your quick vitals to a coal—              40
      If measured by a glass,
How long would it seem burning! Let there pass
A minute, ten, ten trillion; but the blaze
Is infinite, eternal: this is death,
To die and know it. This is the Black Widow, death.

▶ *Philip Larkin (1922-     )*

# CHURCH GOING

Once I am sure there's nothing going on
I step inside, letting the door thud shut.
Another church: matting, seats, and stone,
And little books; sprawlings of flowers, cut
For Sunday, brownish now; some brass and stuff
Up at the holy end; the small neat organ;
And a tense, musty, unignorable silence,
Brewed God knows how long. Hatless, I take off
My cycle-clips in awkward reverence,

Move forward, run my hand around the font.           10
From where I stand, the roof looks almost new—
Cleaned, or restored? Someone would know: I don't.
Mounting the lectern, I peruse a few
Hectoring large-scale verses, and pronounce
'Here endeth' much more loudly than I'd meant.
The echoes snigger briefly. Back at the door
I sign the book, donate an Irish sixpence,
Reflect the place was not worth stopping for.

Yet stop I did: in fact I often do,                 20
And always end much at a loss like this,
Wondering what to look for; wondering, too,
When churches fall completely out of use
What we shall turn them into, if we shall keep
A few cathedrals chronically on show,
Their parchment, plate and pyx in locked cases,
And let the rest rent-free to rain and sheep.
Shall we avoid them as unlucky places?

Or, after dark, will dubious women come
To make their children touch a particular stone;

Pick simples for a cancer; or on some                                  30
Advised night see walking a dead one?
Power of some sort or other will go on
In games, in riddles, seemingly at random;
But superstition, like belief, must die,
And what remains when disbelief has gone?
Grass, weedy pavement, brambles, buttress, sky,

A shape less recognisable each week,
A purpose more obscure. I wonder who
Will be the last, the very last, to seek
This place for what it was; one of the crew                            40
That tap and jot and know what rood-lofts were?
Some ruin-bibber, randy for antique,
Or Christmas-addict, counting on a whiff
Of grown-and-bands and organ-pipes and myrrh?
Or will he be my representative,

Bored, uninformed, knowing the ghostly silt
Dispersed, yet tending to this cross of ground
Through suburb scrub because it held unspilt
So long and equably what since is found
Only in separation—marriage, and birth,                               50
And death, and thoughts of these—for whom was built
This special shell? For, though I've no idea
What this accoutred frowsty barn is worth,
It pleases me to stand in silence here;

A serious house on serious earth it is,
In whose blent air all our compulsions meet,
Are recognised, and robed as destinies.
And that much never can be obsolete,
Since someone will forever be surprising
A hunger in himself to be more serious,                                60
And gravitating with it to this ground,
Which, he once heard, was proper to grow wise in,
If only that so many dead lie round.


▶  *Allen Ginsberg (1926-       )*

# A SUPERMARKET IN CALIFORNIA

What thoughts I have of you tonight, Walt Whitman, for I walked
down the sidestreets under the trees with a headache self-conscious looking at the full moon.

In my hungry fatigue, and shopping for images, I went into the neon
fruit supermarket, dreaming of your enumerations!

What peaches and what penumbras! Whole families shopping at night!
Aisles full of husbands! Wives in the avocados, babies in the tomatoes!—
and you, Garcia Lorca, what were you doing down by the watermelons?

I saw you, Walt Whitman, childless, lonely old grubber, poking among the meats in the refrigerator and eyeing the grocery boys.                    10

I heard you asking questions of each: Who killed the pork chops? What price bananas? Are you my Angel?

I wandered in and out of the brilliant stacks of cans following you, and followed in my imagination by the store detective.

We strode down the open corridors together in our solitary fancy tasting artichokes, possessing every frozen delicacy, and never passing the cashier.

Where are we going, Walt Whitman? The doors close in an hour. Which way does your beard point tonight?

(I touch your book and dream of our odyssey in the supermarket and     20 feel absurd.)

Will we walk all night through solitary streets? The trees add shade to shade, lights out in the houses, we'll both be lonely.

Will we stroll dreaming of the lost America of love past blue automobiles in driveways, home to our silent cottage?

Ah, dear father, graybeard, lonely old courage-teacher, what America did you have when Charon quit poling his ferry and you got out on a smoking bank and stood watching the boat disappear on the black waters of Lethe?


# AMERICA

America I've given you all and now I'm nothing.
America two dollars and twentyseven cents January 17, 1956.
I can't stand on my own mind.
America when will we end the human war?
Go fuck yourself with your atom bomb.
I don't feel good don't bother me.
I won't write my poem till I'm in my right mind.
America when will you be angelic?
When will you take off your clothes?
When will you look at yourself through the grave?                        10
When will you be worthy of your million Trotskyites?
America why are your libraries full of tears?
America when will you send your eggs to India?
I'm sick of your insane demands.
It occurs to me that I am America.
I am talking to myself again.

Asia is rising against me.
I haven't got a chinaman's chance.
I'd better consider my national resources.
My national resources consist of two joints of marijuana millions of     20
        genitals an unpublishable private literature that goes 1400 miles an
        hour and twentyfive-thousand mental institutions.
I say nothing about my prisons nor the millions of underprivileged who
        live in my flowerpots under the light of five hundred suns.

I have abolished the whorehouses of France, Tangiers is the next to go.

My ambition is to be President despite the fact that I'm a Catholic.

America how can I write a holy litany in your silly mood?

I will continue like Henry Ford my strophes are as individual as his
    automobiles more so they're all different sexes.

America I will sell you strophes $2500 apiece $500 down on your old    30
    strophe

America free Tom Mooney

America save the Spanish Loyalists

America Sacco & Vanzetti must not die

America I am the Scottsboro boys.

America when I was seven Momma took me to Communist Cell meetings
    they sold us garbanzos a handful per ticket a ticket costs a nickel
    and the speeches were free everybody was angelic and sentimental
    about the workers it was all so sincere you have no idea what a good
    thing the party was in 1835 Scott Nearing was a grand old man a    40
    real mensch Mother Bloor made me cry I once saw Israel Amter
    plain. Everybody must have been a spy.

America you don't really want to go to war.

America it's them bad Russians.

Them Russians them Russians and them Chinamen. And them Russians.

The Russia wants to eat us alive. The Russia's power mad. She wants to
    take our cars from out our garages.

When can I go into the supermarket and buy what I need with my good
    looks?

America after all it is you and I who are perfect not the next world.    50

Your machinery is too much for me.

You made me want to be a saint.

There must be some other way to settle this argument.

Burroughs is in Tangiers I don't think he'll come back it's sinister.

Are you being sinister or is this some form of practical joke?

I'm trying to come to the point.

I refuse to give up my obsession.

America stop pushing I know what I'm doing.

America the plum blossoms are falling.

I haven't read the newspapers for months, everyday somebody goes on    60
    trial for murder.

America I feel sentimental about the Wobblies.

America I used to be a communist when I was a kid I'm not sorry.

I smoke marijuana every chance I get.

I sit in my house for days on end and stare at the roses in the closet.

When I go to Chinatown I get drunk and never get laid.

My mind is made up there's going to be trouble.

You should have seen me reading Marx.

My psychoanalyst thinks I'm perfectly right.

I won't say the Lord's Prayer.    70

I have mystical visions and cosmic vibrations.

America I still haven't told you what you did to Uncle Max after he came
    over from Russia.

I'm addressing you.
Are you going to let your emotional life be run by Time Magazine?
I'm obsessed by Time Magazine.
I read it every week.
Its cover stares at me every time I slink past the corner candystore.
I read it in the basement of the Berkeley Public Library.
It's always telling me about responsibility. Businessmen are serious.    80
     Movie producers are serious. Everybody's serious but me.

Her wants to grab Chicago. Her needs a Red Readers' Digest. Her wants
     our auto plants in Siberia. Him big bureaucracy running our filling
     stations.
That no good. Ugh. Him make Indians learn read. Him need big black
     niggers. Hah. Her make us all work sixteen hours a day. Help.
America this is quite serious.
America this is the impression I get from looking in the television set.
America is this correct?
I'd better get right down to the job.    · 90
It's true I don't want to join the Army or turn lathes in precision parts
     factories, I'm nearsighted and psychopathic anyway.
America I'm putting my queer shoulder to the wheel.


▶   *Thom Gunn (1929-     )*

# INNOCENCE

He ran the course and as he ran he grew,
And smelt his fragrance in the field. Already,
Running he knew the most he ever knew,
The egotism of a healthy body.

Ran into manhood, ignorant of the past:
Culture of guilt and guilt's vague heritage,
Self-pity and the soul; what he possessed
Was rich, potential, like the bud's tipped rage.

The Corps developed, it was plain to see,
Courage, endurance, loyalty and skill    10
To a morale firm as morality,
Hardening him to an instrument, until

The finitude of virtues that were there
Bodied within the swarthy uniform
A compact innocence, child-like and clear,
No doubt could penetrate, no act could harm.

When he stood near the Russian partisan
Being burned alive, he therefore could behold
The ribs wear gently through the darkening skin
And sicken only at the Northern cold,    20

Could watch the fat burn with a violet flame
And feel disgusted only at the smell,
And judge that all pain finishes the same
As melting quietly by his boots it fell.


▶ *Gregory Corso (1930-      )*

# MARRIAGE

*for Mr. and Mrs. Mike Goldberg*

Should I get married? Should I be good?
Astound the girl next door
with my velvet suit and faustus hood?
Don't take her to movies but to cemeteries
tell all about werewolf bathtubs and forked clarinets
then desire her and kiss her and all the preliminaries
and she going just so far and I understanding why
not getting angry saying You must feel! It's beautiful to feel!
Instead take her in my arms
lean against an old crooked tombstone                              10
and woo her the entire night the constellations in the sky—

When she introduces me to her parents
back straightened, hair finally combed, strangled by a tie,
should I sit knees together on their 3rd-degree sofa
and not ask Where's the bathroom?
How else to feel other than I am,
a young man who often thinks Flash Gordon soap—
O how terrible it must be for a young man
seated before a family and the family thinking
We never saw him before! He wants our Mary Lou!                   20
After tea and homemade cookies they ask What do you do?
Should I tell them? Would they like me then?
Say All right get married, we're losing a daughter
but we're gaining a son—
And should I then ask Where's the bathroom?

O God, and the wedding! All her family and her friends
and only a handful of mine all scroungy and bearded
just waiting to get at the drinks and food—
And the priest! he looking at me as if I masturbated
asking me Do you take this woman                                  30
for your lawful wedded wife?
And I, trembling what to say, say Pie Glue!
I kiss the bride all those corny men slapping me on the back:
She's all yours, boy! Ha-ha-ha!
And in their eyes you could see
some obscene honeymoon going on—

Then all that absurd rice and clanky cans and shoes
Niagara Falls! Hordes of us! Husbands! Wives! Flowers!
All streaming into cozy hotels
All going to do the same thing tonight                                    40
The indifferent clerk he knowing what was going to happen
The lobby zombies they knowing what
The whistling elevator man he knowing
The winking bellboy knowing
Everybody knows! I'd be almost inclined not to do anything!
Stay up all night! Stare that hotel clerk in the eye!
Screaming: I deny honeymoon! I deny honeymoon!
running rampant into those almost climactic suites
yelling Radio belly! Cat shovel!
O I'd live in Niagara forever! in a dark cave beneath the Falls      50
I'd sit there the Mad Honeymooner
devising ways to break marriages, a scourge of bigamy
a saint of divorce—

But I should get married I should be good
How nice it'd be to come home to her
and sit by the fireplace and she in the kitchen
aproned young and lovely wanting my baby
and so happy about me she burns the roast beef
and comes crying to me and I get up from my big papa chair
saying Christmas teeth! Radiant brains! Apple deaf!                   60
God what a husband I'd make! Yes, I should get married!
So much to do! like sneaking into Mr. Jones' house late at night
and cover his golf clubs with 1920 Norwegian books
Like hanging a picture of Rimbaud on the lawnmower
Like pasting Tannu Tuva postage stamps
all over the picket fence
Like when Mrs. Kindhead comes to collect
for the Community Chest
grab her and tell her There are unfavorable omens in the sky!
And when the mayor comes to get my vote tell him                      70
When are you going to stop people killing whales!
And when the milkman comes leave him a note in the bottle
Penguin dust, bring me penguin dust, I want penguin dust—

Yet if I should get married and it's Connecticut and snow
and she gives birth to a child and I am sleepless, worn,
up for nights, head bowed against the quiet window,
the past behind me,
finding myself in the most common of situations
a trembling man
knowledged with responsibility not twig-smear                         80
nor Roman coin soup —
O what would that be like!
Surely I'd give it for a nipple a rubber Tacitus
For a rattle a bag of broken Bach records

Tack Della Francesca all over its crib
Sew the Greek alphabet on its bib
And build for its playpen a roofless Parthenon—

No, I doubt I'd be that kind of father
not rural not snow no quiet window
but hot smelly tight New York City                                          90
seven flights up, roaches and rats in the walls
a fat Reichian wife screeching over potatoes Get a job!
And five nose-running brats in love with Batman
And the neighbors all toothless and dry haired
like those hag masses of the 18th century
all wanting to come in and watch TV
The landlord wants his rent
Grocery store Blue Cross Gas & Electric Knights of Columbus
Impossible to lie back and dream Telephone snow,
ghost parking—                                                            100
No! I should not get married I should never get married!

But—imagine if I were married to a beautiful
sophisticated woman
tall and pale wearing an elegant black dress
and long black gloves
holding a cigarette holder in one hand
and a highball in the other
and we lived high up in a penthouse with a huge window
from which we could see all of New York
and even farther on clearer days                                          110
No, can't imagine myself married to that pleasant prison dream—

O but what about love? I forget love
not that I am incapable of love
it's just that I see love as odd as wearing shoes—
I never wanted to marry a girl who was like my mother
And Ingrid Bergman was always impossible
And there's maybe a girl now but she's already married
And I don't like men and—
but there's got to be somebody!
Because what if I'm 60 years old and not married,                         120
all alone in a furnished room with pee stains on my underwear
and everybody else is married! All the universe married but me!

Ah, yet well I know that were a woman possible
as I am possible
then marriage would be possible—
Like SHE in her lonely alien gaud waiting her Egyptian lover
so I wait—bereft of 2,000 years and the bath of life.

# BUT I DO NOT NEED KINDNESS

### 1

I have known the strange nurses of Kindness,
I have seen them kiss the sick, attend the old,
give candy to the mad!
I have watched them, at night, dark and sad,
rolling wheelchairs by the sea!
I have known the fat pontiffs of Kindness,
the little old grey-haired lady,
the neighborhood priest,
the famous poet,
the mother,                                          10
I have known them all!
I have watched them, at night, dark and sad,
pasting posters of mercy
on the stark posts of despair.

### 2

I have known Almighty Kindness Herself!
I have sat beside Her pure white feet,
gaining Her confidence!
We spoke of nothing unkind,
but one night I was tormented by those strange nurses,
those fat pontiffs                                    20
The little old lady rode a spiked car over my head!
The priest cut open my stomach, put his hands in me,
and cried:—Where's your soul! Where's your soul!—
The famous poet picked me up
and threw me out of the window!
The mother abandoned me!
I ran to Kindness, broke into Her chamber,
and profaned!
with an unnamable knife I gave Her a thousand wounds,
and inflicted them with filth!                        30
I carried Her away, on my back, like a ghoul!
down the cobble-stoned night!
Dogs howled! Cats fled! All windows closed!
I carried Her ten flights of stairs!
Dropped Her on the floor of my small room,
and kneeling beside Her, I wept. I wept.

### 3

But what is Kindness? I have killed Kindness,
but what is it?
You are kind because you live a kind life.
St. Francis was kind.                                 40
The landlord is kind.
A cane is kind.
Can I say people, sitting in parks, are kinder?

▶ *Sylvia Plath (1932-1963)*

# DADDY

You do not do, you do not do
Any more, black shoe
In which I have lived like a foot
For thirty years, poor and white,
Barely daring to breathe or Achoo.

Daddy, I have had to kill you.
You died before I had time—
Marble-heavy, a bag full of God,
Ghastly statue with one grey toe
Big as a Frisco seal                                    10

And a head in the freakish Atlantic
Where it pours bean green over blue
In the waters off beautiful Nauset.
I used to pray to recover you.
Ach, du.

In the German tongue, in the Polish town
Scraped flat by the roller
Of wars, wars, wars.
But the name of the town is common.
My Polack friend                                       20

Says there are a dozen or two.
So I never could tell where you
Put your foot, your root,
I never could talk to you.
The tongue stuck in my jaw.

It stuck in a barb wire snare.
Ich, ich, ich, ich,
I could hardly speak.
I thought every German was you
And the language obscene                               30

An engine, an engine
Chuffing me off like a Jew.
A Jew to Dachau, Auschwitz, Belsen.
I began to talk like a Jew.
I think I may well be a Jew.

The snows of the Tyrol, the clear beer of Vienna
Are not very pure or true.
With my gypsy ancestress and my weird luck

And my Taroc pack and my Taroc pack
I may be a bit of a Jew.                               40

I have always been scared of *you*,
With your Luftwaffe, your gobbledygoo.
And your neat moustache
And your Aryan eye, bright blue,
Panzer-man, panzer-man, O You—

Not God but a swastika
So black no sky could squeak through.
Every woman adores a Fascist,
The boot in the face, the brute
Brute heart of a brute like you.                       50

You stand at the blackboard, daddy,
In the picture I have of you,
A cleft in your chin instead of your foot
But no less a devil for that, no not
Any less the black man who

Bit my pretty red heart in two.
I was ten when they buried you.
At twenty I tried to die
And get back, back, back to you.
I thought even the bones would do.                     60

But they pulled me out of the sack,
And they stuck me together with glue,
And then I knew what to do.
I made a model of you,
A man in black with a Meinkampf look

And a love of the rack and the screw.
And I said I do, I do.
So daddy, I'm finally through,
The black telephone's off at the root,
The voices just can't worm through.                    70

If I've killed one man, I've killed two—
The vampire who said he was you
And drank my blood for a year,
Seven years, if you want to know.
Daddy, you can lie back now.

There's a stake in your fat black heart
And the villagers never liked you.
They are dancing and stamping on you.
They always *knew* it was you.
Daddy, daddy, you bastard, I'm through.                80

▶ *John Updike (1932-        )*

# EX-BASKETBALL PLAYER

Pearl Avenue runs past the high school lot,
Bends with the trolley tracks, and stops, cut off
Before it has a chance to go two blocks,
At Colonel McComsky Plaza. Berth's Garage
Is on the corner facing west, and there,
Most days, you'll find Flick Webb, who helps Berth out.

Flick stands tall among the idiot pumps—
Five on a side, the old bubble-head style,
Their rubber elbows hanging loose and low.
One's nostrils are two S's, and his eyes                          10
An E and O. And one is squat, without
A head at all—more of a football type.

Once, Flick played for the high school team, the Wizards.
He was good: in fact, the best. In '46,
He bucketed three hundred ninety points,
A county record still. The ball lover Flick.
I sam him rack up thirty-eight or forty
In one home game. His hands were like wild birds.

He never learned a trade; he just sells gas,
Checks oil, and changes flats. Once in a while,                   20
As a gag, he dribbles an inner tube,
But most of us remember anyway.
His hands are fine and nervous on the lug wrench.
It makes no difference to the lug wrench, though.

Off work, he hangs around Mae's Luncheonette.
Grease-grey and kind of coiled, he plays pinball,
Sips lemon cokes, and smokes those thin cigars;
Flick seldom speaks to Mae, just sits and nods
Beyond her face towards the bright applauding tiers
Of Necco Wafers, Nibs, and Juju Beads.                           30

# ►►► METRICS

Rhythm, or measured motion, is an essential part of the structure of poetry; it also, of course, influences the content. Because poetry is the literary genre most often read aloud, sound is a crucial factor. A boring or difficult rhythmic pattern can detract from even the most beautiful or clever lines. While metrics can become an extremely complex and involved subject, knowledge of a few principal terms is enough for the beginning poetry reader; increased knowledge and experience in reading poetry will bring greater understanding of the subject; when the metrical pattern is studied in the context of the poem as a whole, it seems more a natural and integral part, rather than a forcibly abstracted confusion.

First of all, sound patterns involve recurrence, the alternation between accented and non-accented syllables. Meter means, basically, organized recurrence; in other words, accents occurring at equal intervals. This is one element that distinguishes verse from prose. An accented syllable is one which is given greater stress and prominence than its neighbors. Stress means basically the same thing as accent, though it often refers mainly to the force of utterance, to the duration and pitch, and to the transition between sounds.

The accent patterns may be determined by etymological requirements (based on the language used), rhetorical requirements (based on the relative importance of each part of the poem), and metrical requirements. Time intervals are designated by unstressed syllables and pauses.

Meter is measured by the foot, line, and stanza. A foot consists of one accented syllable with one or two, occasionally three or four, unaccented ones. The main types of feet are the iamb, trochee, and spondee, each of which contains two syllables, and the anapest and dactyl, which contain three.

The line is determined by the number of feet; beginning with the one-foot line, they are called the monometer, dimeter, trimeter, tetrameter, pentameter, hexameter, heptameter, and octometer. Caesurae are lines of eight or more syllables divided into units corresponding to natural speech patterns; if placed after a stressed syllable, a caesurea is called masculine, after an unstressed syllable, feminine. An end-stopped line is one in which the end corresponds with the end of a natural sentence or phrase; a run-on is a line in which the main idea extends into the next line.

There are a number of types of rime: end rime, in which the final word of a line rimes with the final word of another line in some sort of regular pattern; internal rime, in which the line is divided into two parts, the last word in the first half riming with the last word in the last; inexact or slant rime, also called half-rime, in which the words rimed sound similar in some way but are not really rimed; and true or exact rime.

A stanza is a group of lines whose metrical pattern is repeated throughout the poem; the number of lines varies greatly from poem to poem. Stanzas generally range from two to nine lines; they are called the couplet, tercet, quatrain, quintrain, sester, seven, eight, and nine-line stanzas. Series of stanzas are described in terms of stanzaic form, of which the main considerations are the rime scheme, position of the refrain, if any, metrical foot prevalent, and the number of feet in each line. Lines without stanzas are said to be in continuous form.

Scansion, the process by which verse is measured, consists in identifying the foot, finding the number of feet in each line, determining whether there is a pattern, and, if so, describing the stanzaic pattern. Scansion tends to be arbitrary, relative, and often inexact. Furthermore, good, smooth, steady meter is no indication of a superior poem, it is merely one aspect of poetry presentation. A too-smooth metric pattern, in fact, can become extremely monotonous, detracting from the poem's other qualities.

Other terms involved in discussing sound patterns include blank verse, which is unrimed iambic pentameter; free verse, which contains no metrical patterns or restrictions (the difference between free verse and rhythmical prose is that the former is structured in lines, the latter is not); parallelism, the repetition of syntax used to add information and increase significance of any particular part of the poem; and various sound devices.

Onomatopoeia is the condition in which sound suggests and reflects meaning; through poetic intensives, through stressed and underplayed words, sounds, and phrases, through use of euphony (pleasant, harmonious sound combinations) and cacophony (discordant sounds), meaning is implied, sometimes subtly, sometimes quite obviously. Assonance is a term meaning repetition of similar vowel sounds within the same word, phrase or line; alliteration means the repetition of similar or identical consonant sounds at the beginning of syllables; consonance is the repetition of two or more consonant sounds within the same word or groups of words.

At its best, meter can underline and re-enforce meaning; as an integral part of the poem's form, it can complement and enrich the content. The difference between the poem's two essential rhythms, that which is expected and that which occurs, may contribute greatly to the excitement, originality, and smoothness of expression; a successful balance between the two will benefit any poem. The type of metrical patterns used naturally has some effect on the message conveyed. Tone and mood are especially affected by sound patterns; happiness, grief, sobriety, and frivolity can all be expressed by certain types of rime, meter, and sound devices. The poet can create a hard, clear, cutting sound or a soft, flowing, languid one; his sound patterns, choppy or smooth, lively or somber, can greatly influence the reader's reception and interpretation of the poem. The poet can create an ironic effect by introducing an obvious discrepancy between the meter, rhythm, and sound patterns and the message they convey. He can increase or modify the prominence and significance of his imagery, figurative language, and symbolism, depending on the pattern of placement. An unusual arrangement of words and lines, affecting the reader visually before he even begins to read and evaluate, will probably affect his reactions and interpretation.

Poetry demands harmony, integration, and balance between unlike elements; it demands that the message be successfully coordinated with the means of presentation to achieve the best possible effect. The major importance of any poem is, of course, its guiding theme or idea, but the impact of this idea depends on skillful presentation; a good metrical arrangement is vital to a good poem.

# LORD RANDAL

"O where ha you been, Lord Randal, my son?
And where ha you been, my handsome young man?"
"I ha been at the greenwood; mother, mak my bed soon,
For I'm wearied wi huntin, and fain wad lie down."

"An wha met ye there, Lord Randal, my son?
An wha met you there, my handsome young man?"
"O I met wi my true-love; mother, mak my bed soon,
For I'm wearied wi huntin, and fain wad lie down."

"And what did she give you, Lord Randal, my son?
And what did she give you, my handsome young man?"                    10
"Eels fried in a pan, mother, mak my bed soon,
For I'm wearied wi' hunting and fain wad lie down."

"And wha gat your leavins, Lord Randal, my son?
And wha gat your leavins, my handsome young man?"
"My hawks and my hounds, mother, mak my bed soon,
For I'm wearied wi' hunting and fain wad lie down."

"And what becam of them, Lord Randal, my son?
And what becam of them, my handsome young man?"
"They stretched their legs out an died, mother, mak my bed soon,
For I'm wearied wi' hunting and fain wad lie down."                   20

"O I fear you are poisoned, Lord Randal, my son.
I fear you are poisoned, my handsome young man."
"O yes, I am poisoned, mother, mak my bed soon,
For I'm sick at the heart and I fain wad lie down."

"What d' ye leave to your mother, Lord Randal, my son?
What d' ye leave to your mother, my handsome young man?"
"Four and twenty milk kye, mother, mak my bed soon,
For I'm sick at the heart and I fain wad lie down."

"What d' ye leave to your sister, Lord Randal, my son?
What d' ye leave to your sister, my handsome young man?"              30
"My gold and my silver, mother, mak my bed soon,
For I'm sick at the heart an I fain wad lie down."

"What d' ye leave to your brother, Lord Randal, my son?
What d' ye leave to your brother, my handsome young man?"
"My houses and my lands, mother, mak my bed soon,
For I'm sick at the heart and I fain wad lie down."

"What d' ye leave to your true-love, Lord Randal, my son?
What d' ye leave to your true-love, my handsome young man?"
"I leave her hell and fire, mother, mak my bed soon,
For I'm sick at the heart and I fain wad lie down."                   40

## WESTERN WIND

O Western wind, when wilt thou blow
   That the small rain down can rain?
Christ, that my love were in my arms,
   And I in my bed again!

▶ *Edmund Spenser (1522-1599)*

## from *AMORETTI*

SONNET 79

Men call you fair, and you do credit it,
For that yourself ye daily such do see;
But the true fair, that is the gentle wit,
And virtuous mind, is much more praised of me.
For all the rest, however fair it be,
Shall turn to nought, and lose that glorious hue;
But only that is permanent and free
From frail corruption that doth flesh ensue.
That is true beauty; that doth argue you
To be divine and born of heavenly seed,         10
Derived from that fair Spirit, from whom all true
And perfect beauty did at first proceed.
He only fair, and what he fair hath made;
And other fair, like flowers, untimely fade.

▶ *Sir Edward Dyer (1543-1607)*

## MY MIND TO ME A KINGDOM IS

My mind to me a kingdom is;
   Such present joys therein I find
That it excels all other bliss
   That earth affords or grows by kind.
Though much I want which most would have,
Yet still my mind forbids to crave.

No princely pomp, no wealthy store,
   No force to win the victory,
No wily wit to salve a sore,
   No shape to feed a loving eye;         10
To none of these I yield as thrall,—
For why? My mind doth serve for all.

I see how plenty surfeits oft,
    And hasty climbers soon do fall;
I see that those which are aloft
    Mishap doth threaten most of all;
They get with toil, they keep with fear.
Such cares my mind could never bear.


▶ *William Shakespeare (1564-1616)*

# SONNET 104

To me, fair friend, you never can be old,
For as you were when first your eye I eyed
Such seems your beauty still. Three winters cold
Have from the forests shook three summer's pride,
Three beauteous springs to yellow autumn turned
In process of the seasons have I seen,
Three April perfumes in three hot Junes burned,
Since first I saw you fresh, which yet are green.
Ah, yet doth beauty, like a dial-hand,
Steal from his figure, and no pace perceived;                    10
So your sweet hue, which methinks still doth stand,
Hath motion, and mine eye may be deceived:
For fear of which, hear this, thou age unbred:
Ere you were born was beauty's summer dead.


▶ *Thomas Campion (1567-1620)*

# MY SWEETEST LESBIA

My sweetest Lesbia, let us live and love,
And though the sager sort our deeds reprove,
Let us not weigh them. Heaven's great lamps do dive
Into their west, and straight again revive,
But soon as once set is our little light,
Then must we sleep one ever-during night.

If all would lead their lives in love like me,
Then bloody swords and armor should not be,
No drum nor trumpet peaceful sleeps should move,
Unless alarm came from the camp of love.                        10
But fools do live and waste their little light,
And seek with pain their ever-during night.

When timely death my life and fortune ends,
Let not my hearse be vexed with mourning friends,

But let all lovers, rich in triumph, come
And with sweet pastimes grace my happy tomb;
And Lesbia, close up thou my little light,
And crown with love my ever-during night.


▶ *John Donne (1573-1631)*

# SONG

Go and catch a falling star,
  Get with child a mandrake root,
Tell me where all past years are,
  Or who cleft the devil's foot,
Teach me to hear mermaids singing,
Or to keep off envy's stinging,
      And find
      What wind
Serves to advance an honest mind.

If thou be'st born to strange sights,           10
  Things invisible to see,
Ride ten thousand days and nights,
  Till age snow white hairs on thee,
Thou, when thou return'st, wilt tell me
All strange wonders that befell thee,
      And swear
      No where
Lives a woman true and fair.

If thou find'st one, let me know;
  Such a pilgrimage were sweet;                20
Yet do not, I would not go,
  Though at next door we might meet:
Though she were true when you met her,
And last till you write your letter,
      Yet she
      Will be
False, ere I come, to two or three.


▶ *Robert Herrick (1591-1674)*

# THE NIGHT-PIECE, TO JULIA

Her eyes the glow-worm lend thee,
The shooting stars attend thee:
    And the elves also,
    Whose little eyes glow
Like the sparks of fire, befriend thee.

No will-o'-th'-wisp mislight thee;
Nor snake, or slow-worm bite thee:
    But on, on thy way,
    Not making a stay,
Since ghost there's none to affright thee.     10

Let not the dark thee cumber;
What though the moon does slumber:
    The stars of the night
    Will lend thee their light,
Like tapers clear without number.

Then, Julia, let me woo thee,
Thus, thus to come unto me:
    And when I shall meet
    Thy silv'ry feet,
My soul I'll pour into thee.                    20

▶ *George Herbert (1593-1633)*

# THE ALTAR

     A broken altar, Lord, Thy servant rears,
     Made of a heart and cemented with tears;
       Whose parts are as Thy hand did frame;
       No workman's tool hath touched the same.
             A     heart     alone
             Is     such    a     stone
             As     nothing     but
             Thy power doth cut.
             Wherefore each part
             Of my hard heart         10
             Meets in this frame
             To praise Thy name:
    That, if I chance to hold my peace,
    These stones to praise Thee may not cease.
  Oh, let Thy blessed sacrifice be mine
  And sanctify this altar to be thine!

# EASTER WINGS

     Lord, who createdst man in wealth and store,
       Though foolishly he lost the same,
         Decaying more and more
            Till he became
             Most poor:
             With Thee
           O let me rise
       As larks, harmoniously.
     And sing this day Thy victories:
    Then shall the fall further the flight in me.   10

▶ *Alexander Pope (1688-1744)*

# SOUND AND SENSE

     True ease in writing comes from art, not chance,
     As those move easiest who have learned to dance.
     'Tis not enough no harshness gives offense,
     The sound must seem an echo to the sense:
     Soft is the strain when Zephyr gently blows,
     And the smooth stream in smoother numbers flows;
     But when loud surges lash the sounding shore,
     The hoarse, rough verse should like the torrent roar;
     When Ajax strives some rock's vast weight to throw,
     The line too labors, and the words move slow;     10

Not so, when swift Camilla scours the plain,
Flies o'er the unbending corn, and skims along the main.
Hear how Timotheus' varied lays surprise,
And bid alternate passions fall and rise!

▶ *Thomas Gray (1716-1771)*

## ELEGY WRITTEN IN A COUNTRY CHURCHYARD

The curfew tolls the knell of parting day,
The lowing herd winds slowly o'er the lea,
The plowman homeward plods his weary way,
And leaves the world to darkness and to me.

Now fades the glimmering landscape on the sight,
And all the air a solemn stillness holds,
Save where the beetle wheels his droning flight,
And drowsy tinklings lull the distant folds;

Save that from yonder ivy-mantled tow'r
The moping owl does to the moon complain                    10
Of such, as wand'ring near her secret bow'r,
Molest her ancient solitary reign.

Beneath those rugged elms, that yew-tree's shade,
Where heaves the turf in many a mould'ring heap,
Each in his narrow cell for ever laid,
The rude forefathers of the hamlet sleep.

The breezy call of incense-breathing morn,
The swallow twitt'ring from the straw-built shed,
The cock's shrill clarion, or the echoing horn,
No more shall rouse them from their lowly bed.             20

For them no more the blazing hearth shall burn,
Or busy housewife ply her evening care:
No children run to lisp their sire's return,
Or climb his knees the envied kiss to share.

Oft did the harvest to their sickle yield,
Their furrow oft the stubborn glebe has broke;
How jocund did they drive their team afield!
How bowed the woods beneath their sturdy stroke!

Let not Ambition mock their useful toil,
Their homely joys, and destiny obscure;                    30
Nor Grandeur hear with a disdainful smile,
The short and simple annals of the poor.

The boast of heraldry, the pomp of pow'r,
And all that beauty, all that wealth e'er gave

Awaits alike th' inevitable hour.
The paths of glory lead but to the grave.

Nor you, ye Proud, impute to These the fault,
If Memory o'er their Tomb no Trophies raise,
Where through the long-drawn aisle and fretted vault
The pealing anthem swells the note of praise.                    40

Can storied urn or animated bust
Back to its mansion call the fleeting breath?
Can Honor's voice provoke the silent dust,
Or Flattery sooth the dull cold ear of Death?

Perhaps in this neglected spot is laid
Some heart once pregnant with celestial fire;
Hands, that the rod of empire might have swayed,
Or waked to ecstasy the living lyre.

But Knowledge to their eyes her ample page
Rich with the spoils of time did ne'er unroll;                   50
Chill Penury repressed their noble rage,
And froze the genial current of the soul.

Full many a gem of purest ray serene,
The darkness unfathomed caves of ocean bear:
Full many a flower is born to blush unseen,
And waste its sweetness on the desert air.

Some village-Hampden, that with dauntless breast
The little Tyrant of his fields withstood;
Some mute inglorious Milton here may rest,
Some Cromwell guiltless of his country's blood.                  60

The applause of listening senates to command,
The threats of pain and ruin to despise,
To scatter plenty o'er a smiling land,
And read their history in a nation's eyes,

Their lot forbade: nor circumscribed alone
Their growing virtues, but their crimes confin'd;
Forbade to wade through slaughter to a throne,
And shut the gates of mercy on mankind,

The struggling pangs of conscious truth to hide,
To quench the blushes of ingenuous shame,                        70
Or heap the shrine of Luxury and Pride
With incense kindled at the Muse's flame.

Far from the madding crowd's ignoble strife,
Their sober wishes never learned to stray;
Along the cool sequestered vale of life
They kept the noiseless tenor of their way.

Yet even these bones from insult to protect,
Some frail memorial still erected nigh,

With uncouth rhymes and shapeless sculpture decked,
Implores the passing tribute of a sigh.                    80

Their name, their years, spelt by the unlettered muse,
The place of fame and elegy supply:
And many a holy text around she strews,
That teach the rustic moralist to die.

For who to dumb forgetfulness a prey,
This pleasing anxious being e'er resigned,
Left the warm precincts of the cheerful day,
Nor cast one longing lingering look behind?

On some fond breast the parting soul relies,         90
Some pious drops the closing eye requires;
E'en from the tomb the voice of Nature cries,
E'en in our ashes live their wonted fires.

For thee, who mindful of the unhonored dead
Dost in these lines their artless tale relate,
If chance, by lonely contemplation led,
Some kindred spirit shall inquire thy fate,

Haply some hoary-headed swain may say,
"Oft have we seen him at the peep of dawn
Brushing with hasty steps the dews away
To meet the sun upon the upland lawn.              100

"There at the foot of yonder nodding beech
That wreathes its old fantastic roots so high,
His listless length at noontide would he stretch,
And pore upon the brook that babbles by.

"Hard by yon wood, now smiling as in scorn,
Muttering his wayward fancies he would rove,
Now drooping, woeful wan, like one forlorn,
Or crazed with care, or crossed in hopeless love.

"One morn I missed him on the customed hill,
Along the heath and near his favorite tree;        110
Another came; nor yet beside the rill,
Nor up the lawn, nor at the wood was he;

"The next with dirges due in sad array
Slow through the church-way path we saw him borne.
Approach and read (for thou can'st read) the lay
Graved on the stone beneath yon agéd thorn."


THE EPITAPH

*Here rests his head upon the lap of earth*
*A youth to Fortune and to Fame unknown.*
*Fair Science frowned not on his humble birth,*
*And Melancholy marked him for her own.*            120

*Large was his bounty, and his soul sincere,*
*Heaven did a recompense as largely send:*
*He gave to Misery all he had, a tear,*
*He gained from Heaven ('twas all he wished) a friend.*

*No farther seek his merits to disclose,*
*Or draw his frailties from their dread abode,*
*(There they alike in trembling hope repose)*
*The bosom of his Father and his God.*

▶ *William Wordsworth (1770-1850)*

# A SLUMBER DID MY SPIRIT SEAL

A slumber did my spirit seal;
  I had no human fears:
She seem'd a thing that could not feel
  The touch of earthly years.

No motion has she now, no force;
  She neither hears nor sees;
Roll'd round in earth's diurnal course,
  With rocks, and stones, and trees.

▶ *Walter Savage Landor (1775-1864)*

# TO AGE

Welcome, old friend! These many years
  Have we lived door by door;
The Fates have laid aside their shears
  Perhaps for some few more.

I was indocile at an age
  When better boys were taught,
But thou at length hast made me sage,
  If I am sage in aught.

Little I know from other men,
  Too little they from me,                    10

But thou hast pointed well the pen
  That writes these lines to thee.

Thanks for expelling Fear and Hope,
  One vile, the other vain;
One's scourge, the other's telescope,
  I shall not see again.

Rather what lies before my feet
  My notice shall engage—
He who hath braved Youth's dizzy heat
  Dreads not the frost of Age.               20

▶ *John Keats (1795-1821)*

# ON FIRST LOOKING INTO CHAPMAN'S HOMER

Much have I travelled in the realms of gold,
And many goodly states and kingdoms seen:
Round many western islands have I been
Which bards in fealty to Apollo hold.
Oft of one wide expanse had I been told
That deep-browed Homer ruled as his demesne;

Yet did I never breathe its pure serene
Till I heard Chapman speak out loud and bold:
Then felt I like some watcher of the skies
When a new planet swims into his ken;                    10
Or like stout Cortez when with eagle eyes
He stared at the Pacific—and all his men
Looked at each other with a wild surmise—
Silent, upon a peak in Darien.

▶  *Edward Fitzgerald (1809-1883)*

## *from* THE RUBÁIYÁT OF OMAR KHAYYÁM

### 12

A Book of Verses underneath the Bough,
A Jug of Wine, a Loaf of Bread—and Thou
    Beside me singing in the Wilderness—
Oh, Wilderness were Paradise enow!

### 13

Some for the Glories of This World; and some
Sigh for the Prophet's Paradise to come;
    Ah, take the Cash, and let the Credit go,
Nor heed the rumble of a distant Drum!

### 16

The Worldly Hope men set their Hearts upon
Turns Ashes—or it prospers; and anon,                    10
    Like Snow upon the Desert's dusty Face,
Lighting a little hour or two—is gone.

### 63

Oh, threats of Hell and Hopes of Paradise!
One thing at least is certain—*This* Life flies;
    One thing is certain and the rest is Lies;
The Flower that once has blown for ever dies.

### 66

I sent my Soul through the Invisible,
Some letter of that After-life to spell:
    And by and by Soul return'd to me,
And answer'd "I Myself am Heav'n and Hell."              20

### 71

The Moving Finger writes; and, having writ,
Moves on: nor all your Piety nor Wit
    Shall lure it back to cancel half a Line,
Nor all your Tears wash out a Word of it.

### 72

And that inverted Bowl they call the Sky,
Whereunder crawling coop'd we live and die,
   Lift not your hands to *It* for help—for It
As impotently moves as you or I.

### 99

Ah, Love! could you and I with Him conspire
To grasp this sorry Scheme of Things entire,         30
   Would not we shatter it to bits—and then
Remold it nearer to the Heart's Desire!

### 100

Yon rising Moon that looks for us again—
How oft hereafter will she wax and wane;
   How oft hereafter rising look for us
Through this same Garden—and for *one* in vain!

### 101

And when like her, O Sáki, you shall pass
Among the Guests Star-scattered on the Grass,
   And in your joyous errand reach the spot
Where I made One—turn down an empty Glass!       40

▶ *Edgar Allan Poe (1809-1849)*

# THE BELLS

### I

Hear the sledges with the bells—
Silver bells!
What a world of merriment their melody foretells!
How they tinkle, tinkle, tinkle,
In the icy air of night!
While the stars that oversprinkle
All the heavens, seem to twinkle
With a crystalline delight;
Keeping time, time, time
In a sort of Runic rhyme,       10
To the tintinnabulation that so musically wells
From the bells, bells, bells, bells,
Bells, bells, bells—
From the jingling and the tinkling of the bells.

### II

Hear the mellow wedding bells—
Golden bells!
What a world of happiness their harmony foretells!

Through the balmy air of night
How they ring out their delight!—
From the molten-golden notes,
And all in tune,
What a liquid ditty floats
To the turtle-dove that listens, while she gloats
On the moon!
Oh, from out the sounding cells,
What a gush of euphony voluminously wells!
How it swells!
How it dwells
On the Future—how it tells
Of the rapture that impels
To the swinging and the ringing
Of the bells, bells, bells—
Of the bells, bells, bells, bells,
Bells, bells, bells—
To the rhyming and the chiming of the bells!

### III

Hear the loud alarum bells—
Brazen bells!
What a tale of terror, now, their turbulency tells!
In the startled ear of night
How they scream out their affright!
Too much horrified to speak,
They can only shriek, shriek,
Out of tune,
In a clamorous appealing to the mercy of the fire,
In a mad expostulation with the deaf and frantic fire.
Leaping higher, higher, higher,
With a desperate desire,
And a resolute endeavor
Now—now to sit, or never,
By the side of the pale-faced moon.
Oh, the bells, bells, bells!
What a tale their terror tells
Of Despair!
How they clang, and clash, and roar!
What a horror they outpour
On the bosom of the palpitating air!
Yet the ear, it fully knows,
By the twanging
And the clanging,
How the danger ebbs and flows;
Yet the ear distinctly tells,
In the jangling
And the wrangling,
How the danger sinks and swells,
By the sinking or the swelling in the anger of the bells—
Of the bells,—

Of the bells, bells, bells, bells,
    Bells, bells, bells—
In the clamor and the clangor of the bells!

## IV

    Hear the tolling of the bells—           70
        Iron bells!
What a world of solemn thought their monody compels!
    In the silence of the night,
    How we shiver with affright
At the melancholy menace of their tone!
    For every sound that floats
    From the rust within their throats
        Is a groan.
      And the people—ah, the people—
      They that dwell up in the steeple,     80
        All alone,
    And who tolling, tolling, tolling,
      In that muffled monotone,
    Feel a glory in so rolling
    On the human heart a stone—
They are neither man nor woman—
They are neither brute nor human—
      They are Ghouls:—
    And their king it is who tolls:—
    And he rolls, rolls, rolls,     90
        Rolls
    A paean from the bells!
    And his merry bosom swells
      With the paean of the bells!
    And he dances, and he yells;
Keeping time, time, time,
In a sort of Runic rhyme,
    To the paean of the bells—
      Of the bells:—
Keeping time, time, time,     100
In a sort of Runic rhyme,
    To the throbbing of the bells—
    Of the bells, bells, bells—
    To the sobbing of the bells;
Keeping time, time, time,
    As he knells, knells, knells,
In a happy Runic rhyme,
    To the rolling of the bells—
    Of the bells, bells, bells:—
    To the tolling of the bells—     110
Of the bells, bells, bells, bells,
    Bells, bells, bells—
To the moaning and the groaning of the bells.

▶ *Alfred, Lord Tennyson (1809-1892)*

## ULYSSES

It little profits that an idle king,
By this still hearth, among these barren crags,
Matched with an aged wife, I mete and dole
Unequal laws unto a savage race,
That hoard, and sleep, and feed, and know not me.
I cannot rest from travel; I will drink
Life to the lees. All times I have enjoyed
Greatly, have suffered greatly, both with those
That loved me, and alone; on shore, and when
Thro' scudding drifts the rainly Hyades                          10
Vext the dim sea. I am become a name;
For always roaming with a hungry heart
Much have I seen and known,—cities of men
And manners, climates, councils, governments,
Myself not least, but honored of them all,—
And drunk delight of battle with my peers,
Far on the ringing plains of windy Troy.
I am a part of all that I have met;
Yet all experience is an arch wherethro'
Gleams that untravelled world whose margin fades             20
For ever and for ever when I move.
How dull it is to pause, to make an end,
To rust unburnished, not to shine in use!
As tho' to breathe were life! Life piled on life
Were all too little, and of one to me
Little remains, but every hour is saved
From that eternal silence, something more,
A bringer of new things: and vile it were
For some three suns to store and hoard myself,
And this gray spirit yearning in desire                         30
To follow knowledge like a sinking star,
Beyond the utmost bound of human thought.

This is my son, mine own Telemachus,
To whom I leave the scepter and the isle,—
Well-loved of me, discerning to fulfill
This labor, by slow prudence to make mild
A rugged people, and thro' soft degrees
Subdue them to the useful and the good.
Most blameless is he, centered in the sphere
Of common duties, decent not to fail                            40
In offices of tenderness, and pay
Meet adoration to my household gods,
When I am gone. He works his work, I mine.

There lies the port; the vessel puffs her sail:
There gloom the dark, broad seas. My mariners,
Souls that have toiled, and wrought, and thought with me—

That ever with a frolic welcome took
The thunder and the sunshine, and opposed
Free hearts, free foreheads—you and I are old;
Old age hath yet his honor and his toil.                            50
Death closes all; but something ere the end,
Some work of noble note, may yet be done,
Not unbecoming men that strove with Gods.
The lights begin to twinkle from the rocks;
The long day wanes; the slow moon climbs; the deep
Moans round with many voices. Come, my friends,
'Tis not too late to seek a newer world.
Push off, and sitting well in order smite
The sounding furrows; for my purpose holds
To sail beyond the sunset, and the baths                            60
Of all the western stars, until I die.
It may be that the gulfs will wash us down;
It may be we shall touch the Happy Isles,
And see the great Achilles, whom we knew.
Though much is taken, much abides; and though
We are not now that strength which in old days
Moved earth and heaven, that which we are, we are:
One equal temper of heroic hearts,
Made weak by time and fate, but strong in will
To strive, to seek, to find, and not to yield.                      70


▶  *Robert Browning (1812-1889)*

# HOME-THOUGHTS  FROM  ABROAD

Oh, to be in England
Now that April's there,
And whoever wakes in England
Sees, some morning, unaware,
That the lowest boughs and the brush-wood sheaf
Round the elm-tree bole are in tiny leaf,
While the chaffinch sings on the orchard bough
In England—now!

And after April, when May follows,
And the whitethroat builds, and all the swallows!                   10
Hark, where my blossomed pear-tree in the hedge
Leans to the field and scatters on the clover
Blossoms and dewdrops—at the bent spray's edge—
That's the wise thrush; he sings each song twice over,
Lest you should think he never could recapture
The first fine careless rapture!
And though the fields look rough with hoary dew,
All will be gay when moontide wakes anew
The buttercups, the little children's dower,
—Far brighter than this gaudy melon-flower!                         20

## A NOISELESS PATIENT SPIDER

A noiseless patient spider,
I marked where on a little promontory it stood isolated,
Marked how to explore the vacant vast surrounding,
It launched forth filament, filament, filament, out of itself,
Ever unreeling them, ever tirelessly speeding them.

And you O my soul where you stand,
Surrounded, detached, in measureless oceans of space,
Ceaselessly musing, venturing, throwing, seeking the spheres to connect
    them,
Till the bridge you will need be formed, till the ductile anchor hold,
Till the gossamer thread you fling catch somewhere, O my soul.    10

---

▸ *Emily Dickinson (1830-1886)*

## I LIKE TO SEE IT LAP THE MILES

I like to see it lap the miles,
And lick the valleys up,
And stop to feed itself at tanks;
And then, prodigious, step

Around a pile of mountains,
And, supercilious, peer

In shanties by the sides of roads;
And then a quarry pare

To fit its ribs,
And crawl between,    10
Complaining all the while
In horrid, hooting stanza;
Then chase itself down hill

And neigh like Boanerges;
Then, punctual as a star,
Stop—docile and omnipotent—
At its own stable door.

---

▸ *Gerard Manley Hopkins (1844-1889)*

## PIED BEAUTY

Glory be to God for dappled things—
  For skies of couple-color as a brinded cow;
    For rose-moles all in stipple upon trout that swim;
Fresh-firecoal chestnut-falls; finches' wings;
  Landscape plotted and pieced—fold, fallow, and plough;
    And all trades, their gear and tackle and trim.

All things counter, original, spare, strange;
  Whatever is fickle, freckled (who knows how?)
    With swift, slow, sweet, sour; adazzle, dim;
He fathers-forth whose beauty is past change:
             Praise him.    10

# SPRING AND FALL

*to a young child*

Márgarét, are you gríeving
Over Goldengrove unleaving?
Leáves, líke the thing of man, you
With your fresh thought care for, can you?
Áh! ás the heart grows older
It will come to such sights colder
By and by, nor spare a sigh
Though worlds of wanwood leafmeal lie;
And yet you wíll weep and know why.
Now no matter, child, the name: 10
Sórrow's spríngs áre the same.
Nor mouth had, no nor mind, expressed
What heart heard of, ghost guessed:
It ís the blight man was born for,
It is Margaret you mourn for.

▶ *A. E. Housman (1859-1936)*

# TO AN ATHLETE DYING YOUNG

The time you won your town the race
We chaired you through the market-place;
Man and boy stood cheering by,
And home we brought you shoulder-high.

Today, the road all runners come,
Shoulder-high we bring you home,
And set you at your threshold down,
Townsman of a stiller town.

Smart lad, to slip betimes away
From fields where glory does not stay, 10
And early though the laurel grows
It withers quicker than the rose.

Eyes the shady night has shut
Cannot see the record cut,
And silence sounds no worse than cheers
After earth has stopped the ears:

Now you will not swell the rout
Of lads that wore their honors out,
Runners whom renown outran
And the name died before the man. 20

So set, before its echoes fade,
The fleet foot on the sill of shade,
And hold to the low lintel up
The still-defended challenge-cup.

And round that early-laureled head
Will flock to gaze the strengthless dead,
And find unwithered on its curls
The garland briefer than a girl's.

▶ *Carl Sandburg (1878-1967)*

# CHICAGO

Hog Butcher for the World,
Tool Maker, Stacker of Wheat,
Player with Railroads and the Nation's
    Freight Handler;
Stormy, husky, brawling,
City of the Big Shoulders:
They tell me you are wicked, and I believe
    them; for I have seen your painted
    women under the gas lamps luring the
    farm boys.                         10
And they tell me you are crooked, and I
    answer: Yes, it is true I have seen the
    gunman kill and go free to kill again.

And they tell me you are brutal, and my
    reply is: On the faces of women and
    children I have seen the marks of wanton
    hunger.
And having answered so I turn once more
    to those who sneer at this my city, and I
    give them back the sneer and say to           20
    them:
Come and show me another city with lifted
    head singing so proud to be alive and
    coarse and strong and cunning.
Flinging magnetic curses amid the toil of
    piling job on job, here is a tall bold
    slugger set vivid against the little soft
    cities;
Fierce as a dog with tongue lapping for        30
    action, cunning as a savage pitted against
    the wilderness,
        Bareheaded,
        Shoveling,
        Wrecking,
        Planning,
        Building, breaking, rebuilding,
Under the smoke, dust all over his mouth,
    laughing as a young man laughs,

Laughing even as an ignorant fighter laughs
 who has never lost a battle.
Bragging and laughing that under his wrist
 is the pulse, and under his ribs the heart
 of the people,
                    Laughing!
Laughing the stormy, husky, brawling
 laughter of youth; half-naked, sweating,
 proud to be Hog-butcher, Tool-maker,
 Stacker of Wheat, Player with Railroads,
 and Freight-handler to the Nation.

40

▶ *William Carlos Williams (1883-1963)*

# SPRING AND ALL

## (PART XVIII)

The pure products of America
go crazy—
mountain folk from Kentucky

or the ribbed north end of
Jersey
with its isolate lakes and

valleys, it deaf-mutes, thieves
old names
and promiscuity between                          10

devil-may-care men who have taken
to railroading
out of sheer lust of adventure—

and young slatterns, bathed
in filth
from Monday to Saturday

to be tricked out that night
with gauds
from imaginations which have no

peasant traditions to give them          20
character
but flutter and flaunt

sheer rags—succumbing without
emotion
save numbed terror

under some hedge of choke-cherry
or viburnum—
which they cannot express—

Unless it be that marriage          30
perhaps
with a dash of Indian blood

will throw up a girl so desolate
so hemmed round
with disease or murder

that she'll be rescued by an
agent—
reared by the state and

sent out at fifteen to work in
some hard pressed
house in the suburbs—          40

some doctor's family, some Elsie—
voluptuous water
expressing with broken

brain the truth about us—
her great
ungainly hips and flopping breasts

addressed to cheap
jewelry
and rich young men with fine eyes

as if the earth under our feet          50
were
an excrement of some sky

and we degraded prisoners
destined
to hunger until we eat filth

while the imagination strains
after deer
going by fields of goldenrod in

the stifling heat of September
Somehow
it seems to destroy us

It is only in isolate flecks that
something
is given off

No one
to witness
and adjust, no one to drive the car

60

▶ *Hart Crane (1899-1932)*

## THE BRIDGE: TO BROOKLYN BRIDGE

How many dawns, chill from his rippling rest
The seagull's wings shall dip and pivot him,
Shedding white rings of tumult, building high
Over the chained bay waters Liberty—

Then, with inviolate curve, forsake our eyes
As apparitional as sails that cross
Some page of figures to be filed away;
—Till elevators drop us from our day....

I think of cinemas, panoramic sleights
With multitudes bent toward some flashing scene
Never disclosed, but hastened to again,
Foretold to other eyes on the same screen;

And Thee, across the harbor, silver-paced
As though the sun took step of thee, yet left
Some motion ever unspent in thy stride—
Implicitly thy freedom staying thee!

Out of some subway scuttle, cell or loft
A bedlamite speeds to thy parapets,
Tilting there momently, shrill shirt ballooning,
A jest falls from the speechless caravan.

Down Wall, from girder into street noon leaks,
A rip-tooth of the sky's acetylene;
All afternoon the cloud-flown derricks turn. . .
Thy cables breathe the North Atlantic still.

And obscure as that heaven of the Jews,
Thy guerdon . . . Accolade thou dost bestow
Of anonymity time cannot raise:
Vibrant reprieve and pardon thou dost show.

O harp and altar, of the fury fused,
(How could mere toil align thy choiring strings!)
Terrific threshold of the prophet's pledge,
Prayer of pariah, and the lover's cry,—

10

20

30

Again the traffic lights that skim thy swift
Unfractioned idiom, immaculate sigh of stars,
Beading thy path—condense eternity:
And we have seen night lifted in thine arms.

Under thy shadow by the piers I waited;
Only in darkness is thy shadow clear.
The City's fiery parcels all undone,
Already snow submerges an iron year. . . .          40

O Sleepless as the river under thee,
Vaulting the sea, the prairies' dreaming sod,
Unto us lowliest sometime sweep, descend
And of the curveship lend a myth to God.


▶  *Louis MacNeice (1907-       )*

*from* AUTUMN JOURNAL

PART XIII

Which things being so, as we said when we studied
    The classics, I ought to be glad
That I studied the classics at Marlborough and Merton,
    Not everyone here having had
The privilege of learning a language
    That is incontrovertibly dead,
And of carting a toy-box of hall-marked marmoreal
        phrases
    Around in his head.
We wrote compositions in Greek which they said was a
        lesson
    In logic and good for the brain;                10
We marched, counter-marched to the field-marshal's blue-
        pencil baton,
    We dressed by the right and we wrote out the sentence
        again.
We learned that a gentleman never misplaces his accents,
    That nobody knows how to speak, much less how to
        write
English who has not hob-nobbed with the great-grand-
        parents of English,
    That the boy on the Modern Side is merely a parasite
But the classical student is bred to the purple, his train-
        ing in syntax
    Is also a training in thought
And even in morals; if called to the bar or the barracks
    He always will do what he ought.                20

And knowledge, besides, should be prized for the sake of
    knowledge:
Oxford crowded the mantelpiece with gods—
Scaliger, Heinsius, Dindorf, Bentley and Wilamowitz—
    As we learned our genuflexions for Honor Mods.
And then they taught us philosophy, logic and metaphysics,
    The Negative Judgment and the Ding an Sich,
And every single thinker was powerful as Napoleon
    And crafty as Metternich.
And it really was very attractive to be able to talk about
    tables
    And to ask if the table *is*,                 30
And to draw the cork out of an old conundrum
    And watch the paradoxes fizz.
And it made one confident to think that nothing
    Really was what it seemed under the sun,
That the actual was not real and the real was not with us
    And all that mattered was the One.
And they said "The man in the street is so naïve, he never
    Can see the wood for the trees;
He thinks he knows he sees a thing but cannot
    Tell you how he knows the thing he thinks he sees."    40
And oh how much I liked the Concrete Universal,
    I never thought that I should
Be telling them vice-versa
    That they can't see the trees for the wood.
But certainly it was fun while it lasted
    And I got my honours degree
And was stamped as a person of intelligence and culture
    For ever wherever two or three
Persons of intelligence and culture
    Are gathered together in talk              50
Writing definitions on invisible blackboards
    In non-existent chalk.
But such sacramental occasions
    Are nowadays comparatively rare;
There is always a wife or a boss or a dun or a client
    Disturbing the air.
Barbarians always, life in the particular always,
    Dozens of men in the street,
And the perennial if unimportant problem
    Of getting enough to eat.                 60
So blow the bugles over the metaphysicians,
    Let the pure mind return to the Pure Mind;
I must be content to remain in the world of Appearance
    And sit on the mere appearance of a behind.
But in case you should think my education was wasted
    I hasten to explain
That having once been in the University of Oxford
    You can never really again

Believe anything that anyone says and that of course is
    an asset
    In a world like ours;70
Why bother to water a garden
    That is planted with paper flowers?
O the Freedom of the Press, the Late Night Final,
    To-morrow's pulp;
One should not gulp one's port but as it isn't
    Port, I'll gulp it if I want to gulp
But probably I'll just enjoy the colour
    And pour it down the sink
For I don't call advertisement a statement
    Or any quack medicine a drink.80
Good-bye now, Plato and Hegel,
    The shop is closing down;
They don't want any philosopher-kings in England,
    There ain't no universals in this man's town.

▶ *John Wain (1925-     )*

# POEM WITHOUT A MAIN VERB

Watching oneself
being clever, being clever:
keeping the keen equipoise between *always* and *never*;

delicately divining
(the gambler's sick art)
which of the strands must hold, and which may part;

playing off, playing off
with pointless cunning
the risk of remaining against the risk of running;

balancing, balancing10
(alert and knowing)
the carelessly hidden with the carefully left showing;

endlessly, endlessly
finely elaborating
the filigree threads in the web and the bars in the grating;

at last minutely
and thoroughly lost
in the delta where profit fans into cost;

with superb navigation
afloat on that darkening, deepening sea,20
helplessly, helplessly.

# TERRAIN

The soul is a region without definite
                    boundaries:
    it is not certain a prairie
can exhaust it
                    or a range enclose it:
it floats (self-adjusting) like the continental
                    mass:
    where it towers most
extending its deepest mantling base
                    (exactly proportional):                              10
does not flow all one way: there is a divide:
    river systems thrown like winter tree-
                    shadows
against the hills: branches, runs, high
                    lakes:
    stagnant lily-marshes:

is variable, has weather; floods unbalancing
    gut it, silt altering the
distribution of weight, the nature of
                    content:                                             20
    whirlwinds move through it
or stand spinning like separate orders: the
                    moon comes:
    there are barren spots: bogs, rising
by self-accretion from themselves, a growth
                    into
    destruction of growth,
change of character,
    invasion of peat by poplar and oak:
                    semi-precious                                        30
stones and precious metals drop from
                    muddy-water into mud:

it is an area of poise, really, held from
                    tipping,
    dark wild water, fierce eels, counter-
                    currents:
a habitat, precise ecology of forms
    mutually to some extent
tolerable, not entirely self-destroying: a
                    crust afloat:                                        40
    a scum, foam to the deep and other-
                    natured:
but deeper than depth, too: a vacancy and
                    swirl:

it may be spherical, light and knowledge
      merely
   the iris and opening
to the dark methods of its sight: how it
      comes and
   goes, ruptures and heals,
whirls and stands still: the moon comes:
      terrain

▶ *Robert Creeley (1926-     )*

# THE NAME

Be natural,
wise
as you can be,
my daughter,

let my name
be in you flesh

I gave you
in the act of

loving your mother,
all your days       10
her ways,
the woman in you

brought from
sensuality's measure,
no other,
there was no thought

of it but such
pleasure all women
must be in her,
as you. But not wiser,       20

not more of nature
than her hair,

the eyes
she gives you.

There will not be another
woman such as you
are. Remember
your mother,

the way you came,
the days of waiting.       30
Be natural,
daughter, wise

as you can be,
all my daughters,
be women
for men

when that time comes.
Let the rhetoric
stay with me
your father. Let       40

me talk about it,
saving you such
vicious self-
exposure, let you

pass it on
in you. I cannot
be more than the man
who watches.

# FEVER 103°

Pure? What does it mean?
The tongues of hell
Are dull, dull as the triple

Tongues of dull, fat Cerberus
Who wheezes at the gate. Incapable
Of licking clean

The aguey tendon, the sin, the sin.
The tinder cries.
The indelible smell

Of a snuffed candle!                                                    10
Love, love, the low smokes roll
From me like Isadora's scarves, I'm in a fright

One scarf will catch and anchor in the wheel,
Such yellow sullen smokes
Make their own element. They will not rise,

But trundle round the globe
Choking the aged and the meek,
The weak

Hothouse baby in its crib,
The ghastly orchid                                                     20
Hanging its hanging garden in the air,

Devilish leopard!
Radiation turned it white
And killed it in an hour.

Greasing the bodies of adulterers
Like Hiroshima ash and eating in.
The sin. The sin.

Darling, all night
I have been flickering, off, on, off, on.
The sheets grow heavy as a lecher's kiss.                              30

Three days. Three nights.
Lemon water, chicken
Water, water makes me retch.

I am too pure for you or anyone.
Your body
Hurts me as the world hurts God. I am a lantern—

My head a moon
Of Japanese paper, my gold beaten skin
Infinitely delicate and infinitely expensive.

Does not my heat astound you! And my light!
All by myself I am a huge camellia
Glowing and coming and going, flush on flush.

I think I am going up,
I think I may rise—
The heads of hot metal fly, and I love, I

Am a pure acetylene
Virgin
Attended by roses,

By kisses, by cherubim,
By whatever these pink things mean!  50
Not you, nor him.

Nor him, nor him
(My selves dissolving, old whore petticoats)—
To Paradise.

# ►►► FIGURATIVE LANGUAGE

Poetry involves description; analogies, contrasts, and comparisons are the best means to describe people, objects, feelings, and moods. Figurative language must not only be descriptive, it must be fresh, imaginative, and exciting. It must describe familiar things—ideas, objects, states of being—in new ways; and it must effectively convey new perspectives and insights. Figurative language, then, expresses the poet's ideas in a style unique to him, intensifies the meaning of his poem, and provides beauty and interest.

The basic forms of figurative language, or figures of speech, are the metaphor and the simile. Other terms are analogy, synecdoche, metonymy, personification, antithesis, allusion, and apostrophe. Rhetorical devices, used to create the tone of a poem, are often considered under the general label of figurative language, as is irony.

The metaphor and simile belong to the class of figures of comparison; the simile makes comparison between two things, people, moods, conditions, and so forth—something is *like* something else. The metaphor, the stronger of the two, eliminates the term of comparison—something *is* something else; this term, of course, is not used in any literal sense. The simile is solely a descriptive device, while the metaphor is a means of describing in absolutes, without compromising terms reminding us that the thing being described is *not* really a flower, sunset, and so forth, but merely resembles one. Almost all poetry makes use of these two figures of speech —they are, in fact, the basis of poetic language.

An analogy is simply a resemblance between two unidentical things; this category includes the figures of comparison, the metaphor and simile, and the figures of association, the basic two being the synecdoche and metonymy. The synecdoche is a descriptive term which substitutes a part for the whole or vice versa (for example, ten sails for ten ships, and a creature for a man); the most common type of synecdoche is that which substitutes some aspect or part of something for the thing itself. The metonymy describes or labels something by referring to an attribute of, or something closely connected and associated with, that thing (for example, the crown for king or queen); it expresses something or concept related to or inherent in but not identical to the thing being described.

Personification means endowing non-human things with human characteristics. Whether the thing described is a bird, a tree, a house, or an idea, giving it qualities normally associated with humans is considered personification. This device, a mainstay of allegory, is also useful in approaching familiar things from new perspectives.

Antithesis means connecting drastically opposing ideas, either within the same line or the same sequence of lines, creating a contradictory, sometimes more balanced, sometimes very surprising, effect. Closely related to this is sentence inversion, in which the usual order of speech is reversed, sometimes merely to assure riming or to create a "poetical" effect, sometimes to make a valid point about the relationship between ideas and language, or to make a comparison with another sentence.

An allusion is a reference to a literary or historical person, place, or event. The most common sources of literary allusions in contemporary poetry, and in other literature as well, are Greek and Roman myths, the Bible, and Shakespeare. Allusions often appear in the form of metaphors and similes, connecting people, things, and happenings of the past with the poet's present concerns.

Apostrophe is addressing an inanimate object as if it were alive or addressing someone absent or dead as if he were present. An apostrophe is used mainly in dramatic narratives, odes, elegies, and the like but can be used in any sort of poetry for dramatic effect and emotional emphasis.

Rhetorical devices (the hyperbole, understatement, paradox, oxymoron, ellipsis, ambiguity, and ambivalence) frequently take the form of figures of speech. The diction, placement, frequency, and quality of all figures of speech, of course, greatly influence the poem's tone and the reader's amount of interest, identification, and reaction.

Irony, whether verbal, dramatic, or situation is often involved in figurative language. Saying the opposite of what one really means, developing contrast between the words, phrases, or figures of speech used and the way in which they are intended, creating discrepancies between expectations and outcomes, allusions to various historical and literary events which re-enforce or contrast with one's point—these are some of the uses of irony in figurative language. All of the rhetorical figures of speech can be used ironically; any analogy, contrast, or comparison, in fact, can, through choice of words, arrangement, and relation to the rest of the poem, take on ironic overtones. Irony can be achieved through use of puns, anticlimax, and litotes, stating something as the negative of its contrary (for example, "It wasn't one of the pleasanter things I've seen" instead of "It was one of the worst things I've ever seen.")

These, then, are the standard forms of figurative language; each poet develops his own style, his own types of comparisons and contrasts, his own methods of effectively describing things. In reading poetry, it is important not to pass over metaphors, similes, allusions, and the rest, but to examine them closely, analyzing why the poet makes the particular comparison at that time and in that way. If he uses a trite or hackneyed figure of speech, why does he do so? What point could he be making? Full appreciation of the content and purpose of figurative expression contributes to appreciation and understanding of the poem as a whole. The message may be obtainable without understanding each figure of speech, but the type, amount, and complexity of figurative language always qualifies and changes the basic theme to some degree.

Styles of poetry change, obviously, and with them changes the type of figurative language most commonly used; the apostrophe is much rarer than it was a hundred years ago, ambiguities probably commoner. But as long as poetry remains, figurative language will persist, as it is one of the essentials of the poetic form of expression. It provides a variety of types of expression for the poet, and a richer experience for the reader.

▶ *William Shakespeare (1564-1616)*

## SONNET 73

That time of year thou mayst in me behold
When yellow leaves, or none, or few, do hang
Upon those boughs which shake against the cold,
Bare ruined choirs, where late the sweet birds sang.
In me thou see'st the twilight of such day
As after sunset fadeth in the west,
Which by and by black night doth take away,
Death's second self, that seals up all in rest.
In me thou see'st the glowing of such fire
That on the ashes of his youth doth lie,                        10
As the death-bed whereon it must expire
Consumed with that which it was nourished by.
    This thou perceiv'st, which makes thy love more strong,
    To love that well which thou must leave ere long.

## SONNET 130

My mistress' eyes are nothing like the sun;
Coral is far more red than her lips' red;
If snow be white, why then her breasts are dun;
If hairs be wires, black wires grow on her head.
I have seen roses damasked, red and white,
But no such roses see I in her cheeks,
And in some perfumes is there more delight
Than in the breath that from my mistress reeks.
I love to hear her speak, yet well I know
That music hath a far more pleasing sound.                      10
I grant I never saw a goddess go;
My mistress, when she walks, treads on the ground.
    And yet, by heaven, I think my love as rare
    As any she belied with false compare.

▶ *John Donne (1572-1631)*

## A VALEDICTION: FORBIDDING MOURNING

As virtuous men pass mildly away,
  And whisper to their souls, to go,
Whilst some of their sad friends do say,
  "The breath goes now," and some say, "No":

So let us melt, and make no noise.
  No tear-floods, nor sigh-tempests move.
'Twere profanation of our joys
  To tell the laity our love.

Moving of the earth brings harms and fears,
  Men reckon what it did and meant;                          10
But trepidation of the spheres,
  Though greater far, is innocent.

Dull sublunary lovers' love
  (Whose soul is sense) cannot admit
Absence, because it doth remove
  Those things which elemented it.

But we, by a love so much refined
  That our selves know not what it is,
Inter-assured of the mind,
  Care less, eyes, lips, and hands to miss.                   20

Our two souls therefore, which are one,
  Though I must go, endure not yet
A breach, but an expansion,
  Like gold to airy thinness beat.

If they be two, they are two so
  As stiff twin compasses are two:
Thy soul, the fixed foot, makes no show
  To move, but doth, if the other do.

And though it in the center sit,
  Yet when the other far doth roam,    30
It leans, and hearkens after it,
  And grows erect, as that comes home.

Such wilt thou be to me, who must
  Like the other foot, obliquely run:
Thy firmness makes my circle just,
  And makes me end where I begun.

# HOLY SONNET 14

Batter my heart, three personed God; for you
As yet but knock, breathe, shine, and seek to mend;
That I may rise and stand, o'erthrow me and bend
Your force to break, blow, burn and make me new.
I, like an usurped town, to another due,
Labour to admit you, but Oh, to no end;
Reason, your viceroy in me, me should defend,
But is captived and proves weak or untrue.
Yet dearly I love you and would be loved fain,
But am betrothed unto your enemy:                10
Divorce me, untie or break that knot again,
Take me to you, imprison me, for I
Except you enthrall me, never shall be free,
Nor ever chaste, except you ravish me.

▶  *George Herbert (1593-1633)*

# LOVE

Love bade me welcome; yet my soul drew back,
    Guilty of dust and sin.
But quick-eyed Love, observing me grow slack
    From my first entrance in,
Drew nearer to me, sweetly questioning
    If I lacked anything.

"A guest," I answered, "worthy to be here";
    Love said, "You shall be he."
"I, the unkind, ungrateful? Ah, my dear,
    I cannot look on Thee."                        10
Love took my hand, and smiling did reply,
    "Who made the eyes but I?"

"Truth, Lord, but I have marred them; let my shame
    Go where it doth deserve."
"And know you not," says Love, "who bore the blame?"
    "My dear, then I will serve."
"You must sit down," says Love, "and taste My meat."
    So I did sit and eat.

## HOUSEWIFERY

Make me, O Lord, Thy spinning-wheel complete.
  Thy holy Word my distaff make for me;
Make mine affections Thy swift flyers neat;
  And make my soul Thy holy spool to be;
  My conversation make to be Thy reel,
  And reel the yarn thereon spun of Thy wheel.

Make me Thy loom then; knit therein this twine;
  And make Thy Holy Spirit, Lord, wind quills;
Then weave the web Thyself. The yarn is fine.
  Thine ordinances make my fulling mills.                    10
  Then dye the same in heavenly colors choice,
  All pinked with varnished flowers of paradise.

Then clothe therewith mine understanding, will,
  Affections, judgment, conscience, memory,
My words and actions, that their shine may fill
  My ways with glory and Thee glorify.
  Then mine apparel shall display before Ye
  That I am clothed in holy robes for glory.

▶ *Robert Burns (1759-1796)*

## A RED, RED ROSE

O, my luve is like a red, red rose,
  That's newly sprung in June.
O, my luve is like the melodie,
  That's sweetly play'd in tune.

As fair art thou, my bonie lass,
  So deep in luve am I,
And I will luve thee still, my dear,
  Till a' the seas gang dry.

Till a' the seas gang dry, my dear,
  And the rocks melt wi' the sun!                    10
And I will luve thee still, my dear,
  While the sands o' life shall run.

And fare thee weel, my only luve,
  And fare thee weel a while!
And I will come again, my luve,
  Tho' it were ten thousand mile!

▶ *William Wordsworth (1770-1850)*

## I WANDERED LONELY AS A CLOUD

I wandered lonely as a cloud
That floats on high o'er vales and hills,
When all at once I saw a crowd,
A host, of golden daffodils;
Beside the lake, beneath the trees,
Fluttering and dancing in the breeze.

Continuous as the stars that shine
And twinkle on the milky way,
They stretched in never-ending line                    10
Along the margin of a bay:
Ten thousand saw I at a glance,
Tossing their heads in sprightly dance.

The waves beside them danced; but they
Outdid the sparkling waves in glee;
A poet could not but be gay,
In such a jocund company;
I gazed—and gazed—but little thought
What wealth the show to me had brought:

For oft, when on my couch I lie
In vacant or in pensive mood,                    20
They flash upon that inward eye

Which is the bliss of solitude;
And then my heart with pleasure fills,
And dances with the daffodils.

▶ *John Keats (1795-1821)*

# TO AUTUMN

Season of mists and mellow fruitfulness,
   Close bosom-friend of the maturing sun:
Conspiring with him how to load and bless
   With fruit the vines that round the thatch-eves run;
To bend with apples the mossed cottage-trees,
   And fill all fruit with ripeness to the core;
     To swell the gourd, and plump the hazel shells
With a sweet kernel; to set budding more,
   And still more, later flowers for the bees,
   Until they think warm days will never cease,          10
     For Summer has o'er-brimmed their clammy cells.

Who hath not seen thee oft amid thy store?
   Sometimes whoever seeks abroad may find
Thee sitting careless on a granary floor,
   Thy hair soft-lifted by the winnowing wind;
Or on a half-reaped furrow sound asleep,
   Drowsed with the fume of poppies, while thy hook
     Spares the next swath and all its twinèd flowers:
And sometimes like a gleaner thou dost keep
   Steady thy laden head across a brook;                 20
   Or by a cider-press, with patient look,
     Thou watchest the last oozings hours by hours.

Where are the songs of Spring? Ay, where are they?
   Think not of them, thou hast thy music too,—
While barrèd clouds bloom the soft-dying day,
   And touch the stubble-plains with rosy hue;
Then in a wailful choir the small gnats mourn
   Among the river sallows, borne aloft
     Or sinking as the light wind lives or dies;
And full-grown lambs loud bleat from hilly bourn;        30
   Hedge-crickets sing; and now with treble soft
   The red-breast whistles from a garden-croft;
     And gathering swallows twitter in the skies.

*Emily Dickinson (1830-1886)*

# BECAUSE I COULD NOT STOP FOR DEATH

Because I could not stop for Death,
He kindly stopped for me;
The carriage held but just ourselves
And Immortality.

We slowly drove, he knew no haste,
And I had put away
My labor, and my leisure too,
For his civility.

We passed the school where children played
At wrestling in a ring;                                          10
We passed the fields of gazing grain,
We passed the setting sun;

We paused before a house that seemed
A swelling of the ground;
The roof was scarcely visible,
The cornice but a mound.

Since then 'tis centuries; but each
Feels shorter than the day
I first surmised the horses' heads
Were toward eternity.                                           20

# "HOPE" IS THE THING WITH FEATHERS

"Hope" is the thing with feathers—
That perches in the soul—
And sings the tune without the words—
And never stops—at all—

And sweetest—in the Gale—is heard—
And sore must be the storm—
That could abash the little Bird
That kept so many warm—

I've heard it in the chillest land—
And on the strangest Sea—                                       10
Yet, never, in Extremity,
It asked a crumb—of Me.

► *Thomas Hardy (1840-1928)*

# AH, ARE YOU DIGGING ON MY GRAVE?

"Ah, are you digging on my grave
  My loved one?—planting rue?"
    —*"No: yesterday he went to wed*
    *One of the brightest wealth has bred.*
    *'It cannot hurt her now,' he said,*
      *'That I should not be true.' "*

"Then who is digging on my grave?
  My nearest, dearest kin?"
    —*"Ah, no: they sit and think, 'What*
      *use!*
    *What good will planting flowers*
      *produce?*      10
    *No tendance of her mound can loose*
      *Her spirit from Death's gin.' "*
"But someone digs upon my grave?
  My enemy?—prodding sly?"
    —*"Nay: when she heard you had*
      *passed the Gate*

*That shuts on all flesh soon or late,*
*She thought you no more worth her*
    *hate,*
    *She cares not where you lie."*

"Then, who is digging on my grave?
  Say—since I have not guessed!"    20
    —*"O it is I, my mistress dear,*
    *Your little dog, who still lives near,*
    *And much I hope my movements here*
      *Have not disturbed your rest?"*

"Ah, yes! *You* dig upon my grave. . . .
  Why flashed it not on me
That one true heart was left behind!
What feeling do we ever find
To equal among human kind
  A dog's fidelity!"    30

  *"Mistress, I dug upon your grave*
    *To bury a bone, in case*
*I should be hungry near this spot*
*When passing on my daily trot.*
*I am sorry, but I quite forgot*
  *It was your resting-place."*

► *Gerard Manley Hopkins (1844-1889)*

# GOD'S GRANDEUR

The world is charged with the grandeur of God.
  It will flame out, like shining from shook foil;
  It gathers to a greatness, like the ooze of oil
Crushed. Why do men then now not reck his rod?
Generations have trod, have trod, have trod;
  And all is seared with trade, bleared, smeared with toil;
  And wears man's smudge and shares man's smell: the soil
Is bare now, nor can foot feel, being shod.

And for all this, nature is never spent;
  There lives the dearest freshness deep down things;    10
And though the last lights off the black West went
  Oh, morning, at the brown brink eastward, springs—
Because the Holy Ghost over the bent
  World broods with warm breast and with ah! bright wings.

▶  *A. E. Housman  (1859-1936)*

# WITH RUE MY HEART IS LADEN

With rue my heart is laden
  For golden friends I had,
For many a rose-lipped maiden
  And many a lightfoot lad.

By brooks too broad for leaping
  The lightfoot boys are sleeping
The rose-lipped girls are sleeping
  In fields where roses fade.

▶  *Carl Sandburg  (1878-1967)*

# FOG

The fog comes
on little cat feet.
It sits looking
over harbor and city
on silent haunches
and then moves on.

▶  *W. H. Auden  (1907-    )*

# THE UNKNOWN CITIZEN

*(To JS/07/M/378*
*This Marble Monument*
*Is Erected by the State)*

He was found by the Bureau of Statistics to be
One against whom there was no official complaint,
And all the reports on his conduct agree
That, in the modern sense of an old-fashioned word, he was a
    saint,
For in everything he did he served the Greater Community.
Except for the War till the day he retired
He worked in a factory and never got fired,
But satisfied his employers, Fudge Motors Inc.
Yet he wasn't a scab or odd in his views,
For his Union reports that he paid his dues,        10
(Our report on his Union shows it was sound)
And our Social Psychology workers found
That he was popular with his mates and liked a drink.
The Press are convinced that he bought a paper every day
And that his reactions to advertisements were normal in every way.
Policies taken out in his name prove that he was fully insured,
And his Health-card shows he was once in hospital but left it
    cured.

▶ *Peter Viereck (1916-      )*

# KILROY

### 1

Also Ulysses once—that other war.
      (Is it because we find his scrawl
      Today on every privy door
      That we forget his ancient rôle?)
Also was there—he did it for the wages—
When a Cathay-drunk Genoese set sail.
*Whenever "longen folk to goon on pilgrimages,"*
*Kilroy is there;*
      he tells The Miller's Tale.

### 2

At times he seems a paranoiac king            10
Who stamps his crest on walls and says, "My own!"
But in the end he fades like a lost tune,
Tossed here and there, whom all the breezes sing.
"Kilroy was here"; these words sound wanly gay,
      Haughty yet tired with long marching.
He is Orestes—guilty of what crime?—
      For whom the Furies still are searching;
      When they arrive, they find their prey
(Leaving his name to mock them) went away.
Sometimes he does not flee from them in time:      20
*"Kilroy was—"*
      *(with his blood a dying man*
      *Wrote half the phrase out in Bataan.)*

### 3

Kilroy, beware. "HOME" is the final trap
That lurks for you in many a wily shape:
In pipe-and-slippers plus a Loyal Hound
      Or fooling around, just fooling around.
Kind to the old (their warm Penelope)
But fierce to boys,
      thus "home" becomes that sea,      30
Horribly disguised, where you were always drowned,—
      (How could suburban Crete condone
The yarns you would have V-mailed from the sun?)—
And folksy fishes sip Icarian tea.
*One stab of hopeless wings imprinted your*
      *Exultant Kilroy-signature*
*Upon sheer sky for all the world to stare:*
      "I was there! I was there! I was there!"

### 4

God is like Kilroy; He, too, sees it all;
That's how He knows of every sparrow's fall;      40

That's why we prayed each time the tightropes cracked
On which our loveliest clowns contrived their act.
The G. I. Faustus who was
                              everywhere
Strolled home again. "What was it like outside?"
Asked Can't, with his good neighbors Ought and But
And pale Perhaps and grave-eyed Better Not;
For "Kilroy" means: the world is very wide.
                    He was there, he was there, he was there!
*And in the suburbs Can't sat down and cried.*                    50


▶  *Richard Wilbur (1921-      )*

# MIND

Mind in its purest play is like some bat
That beats about in caverns all alone,
Contriving by a kind of senseless wit
Not to conclude against a wall of stone.

It has no need to falter or explore;
Darkly it knows what obstacles are there,
And so may weave and flitter, dip and soar
In perfect courses through the blackest air.

And has this simile a like perfection?
The mind is like a bat. Precisely. Save                    10
That in the very happiest intellection
A graceful error may correct the cave.


▶  *Allen Ginsberg (1926-      )*

# POEM ROCKET

*'Be a Star-screwer!'   Gregory Corso*

Old moon my eyes are new moon with
      human footprint
no longer Romeo Sadface in drunken river
      Loony Pierre eyebrow, goof moon
O possible moon in Heaven we get to first
      of ageless constellations of names
as God is possible as All is possible so
      we'll reach another life.

Moon politicians earth weeping and
      warring in eternity                              10

tho not one star disturbed by screaming
      madmen from Hollywood
oil tycoons from Romania making secret
      deals with flabby green Plutonians—
slave camps on Saturn Cuban revolutions
      on Mars?
Old life and new side by side, will Catholic
      church find Christ on Jupiter
Mohammed rave in Uranus will Buddha be
      acceptable on the stolid plants              20
or will we find Zoroastrian temples flower-
      ing on Neptune?
What monstrous new ecclesiastical designs
      on the entire universe unfold in the dying
      Pope's brain?

Scientist alone is true poet he gives us the
   moon
he promises the stars he'll make us a new
   universe if it comes to that
O Einstein I should have sent you my        30
   flaming mss.
O Einstein I should have pilgrimaged to
   your white hair!
O fellow travellers I write you a poem in
   Amsterdam in the Cosmos
where Spinoza ground his magic lenses long
   ago
I write you a poem long ago
already my feet are washed in death
Here I am naked without identity        40
with no more body than the fine black
   tracery of pen mark on soft paper
as star talks to star multiple beams of sunlight all the same myriad thought
in one fold of the universe where Whitman
   was
and Blake and Shelley saw Milton dwelling
   as in a starry temple
brooding in his blindness seeing all—
Now at last I can speak to you beloved        50
   brothers of an unknown moon
real Yous squatting in whatever form amidst
   Platonic Vapors of Eternity
I am another Star.
Will you eat my poems or read them
or gaze with aluminum blind plates on
   sunless pages?
do you dream or translate & accept data
   with indifferent droopings of antennae?
do I make sense to your flowery green        60
   receptor eyesockets? do you have visions
   of God?

Which way will the sunflower turn surrounded by millions of suns?

This is my rocket my personal rocket I send
   up my message Beyond
Someone to hear me there
My immortality
without steel or cobalt basalt or diamond
   gold or mercurial fire        70
without passports filing cabinets bits of
   paper warheads
without myself finally
pure thought
message all and everywhere the same
I send up my rocket to land on whatever
   planet awaits it
preferably religious sweet planets no money
fourth dimensional planets where Death
   shows movies        80
plants speak (courteously) of ancient
   physics and poetry itself is manufactured
   by the trees
the final Planet where the Great Brain of
   the Universe sits waiting for a poem to
   land in His golden pocket
joining the other notes mash-notes love-
   sighs complaints-musical shrieks of despair and the million unutterable
   thoughts of frogs        90
I send you my rocket of amazing chemical
more than my hair my sperm or the cells of
   my body
the speeding thought that flies upward
   with my desire as instantaneous as the
   universe and faster than light
and leave all other questions unfinished
   for the moment to turn back to sleep in
   my desk bed on earth.

# ▶ ▶ ▶ TONE

The tone of a poem is the overall attitude expressed, both the poet's attitude toward the work and the atmosphere created, the message transmitted, to the reader. The latter aspect of tone, the feeling created by the particular combination of structure and content, the aspect of the poem which shapes the reader's reactions, is often called mood. Mood, then, is just one aspect of tone; the overall tone of a poem is often more complex than just the atmosphere that the reader immediately perceives. There is frequently a double attitude, a gap between the poet's apparent attitude and his true feelings, which may be complicated and ambiguous. The surface tone or atmosphere sometimes reflects only one level of meaning; further understanding of the poem will lead to appreciation of the subtle distinctions which play such an important role in determining tone.

Tone is revealed in many ways: the poem's diction, sound and rime patterns, figurative language, imagery, metrical patterns, symbolism, and point of view all contribute to and influence the tone. It must be remembered, however, that tone is not a concrete element, one which can be discovered, isolated at least partially, and closely analyzed according to any particular set of standards or rules. Rather, tone cannot be in any way separated from the poem of which it is a part; it can be discussed only in terms of the aspects of the poem which blend to create it.

Four important considerations in the search for a poem's tone are style, rhetorical devices, point of view, and irony. Style is largely determined by diction, the choice, use, and arrangement of words and the manner in which they are presented. The quality of language used often tends to determine whether the tone is one of frivolity or seriousness, gaiety or gloom. The structural pattern, the length and type of lines and stanzas, the type of rime, the sound effects such as alliteration and assonance, this is another aspect of style. Two poets may discuss exactly the same problem or comment upon the same subject; the differences in their approaches, attitudes, intended messages, and overall purposes are revealed by their styles.

Rhetorical devices are another means of creating tone; some of the most commonly used are hyperbole, understatement, paradox, ellipsis, oxymoron, ambiguity, and ambivalence. Hyperbole is, simply, overstatement; it is used most frequently and effectively when the poet wishes to stress a particular idea, sometimes to re-emphasize its value, sometimes to point out its deficiencies. Frequently used ironically, hyperbole is exaggeration with a purpose. Understatement is, of course, the opposite; a fact or idea is played down, given less than the usual importance. This device often has an even stronger ironical purpose and impact than does hyperbole.

Paradox is a statement which seems on the surface to be untrue, contradictory, or simply ridiculous, yet which, when examined closely, reveals a certain truth. This device, more subtle than hyperbole and understatement, is used to present something important in an unusual, contradictory, and imaginative way. A particular kind of paradox, oxymoron, is one in which opposite terms or things usually thought of as opposites are associated in one expression; this is usually used to reveal mixed emotions or conflicting attitudes toward something.

Ellipsis is the omission of necessary words, which are filled in by the reader's imagination and knowledge. This device is used to avoid wordy, cumbersome phrases, to create a more "poetic" effect, and often to create figurative language; a few words or an expression may represent an important concept or idea.

Ambiguity involves double meaning; obvious ambiguities may be expressed by pun, a play on words. Any of the other devices mentioned can also be used to indicate ambiguity. Ambivalence is even more complex, for it involves conflicting attitudes toward something, attitudes which are held simultaneously. What is involved here, then, is not merely double meaning, but double, or multiple, concurrent feelings. Expressions of ambiguity and ambivalence broaden the poem's perspective and enrich its meaning, giving the reader more to ponder and evaluate.

Point of view can be a useful indicator of tone; whether the poet is directly or indirectly addressing someone or something, addressing the reader, musing to himself, or speaking objectively, is significant in determining tone. The approach used, whether objective and detached or subjective and personal, tells us much about the poet's own feelings and the attitude he wishes the reader to take. When a person, a spokesman or character narrating the story, is used, for example, he may directly reflect the views of his creator, the poet, or he may express opposing or conflicting views, creating ambiguity or ambivalence. The reader, sensing disunity, must delve deeper to discover what the poet is doing. A shift in the point of view used, or an obvious multiplicity of attitudes expressed toward the same thing, these are clues to tonal variation, a situation in which the non-uniformity in attitudes and atmosphere is used to reveal, and sometimes to create, meaning.

Irony is a vital aspect of tone; verbal irony, saying the opposite of what one means, and situation irony, in which the thing that is least expected, or which *should* have the least chance of occurring if things are as they should be, does in fact occur,—are shown by contradiction, contrast, and conflict within a poem. Dramatic irony, in the case of poetry, a discrepancy between what the poet or his narrator says and what is meant, is another means of expressing conflicting tones. Multiple meanings and attitudes, discrepancies between *what* is being said and the *way* in which it is said, contrasts between the poet's apparent views and the views of a character or narrator, frequent use of the previously mentioned rhetorical devices—these are all means of expressing irony, of showing that things are not always as they appear, or as they should be or would be if there were perfect order and sense. Irony shows that simplicity and clarity are seldom possible; rather, complexity, duplicity, and confusion rule poetry, as they rule life. Use of irony enables the poet to increase the scope of the poem, which in turn provides the reader with more terrain to explore, more possibilities to consider.

Tone, then modifies, complicates, and enriches meaning; as mentioned earlier, the means and style of expression influence and color what is said. By creating a particular atmosphere through style, rhetorical devices, point of view, and use of irony, the poet patterns the reader's reactions; he determines to a great extent the way in which the reader will receive his message.

# TO EVERYTHING THERE IS A SEASON

To everything there is a season
And a time to every purpose under the heaven:
A time to be born, and a time to die;
A time to plant, and a time to reap;
A time to kill, and a time to heal;
A time to break down, and a time to build up;
A time to mourn, and a time to dance;
A time to cast away stones, and a time to gather
    stones together;
A time to embrace, and a time to refrain from embracing;
A time to get, and a time to lose;              10
A time to keep, and a time to cast away;
A time to rend, and a time to sew;
A time to keep silence, and a time to speak;
A time to love, and a time to hate;
A time of war, and a time of peace.


▶ *Michael Drayton (1563-1631)*

# SINCE THERE'S NO HELP, COME LET US KISS AND PART

Since there's no help, come let us kiss and part.
    Nay, I have done, you get no more of me,
And I am glad, yea, glad with all my heart
    That thus so cleanly I myself can free;
Shake hands for ever, cancel all our vows,
    And when we meet at any time again,
Be it not seen in either of our brows
    That we one jot of former love retain.
Now at the last gasp of Love's latest breath,
    When, his pulse failing, Passion speechless lies,    10
When Faith is kneeling by his bed of death,
    And Innocence is closing up his eyes,
        Now if thou wouldst, when all have given him over,
        From death to life thou mightst him yet recover.

*[handwritten annotation:* Personification *bracketing lines 9-11]*


▶ *Thomas Campion (1567-1620)*

# THOU ART NOT FAIR

Thou art not fair, for all thy red and white,
    For all those rosy ornaments in thee.
Thou art not sweet, though made of mere
    delight,

Nor fair nor sweet unless thou pity me.
I will not soothe thy fancies. Thou shalt
    prove
That beauty is no beauty without love.

Yet love not me, nor seek thou to allure
    My thoughts with beauty, were it more
        divine.
Thy smiles and kisses I can not endure,
    I'll not be wrapped up in those arms of
        thine.                            10
Now show it, if thou be a woman right,
Embrace, and kiss, and love me in despite.

▶  *John Donne (1572-1631)*

# THE FLEA

Mark but this flea, and mark in this,
How little that which thou deny'st me is;
It sucked me first, and now sucks thee,
And in this flea our two bloods mingled be.
Thou know'st that this cannot be said
A sin, nor shame, nor loss of maidenhead,
    Yet this enjoys before it woo,
    And pampered, swells with one blood made of two,
    And this, alas, is more than we would do.

Oh stay, three lives in one flea spare,           10
Where we almost, yea, more than married are,
This flea is you and I, and this
Our marriage bed and marriage temple is;
Though parents grudge, and you, we're met
And cloistered in these living walls of jet.
    Though use make you apt to kill me,
    Let not to that, self-murder added be,
    And sacrilege, three sins in killing three.

Cruel and sudden, hast thou since
Purpled thy nail in blood of innocence?        20
Wherein could this flea guilty be,
Except in that drop which it sucked from thee?
Yet thou triumph'st and say'st that thou
Find'st not thyself nor me the weaker now;
    'Tis true. Then learn how false fears be:
    Just so much honor, when thou yield'st to me,
    Will waste, as this flea's death took life from thee.

# TO LUCASTA, GOING TO THE WARS

Tell me not, Sweet, I am unkind
That from the nunnery
Of thy chaste breast and quiet mind,
To war and arms I fly.

True, a new mistress now I chase,
The first foe in the field;
And with a stronger faith embrace
A sword, a horse, a shield.

Yet this inconstancy is such
As you too shall adore;                                    10
I could not love thee, Dear, so much,
Loved I not honor more.


# TO ALTHEA, FROM PRISON

When Love with unconfinèd wings
    Hovers within my gates;
And my divine Althea brings
    To whisper at the grates:
When I lie tangled in her hair,
    And fettered to her eye;
The birds, that wanton in the air,
    Know no such liberty.

When flowing cups run swiftly round
    With no allaying Thames,                               10
Our careless heads with roses bound,
    Our hearts with loyal flames;
When thirsty grief in wine we steep,
    When healths and draughts go free,
Fishes that tipple in the deep,
    Know no such liberty.

When (like committed linnets) I
    With shriller throat shall sing
The sweetness, mercy, majesty,
    And glories of my King;                                20
When I shall voice aloud, how good
    He is, how great should be;
Enlargèd winds that curl the flood,
    Know no such liberty.

Stone walls do not a prison make,
    Nor iron bars a cage;
Minds innocent and quiet take
    That for an hermitage;

If I have freedom in my Love,
    And in my soul am free;          30
Angels alone that soar above,
    Enjoy such liberty.


▶ *John Milton (1608-1674)*

# WHEN I CONSIDER HOW MY LIGHT IS SPENT

When I consider how my light is spent,
Ere half my days, in this dark world and wide,
And that one talent which is death to hide
Lodged with me useless, though my soul more bent
To serve therewith my Maker, and present
My true account, lest He returning chide,
"Doth God exact day-labor, light denied?"
I fondly ask. But Patience, to prevent
That murmur, soon replies: "God doth not need
Either man's work or his own gifts; who best     10
Bear His mild yoke, they serve Him best. His state
Is kingly: thousands at His bidding speed,
And post o'er land and ocean without rest;
They also serve who only stand and wait."


▶ *John Dryden (1631-1700)*

## *Song from* MARRIAGE À LA MODE

Why should a foolish marriage vow,
    Which long ago was made,
Oblige us to each other now
    When passion is decayed?
We loved, and we loved, as long as we could,
    Till our love was loved out in us both:
But our marriage is dead, when the pleasure is fled:
    'Twas pleasure first made it an oath.

If I have pleasures for a friend,
    And farther love in store,          10
What wrong has he whose joys did end,
    And who could give no more?
'Tis a madness that he should be jealous of me,
    Or that I should bar him of another:
For all we can gain, is to give ourselves pain,
    When neither can hinder the other.

▶ *William Wordsworth (1770-1850)*

# THE SOLITARY REAPER

Behold her, single in the field,
You solitary Highland Lass!
Reaping and singing by herself;
Stop here, or gently pass!
Alone she cuts and binds the grain,
And sings a melancholy strain;
O listen! for the Vale profound
Is overflowing with the sound.

No Nightingale did ever chant
More welcome notes to weary bands          10
Of travellers in some shady haunt,
Among Arabian sands:
A voice so thrilling ne'er was heard
In spring-time from the Cuckoo-bird,
Breaking the silence of the seas
Among the farthest Hebrides.

Will no one tell me what she sings?—
Perhaps the plaintive numbers flow
For old, unhappy, far-off things,
And battles long ago:          20
Or is it some more humble lay,
Familiar matter of today?
Some natural sorrow, loss, or pain,
That has been, and may be again?

Whate'er the theme, the maiden sang
As if her song could have no ending;
I saw her singing at her work,
And o'er the sickle bending;—
I listened, motionless and still;
And, as I mounted up the hill,          30
The music in my heart I bore
Long after it was heard no more.

# COMPOSED UPON WESTMINSTER BRIDGE

Earth has not anything to show more fair:
Dull would he be of soul who could pass by
A sight so touching in its majesty.
This city now doth, like a garment, wear
The beauty of the morning; silent, bare,
Ships, towers, domes, theaters, and temples lie
Open unto the fields, and to the sky—
All bright and glittering in the smokeless air,
Never did sun more beautifully steep
In his first splendor valley, rock, or hill;          10
Ne'er saw I, never felt, a calm so deep!
The river glideth at his own sweet will.
Dear God! the very houses seem asleep,
And all that mighty heart is lying still!

▶ *George Gordon, Lord Byron (1788-1824)*

# *from* DON JUAN

FRAGMENT

I would to heaven that I were so much clay,
    As I am blood, bone, marrow, passion, feeling—
Because at least the past were passed away—
    And for the future—(but I write this reeling,

Having got drunk exceedingly today,
    So that I seem to stand upon the ceiling)
I say—the future is a serious matter—
And so—for God's sake—hock and soda-water!

FROM CANTO I

My poem's epic and is meant to be
    Divided in twelve books; each book containing,
With love, and war, a heavy gale at sea,
    A list of ships, and captains, and kings reigning,
New characters; the episodes are three:
    A panoramic view of Hell's in training,
After the style of Virgil and of Homer,
So that my name of Epic's no misnomer.

All these things will be specified in time,
    With strict regard to Aristotle's rules,
The *Vade Mecum* of the true sublime,
    Which makes so many poets, and some fools:
Prose poets like blank-verse, I'm fond of rime,
    Good workmen never quarrel with their tools;
I've got new mythological machinery,
And very handsome supernatural scenery.

There's only one slight difference between
    Me and my epic brethren gone before,
And here the advantage is my own, I ween
    (Not that I have not several merits more,
But this will peculiarly be seen);
    They so embellish, that 'tis quite a bore
Their labyrinth of fables to thread through,
Whereas this story's actually true.

FROM CANTO II

Oh ye! who teach the ingenuous youth of nations,
    Holland, France, England, Germany, or Spain,
I pray ye flog them upon all occasions;
    It mends their morals, never mind the pain:
The best of mothers and of educations
    In Juan's case were but employed in vain,
Since, in a way that's rather of the oddest, he
Became divested of his native modesty.

Had he but been placed at a public school,
    In the third form, or even in the fourth,
His daily task had kept his fancy cool,
    At least, had he been nurtured in the north;
Spain may prove an exception to the rule,
    But then exceptions always prove its worth—
A lad of sixteen causing a divorce
Puzzled his tutors very much, of course.

I can't say that it puzzles me at all,
    If all things be considered; first, there was          50
His lady-mother, mathematical,
    A——never mind;—his tutor, an old ass;
A pretty woman—(that's quite natural,
    Or else the thing had hardly come to pass)
A husband rather old, not much in unity
With his young wife—a time, and opportunity.

Well—well; the world must turn upon its axis,
    And all mankind turn with it, heads or tails,
And live and die, make love and pay our taxes,
    And as the veering wind shifts, shift our sails;     60
The king commands us, and the doctor quacks us,
    The priest instructs, and so our life exhales,
A little breath, love, wine, ambition, fame
Fighting, devotion, dust—perhaps a name.


▶ *Percy Bysshe Shelley (1792-1822)*

# OZYMANDIAS

I met a traveller from on antique land
Who said: Two vast and trunkless legs of stone
Stand in the desert. Near them, on the sand,
Half sunk, a shattered visage lies, whose frown,
And wrinkled lip, and sneer of cold command,
Tell that its sculptor well those passions read
Which yet survive, stamped on these lifeless things,
The hand that mocked them and the heart that fed;
And on the pedestal these words appear:
"My name is Ozymandias, king of kings:              10
Look on my works, ye Mighty, and despair!"
Nothing beside remains. Round the decay
Of that colossal wreck, boundless and bare
The lone and level sands stretch far away.


▶ *Emily Dickinson (1830-1886)*

# MY LIFE CLOSED TWICE
# BEFORE ITS CLOSE

My life closed twice before its close—
It yet remains to see
If Immortality unveil
A third event to me

So huge, so hopeless to conceive
As these that twice befell.
Parting is all we know of heaven,
And all we need of hell.

► *Thomas Hardy (1840-1928)*

# THE DARKLING THRUSH

I leaned upon a coppice gate
  When Frost was spectre-gray,
And Winter's dregs made desolate
  The weakening eye of day.
The tangled bine-stems scored the sky
  Like strings of broken lyres,
And all mankind that haunted nigh
  Had sought their household fires.

The land's sharp features seemed to be
  The Century's corpse outleant,             10
His crypt the cloudy canopy,
  The wind his death-lament.
The ancient pulse of germ and birth
  Was shrunken hard and dry,
And every spirit upon earth
  Seemed fervorless as I.

At once a voice arose among
  The bleak twigs overhead
In a full-hearted evensong
  Of joy illimited;                          20
An aged thrush, frail, gaunt, and small,
  In blast-beruffled plume,
Had chosen thus to fling his soul
  Upon the growing gloom.

So little cause for carolings
  Of such ecstatic sound
Was written on terrestrial things
  Afar or nigh around,
That I could think there trembled through
  His happy good-night air                   30
Some blessed Hope, whereof he knew
  And I was unaware.

► *Gerard Manley Hopkins (1844-1889)*

# SPRING

Nothing is so beautiful as spring—
  When weeds, in wheels, shoot long and lovely and lush;
  Thrush's eggs look little low heavens, and thrush
Through the echoing timber does so rinse and wring
The ear, it strikes like lightning to hear him sing;
  The glassy peartree leaves and blooms, they brush
  The descending blue; that blue is all in a rush
With richness; the racing lambs too have fair their fling.

What is all this juice and all this joy?
  A strain of the earth's sweet being in the beginning    10
In Eden garden.—Have, get, before it cloy,
  Before it cloud, Christ, lord, and sour with sinning,
Innocent mind and Mayday in girl and boy,
  Most, O maid's child, thy choice and worthy the winning.

▶ *William Ernest Henley (1849-1903)*

# INVICTUS

Out of the night that covers me,
    Black as the Pit from pole to pole,
I thank whatever gods may be
    For my unconquerable soul.

In the fell clutch of circumstance
    I have not winced nor cried aloud.
Under the bludgeonings of chance
    My head is bloody, but unbowed.

Beyond this place of wrath and tears
    Looms but the Horror of the shade,          10
And yet the menace of the years
    Finds, and shall find, me unafraid.

It matters not how strait the gate,
    How charged with punishments the scroll,
I am the master of my fate;
    I am the captain of my soul.

▶ *A. E. Housman (1859-1936)*

# "TERENCE, THIS IS STUPID STUFF"

"Terence, this is stupid stuff:
You eat your victuals fast enough;
There can't be much amiss, 'tis clear,
To see the rate you drink your beer.
But oh, good Lord, the verse you make,
It gives a chap the belly-ache.
The cow, the old cow, she is dead;
It sleeps well, the hornèd head:
We poor lads, 'tis our turn now
To hear such tunes as killed the cow.      10
Pretty friendship 'tis to rhyme
Your friends to death before their time
Moping melancholy mad:
Come, pipe a tune to dance to, lad."

Why, if 'tis dancing you would be,
There's brisker pipes than poetry.
Say, for what were hop-yards meant,
Or why was Burton built on Trent?
Oh, many a peer of England brews
Livelier liquor than the Muse,      20

And malt does more than Milton can
To justify God's ways to man.
Ale, man, ale's the stuff to drink
For fellows whom it hurts to think:
Look into the pewter pot
To see the world as the world't not.
And faith, 'tis pleasant till 'tis past:
The mischief is that 'twill not last.
Oh, I have been to Ludlow fair
And left my necktie God knows
    where,      30
And carried half-way home, or near,
Pints and quarts of Ludlow beer:
Then the world seemed none so bad,
And I myself a sterling lad;
And down in lovely muck I've lain,
Happy till I woke again.
Then I saw the morning sky:
Heigho, the tale was all a lie;
The world, it was the old world yet,
I was I, my things were wet,      40
And nothing now remained to do
But begin the game anew.

Therefore, since the world has still
Much good, but much less good than ill,

And while the sun and moon endure
Luck's a chance, but trouble's sure,
I'd face it as a wise man would,
And train for ill and not for good.
'Tis true, the stuff I bring for sale          50
Is not so brisk a brew as ale:
Out of a stem that scored the hand
I wrung it in a weary land.
But take it: if the smack is sour,

## WHEN I WAS ONE-AND-TWENTY

When I was one-and-twenty
    I heard a wise man say,
'Give crowns and pounds and guineas
    But not your heart away;
Give pearls away and rubies
    But keep your fancy free.'
But I was one-and-twenty,
    No use to talk to me.

When I was one-and-twenty
    I heard him say again,                      10
'The heart out of the bosom
    Was never given in vain;
'Tis paid with sighs a plenty
    And sold for endless rue.'
And I am two-and-twenty,
    And oh, 'tis true, 'tis true.

▶ *Rudyard Kipling (1865-1936)*

## RECESSIONAL

God of our fathers, known of old,
    Lord of our far-flung battle-line,          50
Beneath whose awful Hand we hold
    Dominion over palm and pine—
Lord God of Hosts, be with us yet,
Lest we forget—lest we forget!

The tumult and the shouting dies:
    The Captains and the Kings depart:
Still stands Thine ancient sacrifice,
    An humble and a contrite heart.             10
Lord God of Hosts, be with us yet,
Lest we forget—lest we forget!

Far-called, our navies melt away;
    On dune and headland sinks the fire:
Lo, all our pomp of yesterday
    Is one with Nineveh and Tyre!
Judge of the Nations, spare us yet,
Lest we forget—lest we forget!

If, drunk with sight of power, we loose
    Wild tongues that have not Thee in awe,     20
Such boastings as the Gentiles use,
    Or lesser breeds without the Law—
Lord God of Hosts, be with us yet,
Lest we forget—lest we forget!

For heathen heart that puts her trust
    In reeking tube and iron shard,
All valiant dust that builds on dust,
    And guarding, calls not Thee to guard,
For frantic boast and foolish word—
Thy Mercy on Thy People, Lord!                  30

▶ *Edwin Arlington Robinson (1869-1935)*

## MINIVER CHEEVY

Miniver Cheevy, child of scorn,
    Grew lean while he assailed the seasons;
He wept that he was ever born,
    And he had reasons.

Miniver loved the days of old
    When swords were bright and steeds were prancing,

The vision of a warrior bold
   Would set him dancing.

Miniver sighed for what was not,
   And dreamed, and rested from his labors;           10
He dreamed of Thebes and Camelot,
   And Priam's neighbors.

Miniver mourned the ripe renown
   That made so many a name so fragrant;
He mourned Romance, now on the town,
   And Art, a vagrant.

Miniver loved the Medici,
   Albeit he had never seen one;
He would have sinned incessantly
   Could he have been one.                 20

Miniver cursed the commonplace
   And eyed a khaki suit with loathing;
He missed the mediaeval grace
   Of iron clothing.

Miniver scorned the gold he sought,
   But sore annoyed was he without it;
Miniver thought, and thought, and thought,
   And thought about it.

Miniver Cheevy, born too late,
   Scratched his head and kept on thinking;      30
Miniver coughed, and called it fate,
   And kept on drinking.

# RICHARD CORY

Whenever Richard Cory went down town,
We people on the pavement looked at him:
He was a gentleman from sole to crown,
Clean favored, and imperially slim.

And he was always quietly arrayed,
And he was always human when he talked;
But still he fluttered pulses when he said,
"Good-morning," and he glittered when he walked.

And he was rich—yes, richer than a king—
And admirably schooled in every grace:         10
In fine, we thought he was everything
To make us wish that we were in his place.

So on we worked, and waited for the light,
And went without the meat, and cursed the bread;
And Richard Cory, one calm summer night,
Went home and put a bullet through his head.

▶ *Ezra Pound (1885-    )*

# SALUTATION

O generation of the thoroughly smug
   and thoroughly uncomfortable,
I have seen fishermen picnicking in the sun,
I have seen them with untidy families,
I have seen their smiles full of teeth
   and heard ungainly laughter.
And I am happier than you are,
And they were happier than I am;
And the fish swim in the lake
   and do not even own clothing.    10

▶ *D. H. Lawrence (1885-1930)*

# PIANO

Softly, in the dusk, a woman is singing to me;
Taking me back down the vista of years, till I see
A child sitting under the piano, in the boom of the tingling
    strings
And pressing the small, poised feet of a mother who smiles
    as she sings.

In spite of myself, the insidious mastery of song
Betrays me back, till the heart of me weeps to belong
To the old Sunday evenings at home, with winter outside
And hymns in the cozy parlor, the tinkling piano our guide.

So now it is vain for the singer to burst into clamor
With the great black piano appassionato. The glamor    10
Of childish days is upon me, my manhood is cast
Down in the flood of rememberance, I weep like a child
    for the past.

▶ *Archibald MacLeish (1892-    )*

# "DOVER BEACH" A NOTE TO THAT POEM

The Wave Withdrawing
Withers with seaward rustle of flimsy water
Sucking the sand down: dragging at empty shells:
The roll after it settling: too smooth: smothered . . .

After forty a man's a fool to wait in the
Sea's face for the full force and the roaring of
Surf to come over him: droves of careening water.
After forty the tug's out and the salt and the
Sea follow it: less sound and violence:
Nevertheless the ebb has its own beauty    10
Shells sand and all the whispering rustle.
There's earth in it then and the bubbles of foam gone.

Moreover—and this too has its lovely uses—
It's the outward wave that spills the inward forward
Tripping the proud piled mute virginal
Mountain of water in wallowing welter of light and
Sound enough—thunder for miles back: it's a fine and a
Wild smother to vanish in: pulling down—
Tripping with outward ebb the urgent inward.

Speaking alone for myself it's the steep hill and the          20
Toppling lift of the young men I am toward now—
Waiting for that as the wave for the next wave.
Let them go over us all I say with the thunder of
What's to be next in the world. It's we will be under it!


▶ *Hugh MacDiarmid (1892-        )*

# REFLECTIONS IN A SLUM

A lot of the old folk here—all that's left
Of them after a lifetime's infernal thrall
Remind me of a Bolshie the "whites" buried alive
Up to his nose, just able to breathe, that's all.

Watch them. You'll see when I mean. When found
His eyes had lost their former gay twinkle.
Ants had eaten *that* away; but there was still
Some life in him . . . his forehead *would* wrinkle!
And I remember Gide telling
Of Valéry and himself:                                          10
"It was a long time ago. We were young.
We had mingled with idlers
Who formed a circle
Round a troupe of wretched mountebanks.
It was on a raised strip of pavement
In the boulevard Saint Germain,
In front of the Statue of Broca.
They were admiring a poor woman,
Thin and gaunt, in pink tights, despite the cold.
Her team-mate had tied her, trussed her up,          20
Skilfully from head to foot,
With a rope that went round her
I don't know how many times,
And from which, by a sort of wriggling,
She was to manage to free herself.
Sorry image of the fate of the masses!
But no one thought of the symbol.
The audience merely contemplated
In stupid bliss the patient's efforts.
She twisted, she writhed, slowly freed one arm,          30

Then the other, and when at last
The final cord fell from her
Valéry took me by the arm:
'Let's go now! She has ceased suffering!' "

Oh, if only ceasing to suffer
They were able to become men.
Alas! how many owe their dignity,
Their claim on our sympathy,
Merely to their misfortune.
Likewise, so long as a plant has not blossomed          40
One can hope that its flowering will be beautiful.
What a mirage surrounds what has not yet blossomed!
What a disappointment when one can no longer
Blame the abjection on the deficiency!
It is good that the voice of the indigent,
Too long stifled, should manage
To make itself heard.
But I cannot consent to listen
To nothing but that voice.
Man does not cease to interest me                       50
When he ceases to be miserable.
Quite the contrary!
That it is important to aid him
In the beginning goes without saying,
Like a plant it is essential
To water at first,
But this is in order to get it to flower
And I *am concerned with the blossom.*

▶ *Wilfred Owen (1893-1918)*

# THE NEXT WAR

*War's a joke for me and you,*
*While we know such dreams are true.*
                                        —*Sassoon*

Out there, we've talked quite friendly up to Death;
    Sat down and eaten with him, cool and bland,—
    Pardoned his spilling mess-tins in our hand.
We've sniffed the green thick odour of his breath,—
Our eyes wept, but our courage didn't writhe.
    He's spat at us with bullets and he's coughed
    Shrapnel. We chorussed when he sang aloft;
We whistled while he shaved us with his scythe.

Oh, Death was never an enemy of ours!
    We laughed at him, we leagued with him, old chum.     10

No soldier's paid to kick against his powers.
    We laughed, knowing that better men would come,
And greater wars; when each proud fighter brags
He wars on Death—for Life; not men—for flags.


## ANTHEM FOR DOOMED YOUTH

What passing-bells for these who die as cattle?
    Only the monstrous anger of the guns.
    Only the stuttering rifle's rapid rattle
Can patter out their hasty orisons.
No mockeries for them from prayers or bells,
Nor any voice of mourning save the choirs,—
The shrill, demented choirs of wailing shells;
And bugles calling for them from sad shires.

What candles may be held to speed them all?
    Not in the hands of boys, but in their eyes          10
Shall shine the holy glimmers of good-byes.
    The pallor of girls' brows shall be their pall;
Their flowers the tenderness of silent minds,
And each slow dusk a drawing-down of blinds.


▶ *Dorothy Parker (1893-1967)*

## A FAIRLY SAD TALE

I think that I shall never know
Why I am thus, and I am so.
Around me, other girls inspire
In men the rush and roar of fire,
The sweet transparency of glass,
The tenderness of April grass.
The durability of granite;
But me—I don't know how to plan it.
The lads I've met in Cupid's deadlock
Were—shall we say?—born out of wedlock.   10
They broke my heart, they stilled my song,
And said they had to run along,
Explaining, so to sop my tears.
First came their parents or careers.
But ever does experience
Deny me wisdom, calm, and sense!
Though she's a fool who seeks to capture
The twenty-first fine, careless rapture,

I must go on, till ends my rope,
Who from my birth was cursed with hope.   20
A heart in half is chaste, archaic;
But mine resembles a mosaic—
The thing's become ridiculous!
Why am I so? Why am I thus?


## FIGHTING WORDS

Say my love is easy had,
    Say I'm bitten raw with pride,
Say I am too often sad—
    Still behold me at your side.

Say I'm neither brave nor young,
    Say I woo and coddle care,
Say the devil touched my tongue—
    Still you have my heart to wear.

But say my verses do not scan,
    And I get me another man!          10

# SECOND LOVE

"So surely is she mine," you say, and turn
Your quick and steady mind to harder things—
To bills and bonds and talk of what men earn—
And whistle up the stair, of evenings.
And do you see a dream behind my eyes,
Or ask a simple question twice of me—
"Thus women are," you say; for men are wise
And tolerant, in their security.

How shall I count the midnights I have known
When calm you turn to me, nor feel me start,        10
To find my easy lips upon your own
And know my breast beneath your rhythmic heart.
Your god defer the day I tell you this:
My lad, my lad, it is not you I kiss!


▶ *Hart Crane (1899-1932)*

# CHAPLINESQUE

We make our meek adjustments,
Contented with such random consolations
As the wind deposits
In slithered and too ample pockets.
For we can still love the world, who find
A famished kitten on the step, and know
Recesses for it from the fury of the street,
Or warm torn elbow coverts.

We will sidestep, and to the final smirk
Dally the doom of that inevitable thumb        10
That slowly chafes its puckered index toward us,
Facing the dull squint with what innocence
And what surprise!

And yet these fine collapses are not lies
More than the pirouettes of any pliant cane;
Our obsequies are, in a way, no enterprise.
We can evade you, and all else but the heart:
What blame to us if the heart live on.

The game enforces smirks; but we have seen
The moon in lonely alleys make        20
A grail of laughter of an empty ash can,
And through all sound of gaiety and quest
Have heard a kitten in the wilderness.

# DIRGE

1-2-3 was the number he played but today the number came
    3-2-1;
Bought his Carbide at 30 and it went to 29; had the favorite
    at Bowie but the track was slow—

O executive type, would you like to drive a floating-power,
    knee-action, silk-upholstered six? Wed a Hollywood star?
    Shoot the course in 58? Draw to the ace, king, jack?
O fellow with a will who won't take no, watch out for three
    cigarettes on the same, single match; O democratic voter
    born in August under Mars, beware of liquidated rails—        10

Denouement to denouement, he took a personal pride in the
    certain, certain way he lived his own, private life,
But nevertheless, they shut off his gas; nevertheless, the bank
    foreclosed; nevertheless, the landlord called; neverthe-
    less, the radio broke,

And twelve o'clock arrived just once too often,
Just the same he wore one gray tweed suit, bought one straw
    hat, drank one straight Scotch, walked one short step,
    took one long look, drew one deep breath,
Just one too many,        20

And wow he died as wow he lived,
Going whop to the office and blooie home to sleep and biff
    got married and bam had children and oof got fired,
Zowie did he live and zowie did he die,

With who the hell are you at the corner of his casket, and
    where the hell're we going on the right-hand silver knob,
    and who the hell cares walking second from the end with
    an American Beauty wreath from why the hell not,

Very much missed by the circulation staff of the New York
    Evening Post; deeply mourned by the B.M.T.        30
Wham, Mr. Roosevelt; pow, Sears Roebuck; awk, big dipper;
    bop, summer rain;
Bong, Mr. bong, Mr., bong, Mr., bong.

▶ *C. Day Lewis (1904-    )*

# LET US NOW PRAISE FAMOUS MEN

Let us now praise famous men,
Not your earth-shakers, not the dynamiters,
But who in the Home Counties or the Khyber,
Trimming their nails to meet an ill wind,
Facing the Adversary with a clean collar,
Justified the system.
Admire the venerable pile that bred them,
Bones are its foundations,
The pinnacles are stone abstractions,
Whose halls are whispering-galleries designed          10
To echo voices of the past, dead tongues.
White hopes of England here
Are taught to rule by learning to obey,
Bend over before vested interests,
Kiss the rod, salute the quarter-deck;
Here is no savage discipline
Of peregrine swooping, of fire destroying,
But a civil code; no capital offender
But the cool cad, the man who goes too far.
Ours the curriculum                                    20
Neither of building birds nor wasteful waters,
Bound in book not violent in vein:
Here we inoculate with dead ideas
Against blood-epidemics, against
The infection of faith and the excess of life.
Our methods are up to date; we teach
Through head and not by heart,
Language with gramophones and sex with charts,
Prophecy by deduction, prayer by numbers.
For honors see prospectus: those who leave us          30
Will get a post and pity the poor;
Their eyes glaze at strangeness;
They are never embarrassed, have a word for everything,
Living on credit, dying when the heart stops;
Will wear black armlets and stand a moment in silence
For the passing of an era, at their own funeral.

▶ *W. H. Auden (1907-    )*

## LAY YOUR SLEEPING HEAD, MY LOVE

Lay your sleeping head, my love,
Human on my faithless arm;
Time and fevers burn away
Individual beauty from
Thoughtful children, and the grave
Proves the child ephemeral:
But in my arms till break of day
Let the living creature lie,
Mortal, guilty, but to me
The entirely beautiful.                          10

Soul and body have no bounds:
To lovers as they lie upon
Her tolerant enchanted slope
In their ordinary swoon,
Grave the vision Venus sends
Of supernatural sympathy,
Universal love and hope;
While an abstract insight wakes
Among the glaciers and the rocks
The hermit's sensual ecstasy.                    20

Certainty, fidelity
On the stroke of midnight pass
Like vibrations of a bell,
And fashionable madmen raise
Their pedantic boring cry:
Every farthing of the cost,
All the dreaded cards foretell,
Shall be paid, but from this night
Not a whisper, not a thought,
Not a kiss nor look be lost.                      30

Beauty, midnight, vision dies:
Let the winds of dawn that blow
Softly round your dreaming head
Such a day of sweetness show
Eye and knocking heart may bless,
Find the mortal world enough;
Noons of dryness see you fed
By the involuntary powers,
Nights of insult let you pass
Watched by every human love.                     40

▶ *Theodore Roethke (1908-1963)*

## THE WAKING

I wake to sleep, and take my waking slow.
I feel my fate in what I cannot fear.
I learn by going where I have to go.

We think by feeling. What is there to know?
I hear my being dance from ear to ear.
I wake to sleep, and take my waking slow.

Of those so close beside me, which are you?
God bless the Ground! I shall walk softly there,
And learn by going where I have to go.

Light takes the Tree; but who can tell us how?    10
The lowly worm climbs up a winding stair;
I wake to sleep, and take my waking slow.

Great Nature has another thing to do
To you and me; so take the lively air,
And, lovely, learn by going where to go.

This shaking keeps me steady. I should know.
What falls away is always. And is near.
I wake to sleep, and take my waking slow,
I learn by going where I have to go.


▶  *Henry Reed (1914-       )*

# NAMING OF PARTS

*Vixi duellis nuper idoneus*
*Et militavi non sine gloria**

Today we have naming of parts. Yesterday,
We had daily cleaning. And tomorrow morning,
We shall have what to do after firing. But today,
Today we have naming of parts. Japonica
Glistens like coral in all of the neighbouring gardens,
    And today we have naming of parts.

This is the lower sling swivel. And this
Is the upper sling swivel, whose use you will see,
When you are given your slings. And this is the piling swivel,
Which in your case you have not got. The branches                    10
Hold in the gardens their silent, eloquent gestures,
    Which in our case we have not got.

This is the safety-catch, which is always released
With an easy flick of the thumb. And please do not let me
See anyone using his finger. You can do it quite easy
If you have any strength in your thumb. The blossoms
Are fragile and motionless, never letting anyone see
    Any of them using their finger.

And this you can see is the bolt. The purpose of this
Is to open the breech, as you see. We can slide it                    20
Rapidly backwards and forwards: we call this
Easing the spring. And rapidly backwards and forwards
The early bees are assaulting and fumbling the flowers:
    They call it easing the Spring.

They call it easing the Spring: it is perfectly easy
If you have any strength in your thumb: like the bolt,
And the breech, and the cocking-piece, and the point of balance,
Which in our case we have not got; and the almond-blossom
Silent in all of the gardens and the bees going backwards and forwards,
    For today we have naming of parts.                               30

---

* Not without glory have I of late lived the military life.

▶ *John Ciardi (1916-    )*

# DIVORCED, HUSBAND DEMOLISHES HOUSE

*—News Item*

It is time to break a house.
What shall I say to you
but torn tin and the shriek
of nails pulled orange
from the ridge pole? Rip it
and throw it away. Beam
by beam. Sill, step, and lintel.
Crack it and knock it down.

Brick by brick. (I breathe
the dust of openings. My tongue          10
is thick with plaster. What can I
say to you? The sky has come
through our rafters. Our windows
are flung wide and the wind's
here. There are no doors
in or out.) Tug it
and let it crash. Haul it,
bulldoze it over. What can I say
to you except that nothing
must be left of the nothing          20
I cannot say to you? It's
done with. Let it come down.

▶ *Richard Wilbur (1921-    )*

# STILL, CITIZEN SPARROW

Still, citizen sparrow, this vulture which you call
Unnatural, let him but lumber again to air
Over the rotten office, let him bear
The carrion ballast up, and at the tall

Tip of the sky lie cruising. Then you'll see
That no more beautiful bird is in heaven's height,
No wider more placid wings, no watchfuller flight;
He shoulders nature there, the frightfully free,

The naked-headed one. Pardon him, you
Who dart in the orchard aisles, for it is he          10
Devours death, mocks mutability,
Has heart to make an end, keeps nature new.

Thinking of Noah, childheart, try to forget
How for so many bedlam hours his saw
Soured the song of birds with its wheezy gnaw,
And the slam of his hammer all the day beset

The people's ears. Forget that he could bear
To see the towns like coral under the keel,
And the fields to dismal deep. Try rather to feel
How high and weary it was, on the waters where          20

He rocked his only world, and everyone's.
Forgive the hero, you who would have died
Gladly with all you knew; he rode that tide
To Ararat; all men are Noah's sons.

▶ *John Updike (1932-      )*

# YOUTH'S PROGRESS

> *Dick Schneider of Wisconsin . . . was elected*
> *"Greek God" for an interfraternity ball.*
>                                          —Life

When I was born, my mother taped my ears
So they lay flat. When I had aged ten years,
My teeth were firmly braced and much improved.
Two years went by; my tonsils were removed.

At fourteen, I began to comb my hair
A fancy way. Though nothing much was there,
I shaved my upper lip—next year, my chin.
At seventeen, the freckles left my skin.

Just turned nineteen, a nicely molded lad,
I said goodbye to Sis and Mother; Dad                    10
Drove me to Wisconsin and set me loose.
At twenty-one, I was elected Zeus.

▶ *Rod McKuen (1938-      )*

# HOW CAN WE BE SURE OF ANYTHING

How can we be sure of anything
                          the tide changes.
The wind that made the grain wave gently yesterday
   blows down the trees tomorrow.
And the sea sends sailors crashing on the rocks,
as easily as it guides them safely home.
                          I love the sea
but it doesn't make me less afraid of it.
                          I love you
but I'm not always sure of what you are                  10
and how you feel.

I'd like to crawl behind your eyes
and see me the way you do
   or climb through your mouth
and sit on every word that comes up through your throat.

Maybe I could be sure then
                          maybe I could know
as it is—I hide beneath your frowns
or worry when you laugh too loud.
                          Always sure a storm is rising.   20

▶ *Anne Sexton (1928-    )*

## SOME FOREIGN LETTERS

I knew you forever and you were always old,
soft white lady of my heart. Surely you would scold
me for sitting up late, reading your letters,
as if these foreign postmarks were meant for me.
You posted them first in London, wearing furs
and a new dress in the winter of eighteen-ninety.
I read how London is dull on Lord Mayor's Day,
where you guided past groups of robbers, the sad holes
of Whitechapel, clutching your pocketbook, on the way
to Jack the Ripper dissecting his famous bones.                          10
This Wednesday in Berlin, you say, you will
go to a bazaar at Bismarck's house. And I
see you as a young girl in a good world still,
writing three generations before mine. I try
to reach into your page and breathe it back . . .
but life is a trick, life is a kitten in a sack.

This is the sack of time your death vacates.
How distant you are on your nickel-plated skates
in the skating park in Berlin, gliding past
me with your Count, while a military band                                20
plays a Strauss waltz. I loved you last,
a pleated old lady with a crooked hand.
Once you read *Lohengrin* and every goose
hung high while you practiced castle life
in Hanover. Tonight your letters reduce
history to a guess. The Count had a wife.
You were the old maid aunt who lived with us.
Tonight I read how the winter howled around
the towers of Schloss Schwöbber, how the tedious
language grew in your jaw, how you loved the sound                       30
of the music of the rats tapping on the stone
floors. When you were mine you wore an earphone.

This is Wednesday, May 9th, near Lucerne,
Switzerland, sixty-nine years ago. I learn
your first climb up Mount San Salvatore;
this is the rocky path, the hole in your shoes,
the yankee girl, the iron interior
of her sweet body. You let the Count choose
your next climb. You went together, armed
with alpine stocks, with ham sandwiches                                  40
and seltzer wasser. You were not alarmed.
by the thick woods of briars and bushes,
nor the rugged cliff, nor the first vertigo
up over Lake Lucerne. The Count sweated
with his coat off as you waded through top snow.

He held your hand and kissed you. You rattled
down on the train to catch a steamboat for home;
or other postmarks: Paris, Verona, Rome.

This is Italy. You learn its mother tongue.
I read how you walked over the Palatine among                    50
the ruins of the palaces of the Caesars;
alone in the Roman autumn, alone since July.
When you were mine they wrapped you out of here
with your best hat over your face. I cried
because I was seventeen. I am older now.
I read how your student ticket admitted you
into the private chapel of the Vatican and how
you cheered with the others, as we used to do
on the Fourth of July. One Wednesday in November
you watched a balloon, painted like a silver ball,               60
float up over the Forum, up over the lost emperors,
to shiver its little modern cage in an occasional
breeze. You worked your New England conscience out
beside artisans, chestnut vendors and the devout.

Tonight I will learn to love you twice;
learn your first days, your mid-Victorian face.
Tonight I will speak up and interrupt
your letters, warning you that wars are coming,
that the Count will die, that you will accept
your America back to live like a prim thing                       70
on the farm in Maine. I tell you, you will come
here, to the suburbs of Boston, to see the blue-nose
world go drunk each night, to see the handsome
children jitterbug, to feel your left ear close
one Friday at Symphony. And I tell you,
you will tip your boot feet out of that hall,
rocking from its sour sound, out onto
the crowded street, letting your spectacles fall
and your hair net tangle as you stop passers-by
to mumble your guilty love while your ears die.                   80

▶  *Lawrence Ferlinghetti (1920-      )*

## LOUD PRAYER

Our father whose art's in heaven
hollow be thy name
unless things change
Thy wigdom come and gone
thy will will be undone
on earth as it isn't heaven
Give us this day our daily bread

at least three times a day
and forgive us our trespasses
as we would forgive those lovelies                                10
whom we wish would trespass against us
And lead us not into temptation
too often on weekdays
but deliver us from evil
whose presence remains unexplained
in thy kingdom of power and glory
oh man.

# ▶▶▶▌ IMAGERY

Imagery, the representation of sense experience through language, is a vital part of poetry. Because the poet often attempts to create a mood, to evoke certain emotions and reactions for the reader, vivid and imaginative imagery captures the reader's attention and draws him into the experience the poet wishes to transmit. Imagery not only helps the reader understand the poet's state of mind or message, but also gives the poem increased personal significance for each reader, as the poet's images interact with the reader's memories, his subjective feelings and judgments, likes and dislikes, and individual interpretations. The connotation and denotation of the words used also plays an important part in the image's effect on the reader; a single image may be interpreted in a variety of different ways by different readers.

Imagery may be direct or descriptive, giving the details of a sense experience, or it may be figurative, expressing sensory information by comparison or analogy in the form of a metaphor or simile. The former type is most often used when the poet wishes to relate one particular impression or create a definite emotional, or intellectual response; the latter type is often used when the poet wishes to develop several levels of meaning. Figurative language, of course, is a separate though closely related aspect of poetry; very generally speaking, figurative language tends toward the subtle and complex while imagery deals more straightforwardly with specific impressions.

Physical imagery, which presents impressions of sight, sound, taste, smell, and touch, combines concrete reality with imagination and fantasy in order to give sense experience added significance and dimension, is, when used with moderation and originality, an effective method of connecting the poet's message with the reader's experiences and attitudes. Sights, sounds, smells, feelings, and tastes evoke memories, moods, and various mental connections; each association produced by imagery increases the poem's impact and ultimate value.

Examples of such affective imagery can be found in Robert Browning's "Meeting at Night," including "the startled little waves that leap/in fiery ringlets from their sleep" and "warm sea-scented beach," which create, respectively, the impressions of excitement and pleasure. Urgency and surprise are produced by the opening line of Browning's "Parting at Morning": "Round the cape of a sudden came the sea." Walt Whitman's comparison of the busy spinning spider with his soul, "Ceaselessly musing, venturing, throwing, seeking . . ." in "A Noiseless Patient Spider," A. E. Housman's lines in "To An Athlete Dying Young": "So set, before its echoes fade/The fleet foot on the sill of shade/And hold to the low linter up/The still-defended challenge-cup," and William Butler Yeats' lines in "Among School Children": "Hollow of cheek as though it drank the wind/And took a mess of shadows for its meat?"—these are all examples of well-chosen, skillfully drawn imagery.

Wallace Stevens' lines in "Thirteen Ways of Looking at a Blackbird," "Icicles filled the long window/With barbaric glass," and "At the sight of blackbirds/Flying in a green light,/Even the bawds of euphony/Would cry out sharply," create an aura of uneasiness, while T. S. Eliot achieves a similar effect in "Sweeney Among the Nightingales" through his descriptions of various people, the man with "The zebra stripes along his jaw/Swelling to maculate giraffe," "The silent vertebrate in brown," who "Contracts and concentrates, withdraws"; and the lady who "Tears at the grapes with murderous paws."

Two poems in which imagery plays a vital and indispensable part are Keats' "The Eve of St. Agnes" and Dylan Thomas' "Poem in October"; here, imagery not only creates mood and reinforces impressions but simultaneously shapes and reflects meaning. The beauty of the language used in description and comparison is an essential element of each poem's total significance. The richness and variety of imagery in these works contribute color and life; they also provide the reader with a base from which he can formulate his own impressions, using his individual experiences to add further dimensions to the poets' descriptions.

Thomas' unusual images, "the mussel-pooled and the heron-Priested shore," "the birds of the winged trees flying my mane," "a springful of larks in a rolling/Cloud and the roadside bushes brimming with whistling/Blackbirds and the sun of October/Summery/On the hill's shoulder," ". . . I wandered and listened/To the rain-wringing/Wind blow cold," "Pale rain over the dwindling harbor/And over the sea-wet church the size of a snail," all contribute to the theme of the joyous freedom and innocence summer of childhood giving way to the cool and far less magical autumn of experience. The lines "And the true/Joy of the long dead child sang burning/In the sun," and "the town below lay leaved with October blood" effectively depict the contrast between the two states.

"The Eve of St. Agnes," a narrative which tells a Romeo and Juliet sort of tale of love, intrigue, glamour, and excitement is given added depth and scope by the extensive imagery. The following examples represent only a few of Keats' appeals to the five senses, but they clearly illustrate the effect that skillful use of imagery has on the poem's tone and mood. In Madelaine's room:

A casement high and triple-arched there was,
All garlanded with carven imag'ries
Of fruits, and flowers, and bunches of knot-grass,
And diamonded with panes of quaint device,
Innumerable of stains and splended dyes,
As are the tiger-moth's deep-damasked wings;
And in the midst, 'mong thousand heraldries,
And twilight saints, and dim emblazonings,
A shielded scutcheon blushed with blood of
    queens and kings.

The girl "Unclasps her warmed jewels one by one;/Loosens her fragrant bodice; by degrees/Her rich attire creeps rustling to her knees;/Half-hidden like a mermaid in sea-weed . . ." Then, ". . . trembling in her soft and chilly nest,/In a sort of wakeful swoon, perplexed she lay,/Until the poppied warmth of sleep oppressed/Her soothed limbs, and soul fatigued away." While she sleeps, Porphyro prepares a feast "Of candied apple, quince, and plum, and gourd;/With jellies smoother than the creamy curd,/And lucent syrups, tinct with cinnamon." Outside, ". . . the frost-wind blows/Like Love's alarum pattering the sharp sleet/Against the window-panes."

This tale of secret love could very easily have been told in either a mundane or an overly sentimental manner; Keats' rich and imaginative imagery, however, gives an ethereal quality, an aura of magic and beauty, of delicate yet strong emotion. His emphasis on details, on thorough description of fleeting sensations and impressions of people and things, embroiders the basically simple plot and theme.

Imagery, then, is not only a means of illustrating the poet's ideas, a decorative device, and a determiner of tone, it can also develop and carry meaning. To be effective, imagery should be well-placed and not overdone; when it is used very frequently, it must display the poet's originality, imagination, and his ability to make subtle distinctions, as is apparent in "Poem in October" and "The Eve of St. Agnes."

▶ *Robert Herrick (1591-1674)*

## DELIGHT IN DISORDER

A sweet disorder in the dress
Kindles in clothes a wantonness;
A lawn about the shoulders thrown
Into a fine distraction;
An erring lace, which here and there
Enthralls the crimson stomacher;
A cuff neglectful, and thereby
Ribbands to flow confusedly;
A winning wave deserving note,
In the tempestuous petticoat;                    10
A careless shoestring, in whose tie
I see a wild civility
Do more bewitch me, than when art
Is too precise in every part.

▶ *Henry King (1592-1669)*

## SIC VITA [SUCH IS LIFE]

Like to the falling of a star,
Or as the flights of eagles are,
Or like the fresh spring's gaudy hue,
Or silver drops of morning dew,
Or like a wind that chafes the flood,
Or bubbles which on water stood:

Even such is man, whose borrowed light
Is straight called in, and paid to night.
   The wind blows out, the bubble dies;
   The spring entombed in autumn lies;          10
   The dew dries up, the star is shot;
   The flight is past, and man forgot.

▶ *Jonathan Swift (1667-1745)*

## A DESCRIPTION OF THE MORNING

Now hardly here and there a hackney-coach
Appearing, showed the ruddy morn's approach.
Now Betty from her master's bed had flown,
And softly stole to discompose her own;
The slip-shod 'prentice from his master's door
Had pared the dirt, and sprinkled round the floor.
Now Moll had whirled her mop with dext'rous airs,
Prepared to scrub the entry and the stairs.
The youth with broomy stumps began to trace
The kennel-edge where wheels had worn the place.          10
The small-coal man was heard with cadence deep,
Till drowned in shriller notes of chimney-sweep:
Duns at his lordship's gate began to meet;
And brick-dust Moll had screamed through half the street.
The turnkey now his flock returning sees,
Duly let out a-nights to steal for fees:
The watchful bailiffs take their silent stands,
And schoolboys lag with satchels in their hands.

*William Blake (1757-1827)*

# LONDON

I wander through each chartered street,
Near where the chartered Thames does flow,
And mark in every face I meet
Marks of weakness, marks of woe.

In every cry of every man,
In every infant's cry of fear,
In every voice, in every ban,
The mind-forged manacles I hear.

How the chimney-sweeper's cry
Every black'ning church appalls;                                    10
And the hapless soldier's sigh
Runs in blood down palace walls.

But most through midnight streets I hear
How the youthful harlot's curse
Blasts the new-born infant's tear,
And blights with plagues the marriage hearse.


*Samuel Taylor Coleridge (1772-1834)*

# KUBLA KHAN

In Xanadu did Kubla Khan
A stately pleasure-dome decree:
Where Alph, the sacred river, ran
Through caverns measureless to man
    Down to a sunless sea.
So twice five miles of fertile ground
With walls and towers were girdled round:
And here were gardens bright with sinuous rills,
Where blossomed many an incense-bearing tree;
And here were forests ancient as the hills,                        10
Enfolding sunny spots of greenery.
But oh! that deep romantic chasm which slanted
Down the green hill athwart a cedarn cover!
A savage place! as holy and enchanted
As e'er beneath a waning moon was haunted
By woman wailing for her demon-lover!
And from this chasm, with ceaseless turmoil seething,
As if this earth in fast thick pants were breathing,
A mighty fountain momently was forced:
Amid whose swift half-intermitted burst                           20
Huge fragments vaulted like rebounding hail,
Or chaffy grain beneath the thresher's flail:

And 'mid these dancing rocks at once and ever
It flung up momently the sacred river.
Five miles meandering with a mazy motion
Through wood and dale the sacred river ran,
Then reached the caverns measureless to man,
And sank in tumult to a lifeless ocean:
And 'mid this tumult Kubla heard from far
Ancestral voices prophesying war!                        30

    The shadow of the dome of pleasure
    Floated midway on the waves;
    Where was heard the mingled measure
    From the fountain and the caves.
It was a miracle of rare device,
A sunny pleasure-dome with caves of ice!

    A damsel with a dulcimer
    In a vision once I saw:
    It was an Abyssinian maid,
    And on her dulcimer she played,                 40
    Singing of Mount Abora.
    Could I revive within me
    Her symphony and song,
    To such a deep delight, 'twould win me,

    That with music loud and long,
    I would build that dome in air,
    That sunny dome! those caves of ice!
    And all who heard should see them there,
    And all should cry, Beware! Beware!
    His flashing eyes, his floating hair!            50
    Weave a circle round him thrice,
    And close your eyes with holy dread,
    For he on honey-dew hath fed,
    And drunk the milk of Paradise.

▶ *John Keats (1795-1821)*

# THE EVE OF ST. AGNES

### 1

    St. Agnes' Eve—Ah, bitter chill it was!
    The owl, for all his feathers, was a-cold;
    The hare limped trembling through the frozen grass,
    And silent was the flock in woolly fold:
    Numb were the Beadsman's fingers, while he told
    His rosary, and while his frosted breath,
    Like pious incense from a censer old,
    Seemed taking flight for Heaven, without a death,
Past the sweet Virgin's picture, while his prayer he saith.

His prayer he saith, this patient, holy man;        10
Then takes his lamp, and riseth from his knees,
And back returneth, meagre, barefoot, wan,
Along the chapel aisle by slow degrees:
The sculptured dead on each side seem to freeze,
Imprisoned in black, purgatorial rails:
Knights, ladies, praying in dumb orat'ries,
He passeth by; and his weak spirit fails
To think how they may ache in icy hoods and mails.

3

Northward he turneth through a little door,
And scarce three steps, ere Music's golden tongue    20
Flattered to tears this aged man and poor;
But no—already had his deathbell rung:
The joys of all life were said and sung.
His was harsh penance on St. Agnes Eve:
Another way he went, and soon among
Rough ashes sat he for his soul's reprieve,
And all night kept awake, for sinners' sake to grieve.

4

That ancient Beadsman heard the prelude soft;
And so it chanced, for many a door was wide,
From hurry to and fro. Soon, up aloft,    30
The silver, snarling trumpets 'gan to chide:
The level chambers, ready with their pride,
Were glowing to receive a thousand guests:
The carvèd angels, ever eager-eyed,
Stared, where upon their heads the cornice rests,
With hair blown back, and wings put crosswise on their breasts.

5

At length burst in the argent revelry,
With plume, tiara, and all rich array,
Numerous as shadows haunting faerily
The brain, new stuffed, in youth, with triumphs gay    40
Of old romance. These let us wish away,
And turn, sole-thoughted, to one Lady there,
Whose heard had brooded, all that wintry day,
On love, and winged St. Agnes' saintly care,
As she had heard old dames full many times declare.

6

They told her how, upon St. Agnes' Eve,
Young virgins might have visions of delight,
And soft adorings from their loves receive
Upon the honeyed middle of the night,
If ceremonies due they did aright;    50

As, supperless to bed they must retire,
And couch supine their beauties, lily white;
Nor look behind, nor sideways, but require
Of Heaven with upward eyes for all that they desire.

7

Full of this whim was thoughtful Madeline:
The music, yearning like a God in pain,
She scarcely heard: her maiden eyes divine,
Fixed on the floor, saw many a sweeping train
Pass by—she heeded not at all: in vain
Came many a tiptoe, amorous cavalier,                60
And back retired; not cooled by high disdain,
But she saw not: her heart was otherwhere:
She sighed for Agnes' dreams, the sweetest of the year.

8

She danced along with vague, regardless eyes,
Anxious her lips, her breathing quick and short:
The hallowed hour was near at hand: she sighs
Amid the timbrels, and the thronged resort
Of whisperers in anger, or in sport;
'Mid looks of love, defiance, hate, and scorn,
Hoodwinked with faery fancy; all amort,                70
Save to St. Agnes and her lambs unshorn,
And all the bliss to be before to-morrow morn.

9

So, purposing each moment to retire,
She lingered still. Meantime, across the moors,
Had come young Porphyro, with heart on fire
For Madeline. Beside the portal doors,
Buttressed from moonlight, stands he, and implores
All saints to give him sight of Madeline,
But for one moment in the tedious hours,
That he might gaze and worship all unseen;                80
Perchance speak, kneel, touch, kiss—in sooth such things have been.

10

He ventures in: let no buzzed whisper tell:
All eyes be muffled, or a hundred swords
Will storm his heart, Love's fev'rous citadel:
For him, those chambers held barbarian hordes,
Hyena foemen, and hot-blooded lords,
Whose very dogs would execrations howl
Against his lineage: not one breast affords
Him any mercy, in that mansion foul,
Save one old beldame, weak in body and in soul.                90

## 11

Ah, happy chance! the aged creature came,
Shuffling along with ivory-headed wand,
To where he stood, hid from the torch's flame,
Behind a broad hall-pillar, far beyond
The sound of merriment and chorus bland:
He startled her; but soon she knew his face,
And grasped his fingers in her palsied hand,
Saying, "Mercy, Porphyro! hie thee from this place:
They are all here to-night, the whole blood-thirsty race!

## 12

"Get hence! get hence! there's dwarfish Hildebrand;                          100
He had a fever late, and in the fit
He cursèd thee and thine, both house and land:
Then there's the old Lord Maurice, not a whit
More tame for his gray hairs—Alas me! flit!
Flit like a ghost away."—"Ah, Gossip dear,
We're safe enough; here in this arm chair sit,
And tell me how"—"Good saints! not here, not here;
Follow me, child, or else these stones will be thy bier."

## 13

He followed through a lowly archèd way,
Brushing the cobwebs with his lofty plume,                                   110
And as she muttered "Well-a—well-a-day!"
He found him in a little moonlight room
Pale, latticed, chill, and silent as a tomb.
"Now tell me where is Madeline," said he,
"Oh tell me, Angela, by the holy loom
Which none but secret sisterhood may see,
When they St. Agnes' wool are weaving piously."

## 14

"St. Agnes! Ah! it is St. Agnes' Eve—
Yet men will murder upon holy days:
Thou must hold water in a witch's sieve,                                     120
And be liege-lord of all the Elves and Fays,
To venture so: it fills me with amaze
To see thee, Porphyro—St. Agnes' Eve!
God's help! my lady fair the conjuror plays
This very night: good angels her deceive!
But let me laugh awhile, I've mickle time to grieve.

## 15

Feebly she laugheth in the languid moon
While Porphyro upon her face doth look,
Like puzzled urchin on an aged crone
Who keepeth closed a wond'rous riddle-book,                                  130
As spectacled she sits in chimney nook.

But soon his eyes grew brilliant, when she told
His lady's purpose; and he scarce could brook
Tears, at the thought of those enchantments cold,
And Madeline asleep in lap of legends old.

### 16

Sudden a thought came like a full-blown rose,
Flashing his brow, and in his painèd heart
Made purple riot: then doth he propose
A stratagem, that makes the beldame start:
'A cruel man and impious thou art:                     140
Sweet lady, let her pray, and sleep, and dream
Alone with her good angels, far apart
From wicked men like thee. Go, go!—I deem
Thou canst not surely be the same that thou didst seem.'

### 17

'I will not harm her, by all saints I swear,'
Quoth Porphyro: 'O may I ne'er find grace
When my weak voice shall whisper its last prayer,
If one of her soft ringlets I displace,
Or look with ruffian passion in her face:
Good Angela, believe me by these tears;               150
Or I will, even in a moment's space,
Awake, with horrid shout, my foemen's ears,
And beard them, though they be more fanged than wolves and bears."

### 18

"Ah! why wilt thou affright a feeble soul?
A poor, weak, palsy-stricken, churchyard thing,
Whose passing-bell may ere the midnight toll;
Whose prayers for thee, each morn and evening,
Were never missed."—Thus plaining, doth she bring
A gentler speech from burning Porphyro;
So woful, and of such deep sorrowing,                 160
That Angela gives promise she will do
Whatever he shall wish, betide her weal or woe.

### 19

Which was, to lead him, in close secrecy,
Even to Madeline's chamber, and there hide
Him in a closet, of such privacy
That he might see her beauty unespied,
And win perhaps the night a peerless bride,
While legioned faeries paced the coverlet,
And pale enchantment held her sleepy-eyed.
Never on such a night have lovers met,               170
Since Merlin paid his Demon all the monstrous debt.

## 20

"It shall be as thou wishest," said the Dame:
"All cates and dainties shall be stored there
Quickly on this feast-night: by the tambour frame
Her own lute thou wilt see: no time to spare,
For I am slow and feeble, and scarce dare
On such a catering trust my dizzy head.
Wait here, my child, with patience; kneel in prayer
The while: Ah! thou must needs the lady wed,
Or may I never leave my grave among the dead."          180

21

So saying she hobbled off with busy fear,
The lover's endless minutes slowly passed;
The dame returned, and whispered in his ear
To follow her; with aged eyes aghast
From fright of dim espial. Safe at last,
Through many a dusky gallery, they gain
The maiden's chamber, silken, hushed, and chaste;
Where Porphyro took covert, pleased amain.
His poor guide hurried back with agues in her brain.

22
                                                        190
Her faltering hand upon the balustrade,
Old Angela was feeling for the stair,
When Madeline, St. Agnes' charmèd maid,
Rose, like a missioned spirit, unaware:
With silver taper's light, and pious care,
She turned, and down the aged gossip led
To a safe level matting. Now prepare,
Young Porphyro, for gazing on that bed;
She comes, she comes again, like ring-dove frayed and fled.

23

Out went the taper as she hurried in;
Its little smoke, in palid moonshine, died:          200
She closed the door, she panted, all akin
To spirits of the air, and visions wide:
No uttered syllable, or, woe betide!
But to her heart, her heart was voluble,
Paining with eloquence her balmy side;
As though a tongueless nightingale should swell
Her throat in vain, and die, heart-stifled, in her dell.

24

A casement high and triple-arched there was,
All garlanded with carven imag'ries
Of fruits, and flowers, and bunches of knot-grass,    210
And diamonded with panes of quaint device,
Innumerable of stains and splended dyes,

As are the tiger-moth's deep-damasked wings;
And in the midst, 'mong thouand heraldries,
And twilight saints, and dim emblazonings,
A shielded scutcheon blushed with blood of queens and kings.

25

Full on this casement shone the wintry moon,
And threw warm gules on Madeline's fair breast,
As down she knelt for heaven's grace and boon;
Rose-bloom fell on her hands, together pressed,     220
And on her silver cross soft amethyst,
And on her hair a glory, like a saint:
She seemed a splendid angel, newly dressed,
Save wings, for heaven—Porphyro grew faint:
She knelt, so pure a thing, so free from mortal taint.

26

Anon his heart revives: her vespers done,
Of all its wreathèd pearls her hair she frees;
Unclasps her warmèd jewels one by one;
Loosens her fragrant bodice; by degrees
Her rich attire creeps rustling to her knees:     230
Half-hidden, like a mermaid in sea-weed,
Pensive awhile she dreams awake, and sees,
In fancy, fair St. Agnes in her bed,
But dares not look behind, or all the charm is fled.

27

Soon, trembling in her soft and chilly nest,
In sort of wakeful swoon, perplexed she lay,
Until the poppied warmth of sleep oppressed
Her soothèd limbs and soul fatigued away;
Flown, like a thought, until the morrow-day;
Blissfully havened both from joy and pain;     240
Clasped like a missal where swart Paynims pray;
Blinded alike from sunshine and from rain,
As though a rose should shut, and be a bud again.

28

Stolen to this paradise, and so entranced,
Porphyro gazed upon her empty dress,
And listened to her breathing, if it chanced
To wake into a slumberous tenderness;
Which when he heard, that minute did he bless,
And breathed himself: then from the closet crept,
Noiseless as fear in a wide wilderness,     250
And over the hushed carpet, silent stept,
And 'tween the curtains peeped, where lo!—how fast she slept.

## 29

Then by the bedside, where the faded moon
Made a dim, silver twilight, soft he set
A table, and, half anguished, threw thereon
A cloth of woven crimson, gold, and jet:—
O for some drowsy Morphean amulet!
The boisterous, midnight, festive clarion,
The kettle-drum, and far-heard clarinet,
Affray his ears, though but in dying tone:—      260
The hall door shuts again, and all the noise is gone.

30

And still she slept an azure-lidded sleep,
In blanchèd linen, smooth, and lavendered,
While he from forth the closet brought a heap
Of candied apple, quince, and plum, and gourd;
With jellies soother than the creamy curd,
And lucent syrups, tinct with cinnamon;
Manna and dates, in argosy transferred
From Fez; and spicèd dainties, every one,
From silken Samarcand to cedared Lebanon.      270

31

These delicates he heaped with glowing hand
On golden dishes and in baskets bright
Of wreathèd silver: sumptuous they stand
In the retirèd quiet of the night,
Filling the chilly room with perfume light.—
"And now, my love, my seraph fair, awake!
Thou art my heaven, and I thine eremite:
Open thine eyes for meek St. Agnes' sake,
Or I shall drowse beside thee, so my soul doth ache."

32

Thus whispering, his warm, unnervèd arm      280
Sank in her pillow. Shaded was her dream
By the dusk curtains:—'twas a midnight charm
Impossible to melt as icèd stream:
The lustrous salvers in the moonlight gleam;
Broad golden fringe upon the carpet lies:
It seemed he never, never could redeem
From such a steadfast spell his lady's eyes;
So mused awhile, entoiled in woofèd phantasies.

33

Awakening up, he took her hollow lute,—
Tumultuous,—and, in chords that tenderest be,      290
He played an ancient ditty, long since mute,
In Provence called, 'La belle dame sans mercy':
Close to her ear touching the melody;—

Wherewith disturbed, she uttered a soft moan:
He ceased—she panted quick—and suddenly
Her blue affrayèd eyes wide open shone:
Upon his knees he sank, pale as smooth-sculptured stone.

34

Her eyes were open, but she still beheld,
Now wide awake, the vision of her sleep:
There was a painful change, that nigh expelled          300
The blisses of her dream so pure and deep;
At which fair Madeline began to weep,
And moan forth witless words with many a sigh;
While still her gaze on Porphyro would keep;
Who knelt, with joined hands and piteous eye,
Fearing to move or speak, she looked so dreamingly.

35

'Ah, Porphyro!' said she, 'but even now
Thy voice was at sweet tremble in mine ear,
Made tuneable with every sweetest vow;
And those sad eyes were spiritual and clear:          310
How changed thou are! how pallid, chill, and drear!
Give me that voice again, my Porphyro,
Those looks immortal, those complainings dear!
Oh leave me not in this eternal woe,
For if thou diest, my Love, I know not where to go.'

36

Beyond a mortal man impassioned far
At these voluptuous accents, he arose,
Ethereal, flushed, and like a throbbing star
Seen mid the sapphire heaven's deep repose;
Into her dream he melted, as the rose          320
Blendeth its odour with the violet,—
Solution sweet: meantime the frost-wind blows
Like Love's alarum pattering the sharp sleet
Against the window-panes; St. Agnes' moon hath set.

37

'Tis dark: quick pattereth the flaw-blown sleet:
'This is no dream, my bride, my Madeline!'
'Tis dark: the iced gusts still rave and beat:
'No dream, alas! alas! and woe is mine!
Porphyro will leave me here to fade and pine.—
Cruel! what traitor could thee hither bring?          330
I curse not, for my heart is lost in thine,
Though thou forsakest a deceivèd thing;—
A dove forlorn and lost with sick unprunèd wing.'

## 38

'My Madeline! sweet dreamer! lovely bride!
Say, may I be for ay thy vassal blest?
Thy beauty's shield, heart-shaped and vermeil dyed?
Ah, silver shrine, here will I take my rest
After so many hours of toil and quest,
A famished pilgrim,—saved by miracle.
Though I have found, I will not rob thy nest        340
Saving of thy sweet self; if thou think'st well
To trust, fair Madeline, to no rude infidel.

39

"Hark! 'tis an elfin-storm from faery land,
Of haggard seeming, but a boon indeed:
Arise—arise! the morning is at hand;—
The bloated wassaillers will never heed:—
Let us away, my love, with happy speed;
There are no ears to hear, or eyes to see,—
Drowned all in Rhenish and the sleepy mead:
Awake! arise! my love, and fearless be,        350
For o'er the southern moors I have a home for thee."

40

She hurried at his words, beset with fears,
For there were sleeping dragons all around,
At glaring watch, perhaps, with ready spears—
Down the wide stairs a darkling way they found.—
In all the house was heard no human sound.
A chain-drooped lamp was flickering by each door;
The arras, rich with horseman, hawk, and hound,
Fluttered in the besieging wind's uproar;
And the long carpets rose along the gusty floor.        360

41

They glide, like phantoms, into the wide hall;
Like phantoms, to the iron porch they glide;
Where lay the Porter, in uneasy sprawl,
With a huge empty flagon by his side:
The wakeful bloodhound rose, and shook his hide,
But his sagacious eye an inmate owns:
By one, and one, the bolts full easy slide:—
The chains lie silent on the footworn stones;—
The key turns, and the door upon its hinges groans.

42

And they are gone: aye, ages long ago        370
These lovers fled away into the storm.
That night the Baron dreamt of many a woe,
And all his warrior-guests, with shade and form
Of witch, the demon, and large coffin-worm

Were long be-nightmared. Angela the old
Died palsy-twitched, with meagre face deform;
The Beadsman, after thousand aves told,
For ay unsought for slept among his ashes cold.


▶ *Ralph Waldo Emerson (1803-1882)*

## THE SNOW-STORM

Announced by all the trumpets of the sky,
Arrives the snow, and, driving o'er the fields,
Seems nowhere to alight: the whited air
Hides hills and woods, the river, and the heaven,
And veils the farm-house at the garden's end.
The sled and traveller stopped, the courier's feet
Delayed, all friends shut out, the housemates sit
Around the radiant fireplace, enclosed
In a tumultuous privacy of storm.

Come see the north wind's masonry.                          10
Out of an unseen quarry evermore
Furnished with tile, the fierce artificer
Curves his white bastions with projected roof
Round every windward stake, or tree, or door.
Speeding, the myriad-handed, his wild work
So fanciful, so savage, nought cares he
For number or proportion. Mockingly,
On coop or kennel he hangs Parian wreaths;
A swan-like form invests the hidden thorn;
Fills up the farmer's lane from wall to wall,                  20
Maugre the farmer's sighs; and at the gate
A tapering turret overtops the work.
And when his hours are numbered, and the world
Is all his own, retiring, as he were not,
Leaves, when the sun appears, astonished Art
To mimic in slow structures, stone by stone,
Built in an age, the mad wind's night-work,
The frolic architecture of the snow.


▶ *Robert Browning (1812-1889)*

## MEETING AT NIGHT

The gray sea and the long black land;
And the yellow half-moon large and low;
And the startled little waves that leap
In fiery ringlets from their sleep,

As I gain the cove with pushing prow,
And quench its speed i' the slushy sand.

Then a mile of warm sea-scented beach;
Three fields to cross till a farm appears;
A tap at the pane, the quick sharp scratch
And blue spurt of a lighted match,
And a voice less loud, through its joys and fears,
Than the two hearts beating each to each!

10

## PARTING AT MORNING

Round the cape of a sudden came the sea,
And the sun looked over the mountain's rim:
And straight was a path of gold for him,
And the need of a world of men for me.


▶ *George Meredith  (1828-1909)*

## LUCIFER IN STARLIGHT

On a starred night Prince Lucifer uprose.
Tired of his dark dominion, swung the fiend
Above the rolling ball, in cloud part screened,
Where sinners hugged their specter of repose.
Poor prey to his hot fit of pride were those.
And now upon his western wing he leaned,
Now his huge bulk o'er Afric's sands careened,
Now the black planet shadowed Arctic snows.
Soaring through wider zones that pricked his scars
With memory of the old revolt from Awe,
He reached a middle height, and at the stars,
Which are the brain of heaven, he looked, and sank.
Around the ancient track marched rank on rank,
The army of unalterable law.

10


▶ *Emily Dickinson  (1830-1886)*

## I HEARD A FLY BUZZ
WHEN I DIED

I heard a fly buzz when I died;
　The stillness round my form
Was like the stillness in the air
　Between the heaves of storm.

The eyes beside had wrung them dry,
　And breaths were gathering sure
For the last onset, when the king
　Be witnessed in his power.

I willed my keepsakes, signed away
　What portion of me I
Could make assignable—and then
　There interposed a fly,

10

With blue, uncertain, stumbling buzz,
　Between the light and me;
And then the windows failed, and then
　I could not see to see.

▶ *Algernon Charles Swinburne*
*(1837-1909)*

# THE GARDEN OF PROSERPINE

Here, where the world is quiet;
  Here, where all trouble seems
Dead winds' and spent waves' riot
  In doubtful dreams of dreams;
I watch the green field growing
For reaping folk and sowing,
For harvest-time and mowing,
  A sleepy world of streams.

I am tired of tears and laughter,
  And men that laugh and weep;          10
Of what may come hereafter
  For men that sow to reap;
I am weary of days and hours,
Blown buds of barren flowers,
Desires and dreams and powers
  And everything but sleep.

Here life has death for neighbor,
  And far from eye or ear
Wan waves and wet winds labor,
  Weak ships and spirits steer;          20
They drive adrift, and whither
They wot not who make thither;
But no such winds blow hither,
  And no such things grow here.

No growth of moor or coppice,
  No heather flower or vine,
But bloomless buds of poppies,
  Green grapes of Proserpine,
Pale beds of blowing rushes,
Where no leaf blooms or blushes          30
Save this whereout she crushes
  For dead men deadly wine.

Pale, without name or number,
  In fruitless fields of corn,
They bow themselves and slumber
  All night till light is born;
And like a soul belated,
In hell and heaven unmated,
By cloud and mist abated
  Comes out of darkness morn.          40

Though one were strong as seven,
  He too with death shall dwell,

Nor wake with wings in heaven,
  Nor weep for pains in hell;
Though one were fair as roses,
His beauty clouds and closes;
And well though love reposes,
  In the end it is not well.

Pale, beyond porch and portal,
  Crowned with calm leaves, she stands          50
Who gathers all things mortal
  With cold immortal hands;
Her languid lips are sweeter
Than love's who fears to greet her
To men that mix and meet her
  From many times and lands.

She waits for each and other,
  She waits for all men born;
Forgets the earth her mother,
  The life of fruits and corn;          60
And spring and seed and swallow
Take wing for her and follow
Where summer song rings hollow
  And flowers are put to scorn.

There go the loves that wither,
  The old loves with wearier wings;
And all dead years draw thither,
  And all disastrous things;
Dead dreams of days forsaken,
Blind buds that snows have shaken,          70
Wild leaves that winds have taken,
  Red strays of ruined springs.

We are not sure of sorrow,
  And joy was never sure;
To-day will die to-morrow;
  Time stoops to no man's lure;
And love-grown faint and fretful,
With lips but half regretful
Sighs, and with eyes forgetful
  Weeps that no loves endure.          80

From too much love of living,
  From hope and fear set free,
We thank with brief thanksgiving
  Whatever gods may be
That no life lives for ever;
That dead men rise up never;
That even the weariest river
  Winds somewhere safe to sea.

Then star nor sun shall waken,
  Nor any change of light;
Nor sound of waters shaken,
  Nor any sound or sight;

Nor wintry leaves nor vernal,
<sup>90</sup> Nor days nor things diurnal;
Only the sleep eternal
  In an eternal night.

▸ *Thomas Hardy (1840-1928)*

# SNOW IN THE SUBURBS

Every branch big with it,
  Bent every twig with it;
Every fork like a white web-foot;
Every street and pavement mute;
Some flakes have lost their way, and grope back upward, when
Meeting those meandering down they turn and descend again.
  The palings are glued together like a wall,
  And there is no waft of wind with the fleecy fall.

A sparrow enters the tree,
  Whereon immediately
A snow-lump thrice his own slight size
Descends on him and showers his head and eyes,

And overturns him,
  And near inurns him,
And lights on a nether twig, when its brush
Starts off a volley of other lodging lumps with a rush.

The steps are a blanched slope,
  Up which, with feeble hope,
A black cat comes, wide-eyed and thin;
  And we take him in.

▸ *Robert Bridges (1844-1930)*

# LONDON SNOW

When men were all asleep the snow came flying,
In large white flakes falllng on the city brown,
Stealthily and perpetually settling and loosely lying,
  Hushing the latest traffic of the drowsy town;
Deadening, muffling, stifling its murmurs failing;
Lazily and incessantly floating down and down;
  Silently sifting and veiling road, roof and railing;
Hiding difference, making unevenness even,
Into angles and crevices softly drifting and sailing.
  All night it fell, and when full inches seven
It lay in the depth of its uncompacted lightness,

The clouds blew off from a high and frosty heaven;
  And all awoke earlier for the unaccustomed brightness
Of the winter dawning, the strange unheavenly glare:
The eye marvelled—marvelled at the dazzling whiteness;
  The ear harkened to the stillness of the solemn air;
No sound of wheel rumbling nor of foot falling,
And the busy morning cries came thin and spare.
  Then boys I heard, as they went to school, calling;
They gathered up the crystal manna to freeze          20
Their tongues with tasting, their hands with snow-balling;
  Or rioted in a drift, plunging up to the knees;
Or peering up from under the white-mossed wonder,
'O look at the trees!' they cried. 'O look at the trees!'
  With lessened load, a few carts creak and blunder,
Following along the white deserted way,

A country company long dispersed asunder:
  When now already the sun, in pale display
Standing by Paul's high dome, spread forth below
His sparkling beams, and awoke the stir of the day.    30
  For now doors open, and war is waged with the snow;
And trains of somber men, past tale of number,
Tread long brown paths, as toward their toil they go:
  But even for them awhile no cares encumber
Their minds diverted; the daily word is unspoken,
The daily thoughts of labor and sorrow slumber
At the sight of the beauty that greets them, for the charm they have broken.

▶ *William Ernest Henley (1849-1903)*

## DISCHARGED

Carry me out
Into the wind and the sunshine,
Into the beautiful world.
O the wonder, the spell of the streets!
The stature and strength of the horses,
The rustle and echo of footfalls,
The flat roar and rattle of wheels!
A swift tram floats huge on us . . .
It's a dream?
The smell of the mud in my nostrils          10
Blows brave—like a breath of the sea!

As of old,
Ambulant, undulant drapery,
Vaguely and strangely provocative,
Flutters and beckons. O yonder—
Is it?—the gleam of a stocking!

Sudden, a spire
Wedged in the mist! O the houses,
The long lines of lofty, gray houses,
Cross-hatched with shadow and light!        20
These are the streets . . .
Each is an avenue leading
Whither I will!

Free . . . !
Dizzy, hysterical, faint,
I sit, and the carriage rolls on with me
Into the wonderful world.

▶ *A. E. Housman (1859-1936)*

## LOVELIEST OF TREES

Loveliest of trees, the cherry now
Is hung with bloom along the bough,

And stands about the woodland ride,
Wearing white for Eastertide.

Now, of my threescore years and ten,
Twenty will not come again,
And take from seventy springs a score,

It only leaves me fifty more.

And since to look at things in bloom
Fifty springs are little room,                    10
About the woodlands I will go
To see the cherry hung with snow.


▶ *William Butler Yeats (1865-1939)*

# AMONG SCHOOL CHILDREN

I walk through the long schoolroom questioning,
A kind old nun in a white hood replies;
The children learn to cipher and to sing,
To study reading-books and history,
To cut and sew, be neat in everything
In the best modern way—the children's eyes
In momentary wonder stare upon
A sixty year old smiling public man.

I dream of a Ledæan body, bent
Above a sinking fire, a tale that she               10
Told of a harsh reproof, or trivial event
That changed some childish day to tragedy—
Told, and it seemed that our two natures blent
Into a sphere from youthful sympathy,
Or else, to alter Plato's parable,
Into the yolk and white of the one shell.

And thinking of that fit of grief or rage
I look upon one child or t'other there
And wonder if she stood so at that age —
For even daughters of the swan can share          20
Something of every paddler's heritage—
And had that color upon cheek or hair;
And thereupon my heart is driven wild:
She stands before me as a living child.

Her present image floats into the mind—
Did quattrocento finger fashion it
Hollow of cheek as though it drank the wind
And took a mess of shadows for its meat?
And I thought never of Ledæan kind
Had pretty plumage once—enough of that,           30
Better to smile on all that smile, and show
There is a comfortable kind of old scarecrow.

What youthful mother, a shape upon her lap
Honey of generation had betrayed,

And that must sleep, shriek, struggle to escape
As recollection or the drug decide,
Would think her son, did she but see that shape
With sixty or more winters on its head,
A compensation for the pang of his birth,
Or the uncertainty of his setting forth?

40

Plato thought nature but a spume that plays
Upon a ghostly paradigm of things;
Solider Aristotle played the taws
Upon the bottom of a king of kings;
World-famous golden-thighed Pythagoras
Fingered upon a fiddle stick or strings
What a star sang and careless Muses heard:
Old clothes upon old sticks to scare a bird.

Both nuns and mothers, worship images,
But those the candles light are not as those

50

That animate a mother's reveries,
But keep a marble or a bronze repose.
And yet they too break hearts—O Presences
That passion, piety or affection knows
And that all heavenly glory symbolize —
O self-born mockers of man's enterprise;

Labor is blossoming or dancing where
The body is not bruised to pleasure soul,
Nor beauty born out of its own despair,
Nor blear-eyed wisdom out of midnight oil.

60

O chestnut-tree, great-rooted blossomer,
Are you the leaf, the blossom or the bole?
O body swayed to music, O brightening glance,
How can we know the dancer from the dance?

*Wallace Stevens (1879-1955)*

# THIRTEEN WAYS OF LOOKING AT A BLACKBIRD

### I

Among twenty snowy mountains,
The only moving thing
Was the eye of the blackbird.

### II

I was of three minds
Like a tree
In which there are three blackbirds.

### III

The blackbird whirled in the autumn winds.
It was a small part of the pantomime.

## IV

A man and a woman
Are one.
A man and a woman and a blackbird
Are one.

## V

I do not know which to prefer,
The beauty of inflections
Or the beauty of innuendoes,
The blackbird whistling
Or just after.

## VI

Icicles filled the long window
With barbaric glass.
The shadow of the blackbird
Crossed it, to and fro.
The mood
Traced in the shadow
An indecipherable cause.

## VII

O thin men of Haddam,
Why do you imagine golden birds?
Do you not see how the blackbird
Walks around the feet
Of the women about you?

## VIII

I know noble accents
And lucid, inescapable rhythms;
But I know, too,
That the blackbird is involved
In what I know.

## IX

When the blackbird flew out of sight,
It marked the edge
Of one of many circles.

## X

At the sight of blackbirds
Flying in a green light,
Even the bawds of euphony
Would cry out sharply.

## XI

He rode over Connecticut
In a glass coach.
Once, a fear pierced him,
In that he mistook
The shadow of his equipage
For blackbirds.

## XII

The river is moving.
The blackbird must be flying.

## XIII

It was evening all afternoon.
It was snowing
And it was going to snow.
The blackbird sat
In the cedar-limbs.

▶ *Ezra Pound (1885-    )*

# IN A STATION OF THE METRO

The apparition of these faces in the crowd;
Petals on a wet, black bough.

> ▶ *T. S. Eliot (1888-1965)*

## PRELUDES

### I

The winter evening settles down
With smell of steaks in passageways.
Six o'clock.
The burnt-out ends of smoky days.
And now a gusty shower wraps
The grimy scraps
Of withered leaves about your feet
And newspapers from vacant lots;
The showers beat
On broken blinds and chimney-pots,          10
And at the corner of the street
A lonely cab-horse steams and stamps.
And then the lighting of the lamps.

### II

The morning comes to consciousness
Of faint stale smells of beer
From the sawdust-trampled street
With all its muddy feet that press
To early coffee-stands.
With the other masquerades
That time resumes,                          20
One thinks of all the hands
That are raising dingy shades
In a thousand furnished rooms.

### III

You tossed a blanket from the bed,
You lay upon your back, and waited;
You dozed, and watched the night revealing
The thousand sordid images
Of which your soul was constituted;
They flickered against the ceiling.
And when all the world came back            30
And the light crept up between the shutters
And you heard the sparrows in the gutters,
You had such a vision of the street
As the street hardly understands;
Sitting along the bed's edge, where
You curled the papers from your hair,
Or clasped the yellow soles of feet
In the palms of both soiled hands.

### IV

His soul stretched tight across the skies
That fade behind a city block,              40
Or trampled by insistent feet

At four and five and six o'clock;
And short square fingers stuffing pipes,
And evening newspapers, and eyes
Assured of certain certainties,
The conscience of a blackened street
Impatient to assume the world.
I am moved by fancies that are curled
Around these images, and cling:
The notion of some infinitely gentle                    50
Infinitely suffering thing.
Wipe your hand across your mouth, and laugh;
The worlds revolve like ancient women
Gathering fuel in vacant lots.


# SWEENEY AMONG THE NIGHTINGALES

ὤμοι, πέπληγμαι καιρίαν πληγὴν ἔσω*

Apeneck Sweeney spreads his knees
Letting his arms hang down to laugh,
The zebra stripes along his jaw
Swelling to maculate giraffe.

The circles of the stormy moon
Slide westward toward the River Plate,
Death and the Raven drift above
And Sweeney guards the hornèd gate.

Gloomy Orion and the Dog
Are veiled; and hushed the shrunken seas;                10
The person in the Spanish cape
Tries to sit on Sweeney's knees

Slips and pulls the table cloth
Overturns a coffee-cup,
Reorganized upon the floor
She yawns and draws a stocking up:

The silent man in mocha brown
Sprawls at the window-sill and gapes;
The waiter brings in oranges
Bananas figs and hothouse grapes;                        20

The silent vertebrate in brown
Contracts and concentrates, withdraws;
Rachel née Rabinovitch
Tears at the grapes with murderous paws;

She and the lady in the cape
Are suspect, thought to be in league;
Therefore the man with heavy eyes
Declines the gambit, shows fatigue,

---

* Woe is me! I am fatally wounded. Aeschylus, *Agamemnon*

Leaves the room and reappears
Outside the window, leaning in,
Branches of wistaria
Circumscribe a golden grin;                                    30

The host with someone indistinct
Converses at the door apart,
The nightingales are singing near
The Convent of the Sacred Heart,

And sang within the bloody wood
When Agamemnon cried aloud,
And let their liquid siftings fall
To stain the stiff dishonoured shroud.                          40

▶  *John Crowe Ransom (1888-     )*

# BELLS FOR JOHN WHITESIDE'S DAUGHTER

There was such speed in her little body,
And such lightness in her footfall,
It is no wonder her brown study
Astonishes us all.

Her wars were bruited in our high window.
We looked among orchard trees and beyond
Where she took arms against her shadow,
Or harried unto the pond

The lazy geese, like a snow cloud
Dripping their snow on the green grass,                         10
Tricking and stopping, sleepy and proud,
Who cried in goose, Alas,

For the tireless heart within the little
Lady with rod that made them rise
From their noon apple-dreams and scuttle
Goose-fashion under the skies!

But now go the bells, and we are ready,
In one house we are sternly stopped
To say we are vexed at her brown study,
Lying so primly propped.                                         20

▶  *Langston Hughes (1902-1967)*

# DREAM DEFERRED

What happens to a dream deferred?
Does it dry up
like a raisin in the sun?
Or fester like a sore—
And then run?

Does it stink like rotten meat?
Or crust and sugar over—
like a syrupy sweet?

Maybe it just sags
like a heavy load.                                              10

*Or does it explode?*

▶ *Richard Eberhart (1904-     )*

# THE GROUNDHOG

In June, amid the golden fields,
I saw a groundhog lying dead.
Dead lay he; my senses shook,
And mind outshot our naked frailty.
There lowly in the vigorous summer
His form began its senseless change,
And made my senses waver dim
Seeing nature ferocious in him.
Inspecting close his maggots' might
And seething cauldron of his being,                    10
Half with loathing, half with a strange love,
I poked him with an angry stick.
The fever arose, became a flame
And Vigour circumscribed the skies,
Immense energy in the sun,
And through my frame a sunless trembling.
My stick had done nor good nor harm.
Then stood I silent in the day
Watching the object, as before;
And kept my reverence for knowledge        20
Trying for control, to be still,
To quell the passion of the blood;
Until I had bent down on my knees
Praying for joy in the sight of decay.
And so I left; and I returned

In Autumn strict of eye, to see
The sap gone out of the groundhog,
But the bony sodden hulk remained.
But the year had lost its meaning,
And in intellectual chains
I lost both love and loathing,                    30
Mured up in the wall of wisdom.
Another summer took the fields again
Massive and burning, full of life,
But when I chanced upon the spot
There was only a little hair left,
And bones bleaching in the sunlight
Beautiful as architecture;
I watched them like a geometer,
And cut a walking stick from a birch.
It has been three years, now.
There is no sign of the groundhog.                    40
I stood there in the whirling summer,
My hand capped a withered heart,
And thought of China and of Greece,
Of Alexander in his tent;
Of Montaigne in his tower,
Of Saint Theresa in her wild lament.

▶ *Theodore Roethke (1908-1963)*

# DOLOR

I have known the inexorable sadness of pencils,
Neat in their boxes, dolor of pad and paper-weight,
All the misery of manilla folders and mucilage,
Desolation in immaculate public places,
Lonely reception room, lavatory, switchboard,
The unalterable pathos of basin and pitcher,
Ritual of multigraph, paper-clip, comma,
Endless duplication of lives and objects.
And I have seen dust from the walls of institutions,
Finer than flour, alive, more dangerous than silica,                    10
Sift, almost invisible through long afternoons of tedium,
Dropping a fine film on nails and delicate eyebrows,
Glazing the pale hair, the duplicate gray standard faces.

# POEM IN OCTOBER

It was my thirtieth year to heaven
Woke to my hearing from harbor and neighbor wood
  And the mussel-pooled and the heron-
      Priested shore
    The morning beckon
With water paying and call of seagull and rook
And the knock of sailing boats on the net-webbed wall
    Myself to set foot
      That second
In the still sleeping town and set forth.          10

  My birthday began with the water-
Birds and the birds of the winged trees flying my name
  Above the farms and the white horses
      And I rose
    In rainy autumn
And walked abroad in a shower of all my days.
High tide and the heron dived when I took the road
    Over the border
      And the gates
Of the town closed as the town awoke.        20

  A springful of larks in a rolling
Cloud and the roadside bushes brimming with whistling
  Blackbirds and the sun of October
      Summery
    On the hill's shoulder,
Here were fond climates and sweet singers suddenly
Come in the morning where I wandered and listened
    To the rain-wringing
      Wind blow cold
In the woods faraway under me.        30

  Pale rain over the dwindling harbor
And over the sea-wet church the size of a snail
  With its horns through mist and the castle
      Brown as owls
    But all the gardens
Of spring and summer were blooming in the tall tales
Beyond the border and under the lark-full cloud.
    There could I marvel
      My birthday
Away but the weather turned around.        40

  It turned away from the blithe country
And down the other air and the blue altered sky
  Streamed again a wonder of summer
      With apples

      Pears and red currants
And I saw in the turning so clearly a child's
Forgotten mornings when he walked with his mother
      Through the parables
        Of sunlight
And the legends of the green chapels               50

      And the twice-told fields of infancy
That his tears burned my cheeks and his heart moved in mine.
    These were the woods the river and sea
        Where a boy
      In the listening
Summertime of the dead whispered the truth of his joy
To the trees and the stones and the fish in the tide.
      And the mystery
        Sang alive
Still in water and singingbirds.               60

      And there could I marvel my birthday
Away but the weather turned around. And the true
    Joy of the long dead child sang burning
        In the sun.
    It was my thirtieth
Year to heaven stood there then in the summer noon
Though the town below lay leaved with October blood.
      O may my heart's truth
        Still be sung
On this high hill in a year's turning.          70

▶ *Richard Wilbur (1921-    )*

# THE PARDON

    My dog lay dead five days without a grave
    In the thick of summer, hid in a clump of pine
    And a jungle of grass and honeysuckle-vine.
    I who had loved him while he kept alive

    Went only close enough to where he was
    To sniff the heavy honeysuckle-smell
    Twined with another odor heavier still
    And hear the flies' intolerable buzz.

    Well, I was ten and very much afraid.
    In my kind world the dead were out of range        10
    And I could not forgive the sad or strange
    In beast or man. My father took the spade

    And buried him. Last night I saw the grass
    Slowly divide (it was the same scene

But now it glowed a fierce and mortal green)
And saw the dog emerging. I confess

I felt afraid again, but still he came
In the carnal sun, clothed in a hymn of flies,
And death was breeding in his lively eyes.
I started in to cry and call his name,

20

Asking forgiveness of his tongueless head.
. . . I dreamt the past was never past redeeming:
But whether this was false or honest dreaming
I beg death's pardon now. And mourn the dead.


▶ *W. D. Snodgrass (1926-     )*

# RETURNED TO FRISCO, 1946

We shouldered like pigs along the rail to try
And catch that first gray outline of the shore
Of our first life. A plane hung in the sky
From which a girl's voice sang: ". . . you're home once more."

For that one moment, we were dulled and shaken
By fear. What could still catch us by surprise?
We had known all along we would be taken
By hawkers, known what authoritative lies

Would plan us as our old lives had been planned.
We had stood years and, then, scrambled like rabbits
Up hostile beaches; why should we fear this land
Intent on luxuries and its old habits?

10

A seagull shrieked for garbage. The Bay Bridge,
Busy with noontime traffic, rose ahead.
We would have liberty, the privilege
Of lingering over steak and white, soft bread

Served by women, free to get drunk or fight,
Free, if we chose, to blow in our back pay
On smart girls or trinkets, free to prowl all night
Down streets giddy with lights, to sleep all day,

20

Pay our own way and make our own selections;
Free to choose just what they meant we should;
To turn back finally to our old affections,
The ties that lasted and which must be good.

Off the port side, through haze, we could discern
Alcatraz, lavender with flowers. Barred,
The Golden Gate, fading away astern,
Stood like the closed gate of your own backyard.

▶ *Karl Shapiro (1913-     )*

# AUTO WRECK

Its quick soft silver bell beating, beating,
And down the dark one ruby flare
Pulsing out red light like an artery,
The ambulance at top speed floating down
Past beacons and illuminated clocks
Wings in a heavy curve, dips down,
And brakes speed, entering the crowd.
The doors leap open, emptying light;
Stretches are laid out, the mangled lifted
And stowed into the little hospital.                                    10
Then the bell, breaking the hush, tolls once,
And the ambulance with its terrible cargo
Rocking, slightly rocking, moves away,
As the doors, an afterthought, are closed.

We are deranged, walking among the cops
Who sweep glass and are large and composed.
One still making notes under the light.
One with a bucket douches ponds of blood
Into the street and gutter.
One hangs lanterns on the wrecks that cling,                           20
Empty husks of locusts, to iron poles.

Our throats were tight as tourniquets,
Our feet were bound with splints, but now
Like convalescents intimate and gauche,
We speak through sickly smiles and warn
With the stubborn saw of common sense,
The grim joke and the banal resolution.
The traffic moves around with care,
But we remain, touching a wound
That opens to our richest horror.                                      30

Already old, the question Who shall die?
Becomes unspoken Who is innocent?
For death in war is done by hands;
Suicide has cause and stillbirth, logic
But this invites the occult mind,
Cancels our physics with a sneer,
And spatters all we knew of dènouement
Across the expedient and wicked stones.

▶ *May Swenson (1919-    )*

## SNOW IN NEW YORK

It snowed in New York. I walked on Fifth
Avenue and saw the orange snowplow cut the drifts
with rotary sickles, suck up celestial clods into its turning neck,
a big flue that spewed them into a garbage truck.
This gift from the alps was good for nothing, though scarcely gray.
The bright apparatus, with hungry noise,
crumbled and mauled the new hills. Convoys
of dump-cars hauled them away.

I went to Riker's to blow my nose
in a napkin and drink coffee for its steam. Two rows                10
of belts came and went from the kitchen, modeling scrambled
eggs, corn muffins, bleeding triangles of pie.
Tubs of dirty dishes slid by.
Outside the fogged window black bulking people stumbled
cursing the good-for-nothing whiteness. I thought
of Rilke, having read how he wrote

to Princess Marie von Thurn und Taxis,
        saying: "The idea haunts me—
it keeps on calling—I must make a poem for Nijinski                20
that could be, so to say, swallowed and then danced." Printed
as on the page, in its
remembered place in the paragraph, that odd name with three dots
over the *iji,* appeared—as I squinted
through the moist window past the traveling
dishes—against the snow. There unraveled

from a file in my mind a magic notion
I, too, used to play with: from chosen words a potion
could be wrung; pickings of them, eaten, could make you fly, walk
on water, be somebody else, do or undo anything, go back          30
or forward on belts of time. But then I thought:
Snow in New York is like poetry, or clothes made of roses.
Who needs it, what can you build with snow, who can you feed? Hoses
were coming to whip back to water, wash
        to the sewers the nuisance-freight.


▶ *James Dickey (1923-    )*

## A DOG SLEEPING ON MY FEET

Being his resting place,
I do not even tense
The muscles of a leg
Or I would seem to be changing.

Instead, I turn the page
Of the notebook, carefully not

Remembering what I have written,
For now, with my feet beneath him
Dying like embers,
The poem is beginning to move          10
Up through my pine-prickling legs
Out of the night wood,

Taking hold of the pen by my fingers.
Before me the fox floats lightly,
On fire with his holy scent.
All, all are running.
Marvelous is the pursuit,
Like a dazzle of nails through the ankles,

Like a twisting shout through the trees
Sent after the flying fox                          20
Through the holes of logs, over streams
Stock-still with the pressure of moonlight.
My killed legs,
My legs of a dead thing, follow,

Quick as pins, through the forest,
And all rushed on into dark
And ends on the brightness of paper.

When my hand, which speaks in a daze
The hypnotized language of beasts,
Shall falter, and fail                             30

Back into the human tongue,
And the dog gets up and goes out
To wander the dawning yard,
I shall crawl to my human bed
And lie there smiling at sunrise,
With the scent of the fox

Burning my brain like an incense,
Floating out of the night wood,
Coming home to my wife and my sons
From the dream of an animal,                        40
Assembling the self I must wake to,
Sleeping to grow back my legs.

# IN THE TREE HOUSE AT NIGHT

And now the green household is dark.
The half-moon completely is shining
On the earth-lighted tops of the trees.
To be dead, a house must be still.
The floor and the walls wave me slowly;
I am deep in them over my head.
The needles and pine cones about me

Are full of small birds at their roundest,
Their fists without mercy gripping
Hard down through the tree to the roots            10
To sing back at light when they feel it.
We lie here like angels in bodies,
My brothers and I, one dead,
The other asleep from much living,

In mid-air huddled beside me.
Dark climbed to us here as we climbed
Up the nails I have hammered all day
Through the sprained, comic rungs of the ladder
Of broom handles, crate slats, and laths
Foot by foot up the trunk to the branches         20
Where we came out at last over lakes

Of leaves, of fields disencumbered of earth
That move with the moves of the spirit.
Each nail in the house is now steadied
By my dead brother's huge, freckled hand.
Through the years, he has pointed his hammer
Up into these limbs, and told us

That we must ascend, and all lie here.

Step after step he has brought me,                                    30
Embracing the trunk as his body,
Shaking its limbs with my heartbeat,
Till the pine cones danced without wind
And fell from the branches like apples.
In the arm-slender forks of our dwelling

I breathe my live brother's light hair.
The blanket around us becomes
As solid as stone, and it sways.
With all my heart, I close                                             40
The blue, timeless eye of my mind.
Wind springs, as my dead brother smiles
And touches the tree at the root;

A shudder of joy runs up
The trunk; the needles tingle;
One bird uncontrollably cries.
The wind changes round, and I stir
Within another's life. Whose life?
Who is dead? Whose presence is living?
When may I fall strangely to earth,

Who am nailed to this branch by a spirit?                             50
Can two bodies make up a third?
To sing, must I feel the world's light?
My green, graceful bones fill the air
With sleeping birds. Alone, alone
And with them I move gently.
I move at the heart of the world.


▶  *Philip Booth (1925-      )*

# MAINE

When old cars get retired, they go to Maine.
Thick as cows in backlots off the blacktop,
East of Bucksport, down the washboard
from Penobscot to Castine,
they graze behind frame barns: a Ford
turned tractor, Hudsons chopped to half-ton
trucks, and Chevy panels, jacked up,
tireless, geared to saw a cord of wood.

Old engines never die. Not in Maine,
where men grind valves the way their wives grind axes.    10
Ring-jobs burned-out down the Turnpike
still make revolutions, turned marine.
If Hardscrabble Hill makes her knock,
Maine rigs the water-jacket salt: a man

can fish forever on converted sixes,
and for his mooring, sink a V-8 block.

When fishing's poor, a man traps what he can.
Even when a one-horse hearse from Bangor fades
away, the body still survives:
painted lobster, baited—off Route 1—
with home preserves and Indian knives,
she'll net a parlor-full of Fords and haul in
transient Cadillacs like crabs. Maine trades
in staying power, not shiftless drives.

20

▶ *George Garrett (1929-     )*

## IN THE HOSPITAL

Here everything is white and clean
as driftwood. Pain's localized
and suffering, strictly routine,
goes on behind a modest screen.

Softly the nurses glide on wheels,
crackle like windy sails, smelling of soap.
I'm needled and the whole room reels.
The Fury asks me how I feel

and grinning turns to the brisk care
of an old man's need, he who awake
is silent, at the window stares,
sleeping, like drowning, cries for air.

10

And finally the fever like a spell
my years cast off. I notice now
nurse's plump buttocks, the ripe swell
of her breasts. It seems I will get well.

Next visitors with magazines;
they come whispering as in church.
The old man looks away and leans
toward light. Dying, too, is a routine.

20

I pack my bag and say goodbyes.
So long to nurse and this Sargossa Sea.
I nod to him and in his eyes
read, raging, the seabird's lonely cry.

▶ *Ted Hughes (1930-     )*

## HAWK ROOSTING

I sit in the top of the wood, my eyes closed.
Inaction, no falsifying dream
Between my hooked head and hooked feet:
Or in sleep rehearse perfect kills and eat.

The convenience of the high trees!
The air's buoyancy and the sun's ray
Are of advantage to me;
And the earth's face upward for my inspection.

My feet are locked upon the rough bark.
It took the whole of Creation
To produce my foot, my each feather;
Now I hold Creation in my foot

10

Or fly up, and revolve it all slowly—
I kill where I please because it is all mine.
There is no sophistry in my body:
My manners are tearing off heads—

The allotment of death.
For the one path of my flight is direct
Through the bones of the living.
No arguments assert my right:                                    20

The sun is behind me.
Nothing has changed since I began.
My eye has permitted no change.
I am going to keep things like this.


▶ *LeRoi Jones (1934-    )*

## THE CLEARING

Trees & brown squares
of shadow. The green
washed out and drained into clumps of mist
that cloak more trees. And trees, outside
the window; or spreading heavy fronds
stepping away from the light. We come
to a forest, or we see it
from the window. We step into it,
spreading the heavy leaves, or drop the blind
& let it clatter in the damp breeze from the yard.        10

Where are the beasts? In a forest,
there are always wild beasts. And the sun, a woman,
goes there to sleep. Brown trunks
their shadows against the white wall, rain
spreading against the glass. Blue rain
outside, and shadows against the wall. A wet wind
moves them. The smells
come in. Leaves & darkness
wetting our faces. Breathing
through the leaves, and disappear.                              20

Trees,
& shadows of trees (the wind
pushes them apart. I am
an animal watching
his forest. Listening
for your breathing, your merest
move in the dark. You wear
a gown of it. The dark
ness. And

we can move naked
through it, through
the forest
if it does not disappear. Who
will remember
the way back. When the blind
flings back
and more smells come in. As sound
or light moving against the wall. Where
are the beasts?

The eye is useless. Sound, Sound,
& what you smell
or feel. I am someone else
who smells you. The lamp
at the corner is bleak
& leafless. Its light
does not even reach
the edge of the trees.

What bird
makes that noise? (If this
were a western place, a temperate hand
could shape it. A western mouth
could make it on this mist. Green mist
settling on our flesh. (if this
were a western place, a bank
of the Marne, Cezanne's greens
& yellows floating unreal
under a bridge. A blue bridge
for a temperate eye. We have
vines. (What bird
makes that noise?

Your voice down the hall. Are
you singing? A shadow song
we lock our movement
in. Were you singing?
down the hall. White plaster
on the walls, our fingers
leave their marks, on
the dust, or tearing
the wall away. Were you
singing? What song
was that?

I love you (& you be
quiet, & feel my wet mouth
on your fingers, I
love you
on your fingers, I

love you
& bring you fish
& oranges. (Before the light fails
we should move to a dryer place,
but not too far from water.) I
Love you & 80
you are singing. What song
is that? (The blinds held up
by a wind, tearing
the shadows. I
Love you
& you hide yourself
in the shadows. The forest is huge
around us. The night
clings to our cries. (I hear
your voice 90
down the hall, through the window, above
all those trees, a light
it seems
& you are singing. What song
is that The words
are beautiful.

▶ *(Translated by*
*Richard McLaughlin, 1971)*

# FIVE HAIKU

## *Matsuo Basho (1644-1694)*

Sudden lightning flash—
And piercing through the blackness
The night-raven's cry.

## *Onitsura (1660-1738)*

The bare skeletons
Hidden beneath festive dress
Ah! Flower-viewing.

## *Kikaku (1661-1707)*

And the beggar—Ah!
Wearing as his summer clothes
The heaven and earth.

## *Taniguchi Buson (1715-1783)*

Drizzles of spring rain—
And soaking on a roof top
An abandoned Ball.

## *Masaoka Shiki (1867-1902)*

The drear autumn wind—
And to me the Gods are not
And Buddhas are not.

# ▶▶▶ SYMBOLISM AND ALLEGORY

Because poetry is a concise and compact mode of expression, it is often many-layered. Many meanings, attitudes, and ideas may be expressed by the same phrase or even the same word. Some poems, of course, are much more complex than others, and there are some which do not transcend their surface meaning. Most poems, however, contain some type of symbolism.

A distinction must, first of all, be made between symbolism and allegory. An allegory is a story or, in the case of poetry, a story in verse, told on two levels, the surface and literal, and the figurative. Allegory is similar to an extended metaphor in that the two, or occasionally more, levels of meaning remain relatively constant throughout the poem; the same symbols mean the same things, there is always a one-to-one correspondence between the levels. While there are some modern allegories, the form is not exceptionally popular today. Rather, it is associated with medieval romances, morality plays, and the like; *Pilgrim's Progress* is perhaps the most famous example of allegory in prose, "Paradise Lost" in poetry.

While there are few modern allegorical poems of this type, allegory does exist in some forms; basically a concrete representation of abstract concepts, ideas, and qualities, allegory is useful when the poet wishes to create a spec-

ific poetical world, in which every surface element corresponds to something else on a second level. This form is most effective when the poet wishes to tell a story with a specific point, a political satire, for example. A more complex, many-faceted theme would be better told with symbolism, rather than within the confining structure of allegory

Symbolism, as opposed to allegory, need not remain uniform throughout the entire poem; a poem containing symbolism may have a variety of levels and the same symbol may have different meanings at different points in the poem. The difference between symbols and allusions, images, and figures of speech should also be clarified at this point. An allusion, a reference to a literary or historical person, place, or event, may serve as a symbol. Poets often refer to certain cultural and societal myths and to archetypes, universal motifs which are present in the dreams, literature, and general consciousness of men in a particular culture; these references may be considered under the category of symbolism.

Images, representations of sense experience, are generally direct description and do not represent anything but the experience they describe; the entire image, of course, may serve as a symbol of something greater than itself. Figures of speech compare, contrast, and analogize rather than represent as such; however, like an image, an entire figure of speech may serve as a symbol.

A symbol, briefly, may be defined as something which represents itself and one or more other things on other levels. There are several types of symbols: traditional or public, more or less agreed upon and understood, and private symbols, which vary from one poem to another. Some poets develop sets of symbols which they use throughout several poems. The former, of which the cross, lightness, darkness, storms, and the changing seasons are examples, are generally easy to recognize, although they must still be carefully evaluated to determine the specific way they are being used, and their purpose in the poem. Symbols unique to a particular poem or poet are more difficult to discover and still more difficult, usually, to comprehend completely. Repetition, emphasis, connotation and denotation of the words used, position of words and phrases, words and phrases which don't seem to make sense on the surface level or which seem to carry further significance and implications—these are all indications of symbols. Once a symbol is discovered and labeled as such, it must be explained in context to determine what it represents; there is no way of labeling and assigning meaning to a symbol outside of the context of the poem in which it appears.

Any meaning decided upon must be tested in terms of the poem's meaning as a whole. Often, several interpretations of a particular symbol are plausible; the poet may in fact have intended it to contain multiple meanings. It may mean one thing at one level, an entirely different thing at another. The first step in discovering and interpreting symbolism is to examine and understand the poem's surface level thoroughly. Sometimes, of course, it is obvious that the poem is symbolic, in which case interpretation on the surface level would be difficult if not impossible. The second step is to look for further meanings, both by examining the poem as a whole and by looking at individual elements which might possibly be symbols.

When interpretations are attempted, each element of the possible meaning must correspond with elements in the poem; there must be a sound basis for each assertion about symbolism. Of course, unless the poet has explained exactly what he means, one can never be absolutely sure that one's interpretation is correct. However, with practice and increasing knowledge of poetry and poetic language, interpretation should become easier.

Poetry's conciseness and brevity and the necessity to say a great deal in a short amount of time and space, make symbolism valuable. A good poem can, in a sense, be taken apart layer by layer, revealing various shades of meaning and perspective until the core idea or theme is reached. Like figurative language, symbolism is a means of expressing feelings and attitude, of transmitting messages, subtly and skillfully. It forces the reader to probe, analyze, consider, and reconsider what he reads, and to question his own preconceptions about poetry and life. Symbolism, when used with skill and imagination, and when blended and integrated with the poem as a whole, is an effective means not only of expressing meaning but of dealing with complexities and ambiguities, of qualifying, broadening, and enriching the basic idea.

*William Blake (1757-1827)*

## THE TIGER

Tiger, Tiger, burning bright,
In the forests of the night;
What immortal hand or eye
Could frame thy fearful symmetry?

In what distant deeps or skies,
Burnt the fire of thine eyes?
On what wings dare he aspire?
What the hand dare seize the fire?

And what shoulder, and what art,
Could twist the sinews of thy heart?          10
And when thy heart began to beat,

What dread hand? and what dread feet?

What the hammer? what the chain,
In what furnace was thy brain?
What the anvil? what dread grasp
Dare its deadly terrors clasp?

When the stars threw down their spears
And watered heaven with their tears:
Did he smile his work to see?
Did he who made the Lamb make thee?          20

Tiger, Tiger, burning bright,
In the forests of the night:
What immortal hand or eye
Dare frame thy fearful symmetry?

*William Wordsworth (1770-1850)*

## THE WORLD IS TOO MUCH WITH US

The world is too much with us; late and soon,
Getting and spending, we lay waste our powers:
Little we see in Nature that is ours;
We have given our hearts away, a sordid boon!
This sea that bares her bosom to the moon;
The winds that will be howling at all hours,
And are up-gathered now like sleeping flowers;
For this, for everything, we are out of tune;
It moves us not.—Great God! I'd rather be
A pagan suckled in a creed outworn;          10
So might I, standing on this pleasant lea,
Have glimpses that would make me less forlorn;
Have sight of Proteus rising from the sea;
Or hear old Triton blow his wreathèd horn.

*Percy Bysshe Shelley (1792-1822)*

## ODE TO THE WEST WIND

### I

O wild West Wind thou breath of Autumn's being,
Thou, from whose unseen presence the leaves dead
Are driven, like ghosts from an enchanter fleeing,

Yellow, and black, and pale and hectic red,
Pestilence-stricken multitudes: O thou,
Who chariotest to their dark wintry bed

The wingèd seeds, where they lie cold and low,
Each like a corpse within its grave, until
Thine azure sister of the spring shall blow

Her clarion o'er the dreaming earth, and fill          10
(Driving sweet buds like flocks to feed in air)
With living hues and odors plain and hill:

Wild Spirit, which art moving everywhere;
Destroyer and preserver; hear, O, hear!

### II

Thou on whose stream, 'mid the steep sky's commotion,
Loose clouds like earth's decaying leaves are shed,
Shook from the tangled boughs of Heaven and Ocean,

Angels of rain and lightning: there are spread
On the blue surface of thine aëry surge,
Like the bright hair uplifted from the head          20

Of some fierce Maenad, even from the dim verge
Of the horizon to the zenith's height,
The locks of the approaching storm. Thou dirge

Of the dying year, to which this closing night
Will be the dome of a vast sepulchre,
Vaulted with all thy congregated might

Of vapours, from whose solid atmosphere
Black rain, and fire, and hail will burst: oh, hear!

### III

Thou who didst waken from his summer dreams
The blue Mediterranean, where he lay,          30
Lulled by the coil of his crystàlline streams,

Beside a pumice isle in Baiae's bay,
And saw in sleep old palaces and towers
Quivering within the wave's intenser day,

All overgrown with azure moss and flowers
So sweet, the sense faints picturing them! Thou
For whose path the Atlantic's level powers

Cleave themselves into chasms, while far below
The sea-blooms and the oozy woods which wear
The sapless foliage of the ocean, know          40

Thy voice, and suddenly grow gray with fear,
And tremble and despoil themselves: oh, hear!

### IV

If I were a dead leaf thou mightest bear;
If I were a swift cloud to fly with thee;
A wave to pant beneath thy power, and share

The impulse of thy strength, only less free
Than thou, O uncontrollable! If even
I were as in my boyhood, and could be

The comrade of thy wanderings over Heaven,
As then, when to outstrip thy skiey speed          50
Scarce seemed a vision; I would ne'er have striven

As thus with thee in prayer in my sore need.
O, lift me as a wave, a leaf, a cloud!
I fall upon the thorns of life! I bleed!

A heavy weight of hours has chained and bowed
One too like thee: tameless, and swift, and proud.

V

Make my thy lyre, even as the forest is:
What if my leaves are falling like its own!
The tumult of thy mighty harmonies

Will take from both a deep, autumnal tone,          60
Sweet though in sadness. Be thou, Spirit fierce,
My spirit! Be thou me, impetuous one!

Drive my dead thoughts over the universe
Like withered leaves to quicken a new birth!
And, by the incantation of this verse,

Scatter, as from an unextinguished hearth
Ashes and sparks, my words among mankind!
Be through my lips to unawakened earth

The trumpet of a prophecy! O, Wind,
If Winter comes, can Spring be far behind?          70

▶ *Alfred, Lord Tennyson (1809-1892)*

## CROSSING THE BAR

Sunset and evening star,
　And one clear call for me!
And may there be no moaning of the bar,
　When I put out to sea,

But such a tide as moving seems asleep,
　Too full for sound and foam,
When that which drew from out the boundless
　deep

Turns again home.

Twilight and evening bell,
　And after that the dark!          10
And may there be no sadness of farewell,
　When I embark;

For though from out our bourne of Time and
　Place
　The flood may bear me far,
I hope to see my Pilot face to face
　When I have crossed the bar.

▶ *Emily Dickinson (1830-1886)*

## MY LIFE HAD STOOD,
## A LOADED GUN

My life had stood, a loaded gun,
In corners, till a day
The owner passed, identified,
And carried me away.

And now we roam in sovereign woods,
And now we hunt the doe,
And every time I speak for him,
The mountains straight reply.

And do I smile, such cordial light
Upon the valley glow,                                    10
It is as a Vesuvian face
Had let its pleasure through.

▶ *Gerard Manley Hopkins (1844-1889)*

## THE WINDHOVER

### TO CHRIST OUR LORD

I caught this morning morning's minion, king-
    dom of daylight's dauphin, dapple-dawn-drawn Falcon, in his riding
    Of the rolling level underneath him steady air, and striding
High there how he rung upon the rein of a wimpling wing
In his ecstasy! then off, off forth on swing,
    As a skate's heel sweeps smooth on a bow-bend: the hurl and gliding
    Rebuffed the big wind. My heart in hiding
Stirred for a bird,—the achieve of, the mastery of the thing!

Brute beauty and valor and act, oh, air, pride, plume, here
    Buckle! AND the fire that breaks from thee then, a billion          10
Times told lovelier, more dangerous, O my chevalier!

    No wonder of it: shéer plód makes plow down sillion
Shine, and blue-bleak embers, ah my dear,
    Fall, gall themselves, and gash gold-vermilion.

▶ *William Butler Yeats (1865-1939)*

## SAILING TO BYZANTIUM

### I

That is no country for old men. The young
In one another's arms, birds in the trees
—Those dying generations—at their song,
The salmon-falls, the mackerel-crowded seas,
Fish, flesh, or fowl, commend all summer long
Whatever is begotten, born, and dies.
Caught in that sensual music all neglect
Monuments of unageing intellect.

## II

An aged man is but a paltry thing,
A tattered coat upon a stick, unless                           10
Soul clap its hands and sing, and louder sing
For every tatter in its mortal dress,
Nor is there singing school but studying
Monuments of its own magnificence;
And therefore I have sailed the seas and come
To the holy city of Byzantium.

## III

O sages standing in God's holy fire
As in the gold mosaic of a wall,
Come from the holy fire, perne in a gyre,
And be the singing-masters of my soul.                        20
Consume my heart away, sick with desire
And fastened to a dying animal
It knows not what it is; and gather me
Into the artifice of eternity.

## IV

Once out of nature I shall never take
My bodily form from any natural thing,
But such a form as Grecian goldsmiths make
Of hammered gold and gold enameling
To keep a drowsy Emperor awake;
Or set upon a golden bough to sing                            30
To lords and ladies of Byzantium
Of what is past, or passing, or to come.

# LEDA AND THE SWAN

A sudden blow: the great wings beating still
Above the staggering girl, her thighs caressed
By the dark webs, her nape caught in his bill,
He holds her helpless breast upon his breast.

How can those terrified vague fingers push
The feathered glory from her loosening thighs?
And how can body, laid in that white rush,
But feel the strange heart beating where it lies?

A shudder in the loins engenders there
The broken wall, the burning roof and tower                   10
And Agamemnon dead.
                        Being so caught up,
So mastered by the brute blood of the air,
Did she put on his knowledge with his power
Before the indifferent beak could let her drop?

▶ *Robert Frost (1874-1963)*

## THE ROAD NOT TAKEN

Two roads diverged in a yellow wood,
And sorry I could not travel both
And be one traveler, long I stood
And looked down one as far as I could
To where it bent in the undergrowth;

Then took the other, as just as fair,
And having perhaps the better claim,
Because it was grassy and wanted wear;
Though as for that the passing there
Had worn them really about the same,             10

And both that morning equally lay
In leaves no step had trodden black.
Oh, I kept the first for another day!
Yet knowing how way leads on to way,
I doubted if I should ever come back.

I shall be telling this with a sigh
Somewhere ages and ages hence:
Two roads diverged in a wood, and I—
I took the one less traveled by,
And that has made all the difference.             20

## THE PASTURE

I'm going out to clean the pasture spring;
I'll only stop to rake leaves away
(And wait to watch the water clear, I may):
I sha'n't be gone long.—You come too.

I'm going out to fetch the little calf
That's standing by the mother. It's so young,
It totters when she licks it with her tongue.
I sha'n't be gone long.—You come too.

## FIRE AND ICE

Some say the world will end in fire,
Some say in ice.
From what I've tasted of desire
I hold with those who favor fire.
But if it had to perish twice,
I think I know enough of hate
To say that for destruction ice
Is also great
And would suffice.

## STOPPING BY WOODS ON A SNOWY EVENING

Whose woods these are I think I know.
His house is in the village though;
He will not see me stopping here
To watch his woods fill up with snow.

My little horse must think it queer
To stop without a farmhouse near
Between the woods and frozen lake
The darkest evening of the year.

He gives his harness bells a shake
To ask if there is some mistake.             10
The only other sound's the sweep
Of easy wind and downy flake.

The woods are lovely, dark and deep,
But I have promises to keep,
And miles to go before I sleep,
And miles to go before I sleep.

▶ *Wallace Stevens (1879-1955)*

## THE IDEA OF ORDER AT KEY WEST

She sang beyond the genius of the sea.
The water never formed to mind or voice,
Like a body wholly body, fluttering
Its empty sleeves; and yet its mimic motion
Made constant cry, caused constantly a cry,

That was not ours although we understood,
Inhuman, of the veritable ocean.

The sea was not a mask. No more was she.
The song and water were not medleyed sound
Even if what she sang was what she heard,
Since what she sang was uttered word by word.
It may be that in all her phrases stirred
The grinding water and the gasping wind;
But it was she and not the sea we heard.

For she was the maker of the song she sang.
The ever-hooded, tragic-gestured sea
Was merely a place by which she walked to sing.
Whose spirit is this? we said, because we knew
It was the spirit that we sought and knew
That we should ask this often as she sang.

If it was only the dark voice of the sea
That rose, or even colored by many waves;
If it was only the outer voice of sky
And cloud, of the sunken coral water-walled,
However clear, it would have been deep air,
The heaving speech of air, a summer sound
Repeated in a summer without end
And sound alone. But it was more than that,
More even than her voice, and ours, among
The meaningless plungings of water and the wind,
Theatrical distances, bronze shadows heaped
On high horizons, mountainous atmospheres
Of sky and sea.
                              It was her voice that made
The sky acutest at its vanishing.
She measured to the hour its solitude.
She was the single artificer of the world
In which she sang. And when she sang, the sea,
Whatever self it had, became the self
That was her song, for she was the maker. Then we,
As we beheld her striding there alone,
Knew that there never was a world for her
Except the one she sang and, singing, made.

Ramon Fernandez, tell me, if you know,
Why, when the singing ended and we turned
Toward the town, tell why the glassy lights,
The lights in the fishing boats at anchor there,
As the night descended, tilting in the air,
Mastered the night and portioned out the sea,
Fixing emblazoned zones and fiery poles,
Arranging, deepening, enchanting night.

Oh! Blessed rage for order, pale Ramon,

10

20

30

40

50

The maker's rage to order words of the sea,
Words of the fragrant portals, dimly-starred,
And of ourselves and of our origins,
In ghostlier demarcations, keener sounds.


## ANECDOTE OF THE JAR

I placed a jar in Tennessee,
And round it was, upon a hill.
It made the slovenly wilderness
Surround that hill.

The wilderness rose up to it,
And sprawled around, no longer wild.
The jar was round upon the ground
And tall and of a port in air.

It took dominion everywhere.
The jar was gray and bare.          10
It did not give a bird or bush,
Like nothing else in Tennessee.


## PETER QUINCE AT
## THE CLAVIER

### I

Just as my fingers on these keys
Make music, so the selfsame sounds
On my spirit make a music, too.

Music is feeling, then, not sound;
And thus it is that what I feel,
Here in this room, desiring you,

Thinking of your blue-shadowed silk,
Is music. It is like the strain
Waked in the elders by Susanna.

Of a green evening, clear and warm,          10
She bathed in her still garden, while
The red-eyed elders watching, felt

The basses of their beings throb
In witching chords, and their thin blood
Pulse pizzicati of Hosanna.

### II

In the green water, clear and warm,
Susanna lay.
She searched
The touch of springs,

And found          20
Concealed imaginings.
She sighed,
For so much melody.

Upon the bank, she stood
In the cool
Of spent emotions.
She felt, among the leaves,
The dew
Of old devotions.

She walked upon the grass,          30
Still quavering.
The winds were like her maids,
On timed feet,
Fetching her woven scarves,
Yet wavering.

A breath upon her hand
Muted the night.
She turned—
A cymbal crashed,
And roaring horns.          40

### III

Soon, with a noise like tambourines,
Came her attendant Byzantines.

They wondered why Susanna cried
Against the elders by her side;

And as they whispered, the refrain
Was like a willow swept by rain.

Anon, their lamps' uplifted flame
Revealed Susanna and her shame.

And then, the simpering Byzantines
Fled, with a noise like tambourines.          50

### IV

Beauty is momentary in the mind—
The fitful tracing of a portal;
But in the flesh it is immortal.

The body dies; the body's beauty lives.
So evenings die, in their green going,

A wave, interminably flowing.
So gardens die, their meek breath scenting
The cowl of winter, done repenting.
So maidens die, to the auroral
Celebration of a maiden's choral.                          60

Susanna's music touched the bawdy strings

Of those white elders; but, escaping,
Left only Death's ironic scraping.
Now, in its immortality, it plays
On the clear viol of her memory,
And makes a constant sacrament of praise.

## THE EMPEROR OF ICE-CREAM

Call the roller of big cigars,
The muscular one, and bid him whip
In kitchen cups concupiscent curds.
Let the wenches dawdle in such dress
As they are used to wear, and let the boys
Bring flowers in last month's newspapers.
Let be be finale of seem.
The only emperor is the emperor of ice-cream.

Take from the dresser of deal,
Lacking the three glass knobs, that sheet          10
On which she embroidered fantails once
And spread it so as to cover her face.
If her horny feet protrude, they come
To show how cold she is, and dumb.
Let the lamp affix its beam.
The only emperor is the emperor of ice-cream.

▶ *William Carlos Williams (1883-1963)*

## THE YACHTS

contend in a sea which the land partly encloses
shielding them from the too heavy blows
of an ungoverned ocean which when it chooses

tortures the biggest hulls, the best man knows
to pit against its beating, and sinks them pitilessly.
Mothlike in mists, scintillant in the minute

brilliance of cloudless days, with broad bellying sails
they glide to the wind tossing green water
from their sharp prows while over them the crew crawls

ant-like, solicitously grooming them, releasing,                    10
making fast as they turn, lean far over and having
caught the wind again, side by side, head for the mark.

In a well guarded arena of open water surrounded by
lesser and greater craft which, sycophant, lumbering
and flittering follow them, they appear youthful, rare

as the light of a happy eye, live with the grace
of all that in the mind is feckless, free and
naturally to be desired. Now the sea which holds them

is moody, lapping their glossy sides, as if feeling
for some slightest flaw but fails completely.                       20
Today no race. Then the wind comes again. The yachts

move, jockeying for a start, the signal is set and they
are off. Now the waves strike at them but they are too
well made, they slip through, though they take in canvas.

Arms with hands grasping seek to clutch at the prows.
Bodies thrown recklessly in the way are cut aside.
It is a sea of faces about them in agony, in despair

until the horror of the race dawns staggering the mind,
the whole sea become an entanglement of watery bodies
lost to the world bearing what they cannot hold. Broken,                    30

beaten, desolate, reaching from the dead to be taken up
they cry out, failing, failing! their cries rising
in waves still as the skillful yachts pass over.


▶  *D. H. Lawrence (1885-1930)*

## SNAKE

A snake came to my water trough
On a hot, hot day, and I in pajamas for the heat,
To drink there.

In the deep, strange-scented shade of the great dark carob tree
I came down the steps with my pitcher
And must wait, must stand and wait, for there he was at the trough before me.

He reached down from a fissure in the earth-wall in the gloom
And trailed his yellow-brown slackness soft-bellied down, over the edge of the
        stone trough
And rested his throat upon the stone bottom,
And where the water had dripped from the tap, in a small clearness,            10
He sipped with his straight mouth,
Softly drank through his straight gums, into his slack long body,
Silently.

Someone was before me at my water trough,
And I, like a second-comer, waiting.

He lifted his head from his drinking, as cattle do,
And looked at me vaguely, as drinking cattle do,
And flickered his two-forked tongue from his lips, and mused a moment,
And stooped and drank a little more,
Being earth-brown, earth-golden from the burning bowels of the earth          20
On the day of Sicilian July, with Etna smoking.

The voice of my education said to me
He must be killed,
For in Sicily the black black snakes are innocent, the gold are venomous.

And voices in me said, If you were a man
You would take a stick and break him now, and finish him off.

But must I confess how I liked him,
How glad I was he had come like a guest in quiet, to drink at my water trough
And depart peaceful, pacified, and thankless
Into the burning bowels of this earth?                                    30

Was it cowardice, that I dared not kill him?
Was it perversity, that I longed to talk to him?
Was it humility, to feel so honored?
I felt so honored.

And yet those voices:
*If you were not afraid, you would kill him!*

And truly I was afraid, I was most afraid,
But even so, honored still more
That he should seek my hospitality
From out the dark door of the secret earth.                              40

He drank enough
And lifted his head, dreamily, as one who has drunken,
And flickered his tongue like a forked night on the air, so black,
Seeming to lick his lips,
And looked around like a god, unseeing, into the air,
And slowly turned his head,
And slowly, very slowly, as if thrice adream
Proceeded to draw his slow length curving round
And climb the broken bank of my wall-face.

And as he put his head into that dreadful hole,                          50
And as he slowly drew up, snake-easing his shoulders, and entered further,
A sort of horror, a sort of protest against his withdrawing into that horrid
    black hole,
Deliberately going into the blackness, and slowly drawing himself after,
Overcame me now his back was turned.

I looked round, I put down my pitcher,
I picked up a clumsy log
And threw it at the water trough with a clatter.

I think it did not hit him;
But suddenly that part of him that was left behind convulsed
    in undignified haste,
Writhered like lightning, and was gone                                   60
Into the black hole, the earth-lipped fissure in the wall-front
At which, in the intense still noon, I stared with fascination.

And immediately I regretted it.
I thought how paltry, how vulgar, what a mean act!
I despised myself and the voices of my accursed human education.

And I thought of the albatross
And I wished he would come back, my snake.

For he seemed to me again like a king,
Like a king in exile, uncrowned in the underworld,
Now due to be crowned again.                                    70

And so, I missed my chance with one of the lords
Of life.
And I have something to expiate:
A pettiness.


▶ *Delmore Schwartz (1906-1967)*

# THE HEAVY BEAR WHO GOES WITH ME

*"the withness of the body"*—Whitehead

The heavy bear who goes with me,
A manifold honey to smear his face,
Clumsy and lumbering here and there,
The central ton of every place,
The hungry beating brutish one
In love with candy, anger, and sleep,
Crazy factotum, dishevelling all,
Climbs the building, kicks the football,
Boxes his brother in the hate-ridden city.

Breathing at my side, that heavy animal,                        10
That heavy bear who sleeps with me,
Howls in his sleep for a world of sugar,
A sweetness intimate as the water's clasp,
Howls in his sleep because the tight-rope
Trembles and shows the darkness beneath.
—The strutting show-off is terrified,
Dressed in his dress-suit, bulging his pants,
Trembles to think that his quivering meat
Must finally wince to nothing at all.

That inescapable animal walks with me,                          20
Has followed me since the black womb held,
Moves where I move, distorting my gesture,
A caricature, a swollen shadow,
A stupid clown of the spirit's motive,
Perplexes and affronts with his own darkness,
The secret life of belly and bone,
Opaque, too near, my private, yet unknown,
Stretches to embrace the very dear
With whom I would walk without him near,
Touches her grossly, although a word                            30
Would bare my heart and make me clear,
Stumbles, flounders, and strives to be fed
Dragging me with him in his mouthing care.

Amid the hundred million of his kind,
The scrimmage of appetite everywhere.

## IN THE NAKED BED, IN PLATO'S CAVE

In the naked bed, in Plato's cave,
Reflected headlights slowly slid the wall,
Carpenters hammered under the shaded window,
Wind troubled the window curtains all night long.
A fleet of trucks strained uphill, grinding
Their freights covered, as usual.
The ceiling lightened again, the slanting diagram
Slid slowly forth.

        Hearing the milkman's chop,
His striving up the stair, the bottle's chink,          10
I rose from bed, lit a cigarette,
And walked to the window. The stony street
Displayed the stillness in which buildings stand,
The street-lamp's vigil and the horse's patience.
The winter sky's pure capital
Turned me back to bed with exhausted eyes.

Strangeness grew in the motionless air. The loose
Film grayed. Shaking wagons, hooves' waterfalls,
Sounded far off, increasing, louder and nearer.
A car coughed, starting. Morning, softly         20
Melting the air, lifted the half-covered chair
From underseas, kindled the looking-glass,
Distinguished the dresser and the white wall.
The bird called tentatively, whistled, called,
Bubbled and whistled, so! Perplexed, still wet
With sleep, affectionate, hungry and cold. So, so,
O son of man, the ignorant night, the travail
Of early morning, the mystery of beginning
Again and again,
        while History is unforgiven.        30

▶ *W. H. Auden (1907-    )*

## IN MEMORY OF W. B. YEATS
## (D. JAN. 1939)

### 1

He disappeared in the dead of winter:
The brooks were frozen, the airports almost deserted,
And snow disfigured the public statues;
The mercury sank in the mouth of the dying day.

O all the instruments agree
The day of his death was a dark cold day.

Far from his illness
The wolves ran on through the evergreen forests,
The peasant river was untempted by the fashionable quays;
By mourning tongues
The death of the poet was kept from his poems.

But for him it was his last afternoon as himself,
An afternoon of nurses and rumors;
The provinces of his body revolted,
The squares of his mind were empty,
Silence invaded the suburbs,
The current of his feeling failed: he became his admirers.

Now he is scattered among a hundred cities
And wholly given over to unfamiliar affections;
To find his happiness in another kind of wood
And be punished under a foreign code of conscience.
The words of a dead man
Are modified in the guts of the living.

But in the importance and noise of tomorrow
When the brokers are roaring like beasts on the floor of the Bourse,
And the poor have the sufferings to which they are fairly accustomed,
And each in the cell of himself is almost convinced of his freedom;
A few thousand will think of this day
As one thinks of a day when one did something slightly unusual.
O all the instruments agree
The day of his death was a dark cold day.

## 2

You were silly like us: your gift survived it all;
The parish of rich women, physical decay,
Yourself; mad Ireland hurt you into poetry.
Now Ireland has her madness and her weather still,
For poetry makes nothing happen: it survives
In the valley of its saying where executives
Would never want to tamper; it flows south
From ranches of isolation and the busy griefs,
Raw towns that we believe and die in; it survives,
A way of happening, a mouth.

## 3

Earth, receive an honoured guest;
William Yeats is laid to rest:
Let the Irish vessel lie
Emptied of its poetry.

Time that is intolerant
Of the brave and innocent,

And indifferent in a week
To a beautiful physique,

Worships language and forgives
Everyone by whom it lives;
Pardons cowardice, conceit,
Lays its honours at their feet.

Time that with this strange excuse
Pardoned Kipling and his views,
And will pardon Paul Claudel,
Pardons him for writing well.

In the nighmare of the dark
All the dogs of Europe bark,
And the living nations wait,
Each sequestered in its hate;

Intellectual disgrace
Stares from every human face,
And the seas of pity lie
Locked and frozen in each eye.

Follow, poet, follow right
To the bottom of the night,
With your unconstraining voice
Still persuade us to rejoice;

With the farming of a verse
Make a vineyard of the curse,
Sing of human unsuccess
In a rapture of distress;

In the deserts of the heart
Let the healing fountain start,
In the prison of his days
Teach the free man how to praise.

▶  *Peter Viereck (1916-      )*

# DON'T LOOK NOW BUT MARY IS EVERYBODY

Mary, long by Boss's kisses bored,
Quit desk and stole His yacht and jumped aboard.
Her lamb took she, for purer were his kisses.
Compass and pistol took she in her purse.
Free sailed she north to eat new freedom up.
And her helped ocean and grew calm and snored.
But when with bleating chum she cuddled up,
Unleased His typoons Boss; therein no bliss is.
Then knew she—by four signs—whose jig was up:

Her buoyed the life-preserver down, not up;
True was the pistol's aim, but in reverse;
The compass steered, but only toward abysses;
The little lamb nipped Mary's thighs and roared.

▶ *Robert Lowell (1917-    )*

## SKUNK HOUR

Nautilus Island's hermit
heiress still lives through winter in her Spartan
cottage;
her sheep still graze above the sea.
Her son's a bishop. Her farmer
is first selectman in our village;
she's in her dotage.

Thirsting for
the hierarchic privacy
of Queen Victoria's century,
she buys up all
the eyesores facing her shore,
and lets them fall.

The season's ill—
we've lost our summer millionaire,
who seemed to leap from an L. L. Bean
catalogue. His nine-knot yawl
was auctioned off to lobstermen.
A red fox stain covers Blue Hill.

And now our fairy
decorator brightens his shop for fall;
his fishnet's filled with orange cork,
orange, his cobbler's bench and awl;
there is no money in his work,
he'd rather marry.

One dark night,
my Tudor Ford climbed the hill's skull;
I watched for love-cars. Lights turned down,
they lay together, hull to hull,
where the graveyard shelves on the town. . . .
My mind's not right.

A car radio bleats,
"Love, O careless Love. . . ." I hear
my ill-spirit sob in each blood cell,
as if my hand were at its throat. . . .
I myself am hell;
nobody's here—

only skunks, that search
in the moonlight for a bite to eat.
They march on their soles up Main Street:
white stripes, moonstruck eyes' red fire
under the chalky-dry and spar spire
of the Trinitarian Church.

I stand on top
of our back steps and breathe the rich air—
a mother skunk with her column of kittens
    swills the garbage pail
She jabs her wedge-head in a cup
of sour cream, drops her ostrich tail,
and will not scare.

▶ *Richard Wilbur (1921-    )*

## THE DEATH OF A TOAD

A toad the power mower caught,
Chewed and clipped of a leg, with a hobbling hop has got
To the garden verge, and sanctuaried him
Under the cineraria leaves, in the shade
Of the ashen heartshaped leaves, in a dim,
Low, and a final glade.

The rare original heartsblood goes,
Spends on the earthen hide, in the folds and wizenings, flows
  In the gutters of the banked and staring eyes. He lies
  As still as if he would return to stone,             10
    And soundlessly attending, dies
      Toward some deep monotone,

    Toward misted and ebullient seas
And cooling shores, toward lost Amphibia's emperies.
  Day dwindles, drowning, and at length is gone
  In the wide and antique eyes, which still appear
    To watch, across the castrate lawn,
      The haggard daylight steer.

# INTRODUCTION
## *to Criticism*

The criticism of poetry starts with the aesthetic experience of reading a poem. Aesthetic faculty involves a degree of experiencing, usually simultaneously, several sensations at a time. Since poetry is the use of language, the aesthetic experience of poetry includes thought. The experience of poetry is both direct and vicarious, the proportion being dependent upon the kind of poem experienced and the language used. The poem often depends on the evocation of previous experience by the means of language. The poem may go beyond that stage and create a more subtle direct experience of a mental or emotional nature.

The surface or direct experience may be sensuous. The second level of experience is reached at a point where the perceiver attempts to distinguish between form and content of a poem. How the poem does its work is the form; what the poem means is the content. The word "theme" is often substituted for the word "content." The critic's task is to point out the presence of both factors in any given poem. His task becomes more difficult as he tries to delineate the part each plays in the aesthetic experience. Often the question shifts and changes shape and becomes a more complicated problem, a sort of *gestalt* experience. Perhaps the words of a great modern poet put it best when he says:

O chestnut tree, great rooted blossomer,
Are you the leaf, the blossom or the bole?
O body swayed to music, O brightening glance,
How can we know the dancer from the dance?
—William Butler Yeats

There are many other problems involved in criticism of poetry. On a practical level criticism is nothing more than paraphrase, explication, analysis, interpretation, and evaluation. On a more theoretical level criticism also involves philosophical considerations about the origin, nature, and basis of poetry.

The question of value often involves the conflicting relationship between personal and social values. If the two value patterns coincide, the conflict does not become a factor; if, however, the personal values contradict the values of a group, the differences become an important aspect of evaluation. The elements of biography, sociology, psychology, religion, and history also may become complicating factors in evaluation. Any one quality by which a poem may be judged is relative to the possible permutations of all of the variables.

How do these variables enter the critical process? The philosophy that the critic holds will in turn determine his values. In aesthetics the values include such concepts as integrity, intensity, originality, truth, content, order, ideas, sound sense, and so forth. These in turn lead into crucial questions that may be applied to poetry in general or to a specific poem. Some of these critical questions are:

Is it possible to evaluate poetry, and is it possible to say that one poem is better than another?

How is a pattern of judgment established?

How is the sense in a poem evaluated and how are the criteria established?

What are the conventions of prosody and what part do they play in the poetic achievement?

What kind of truth does the poem give us? How does this truth fit when juxtaposed with the truths of other disciplines?

What part do feeling and emotion play in the poem? How do they relate to other truths?

Does the poem have any special or self-proclaimed standards which need to be considered in the evaluation?

In *In Defense of Reason* Ivor Winters has succinctly summarized the critical process as follows:

> It will consist of (1) of the statement of such historical or biographical knowledge as may be necessary in order to understand the mind and method of the writer; (2) of such analysis of his literary theories as we may need to understand and evaluate what he is doing; (3) of a rational critique of the paraphraseable content (roughly, the motive) of the poem; (4) of a rational critique of the feeling motivated—that is, of the details of style, as seen in language and technique; and (5) of the final act of judgment, a unique act, the general nature of which can be indicated, but which cannot be communicated precisely, since it consists in receiving from the poet his own final and unique judgment of his matter and in judging that judgment. It should be noted that the purpose of the first four processes is to limit as narrowly as possible the region in which the final unique act is to occur.

Most practical criticism will skip or combine some of the steps indicated by Winters; and to complicate the matter further, most modern critics attempt to use the non-literary disciplines as aids to analyze and evaluate poetry. Psychology, psychiatry, sociology, medicine, anthropology, and philosophy are utilized as aids to poetic analysis. The critics cite figures like Darwin, Marx, Freud, Russell, Ayer, and Sartre in order to drive home a point often developed by an analogy between some aspect of poetry and a salient lesson from the writings of influential thinkers.

Practical criticism may be mere reviewing for popular magazines; serious criticism will usually be intended for publication in periodicals like *PMLA*. Within the extremes of this spectrum, each critic will pick a dominant or key figure of speech which he will use to shape the object of his criticism. The diction and style will, of course, be appropriate to the level of the audience of any given publication. An analysis of a poem written for a Sunday newspaper supplement would in all probability not fit the tone of an academic periodical. The final act of writing criticism will reflect the combination of theory, key metaphor, and individual talent. Stanley Edgar Hyman in *The Armed Vision* summarizes this process effectively:

> Another feature of contemporary criticism worth remarking is that each critic tends to have a master metaphor or series of metaphors in terms of which he sees the critical function, and that this metaphor then shapes, informs, and sometimes limits his work. Thus for R. P. Blackmur the critic is a kind of magical surgeon, who operates without ever cutting living tissue; for George Saintsbury he is a wine-bidder; for Constance Rourke he is a manure-spreader, fertilizing the ground for a good crop; for Waldo Frank he is an obstetrician, bringing new life to birth; for Kenneth Burke, after a number of other images, he has emerged as a wealthy impresario, staging dramatic performances of any work that catches his fancy; for Ezra Pound he is a patient man showing a friend through his library; and so forth.

So much for theory. All the critics agree on the necessary practical steps that need to be taken. One has to read the poem carefully, usually several times. After the careful reading will come an analytic reading or close interpretation which will include whenever appropriate or necessary paraphrase and explication. The logical consequences of the theoretical questions have to be brought down the Hayakawa's ladder of abstraction to the specific rungs at which level they can be answered.

Writing analyses about poetry is no different from writing about prose except in the focus and emphasis that the writer may have to exercise. Since poetry is a more condensed, intensive language, the writing about poetry often has to be more precise and carefully wrought. The beginning critic has to be more careful in selecting his thesis. He has less room to search for his controlling purpose.

Neither are the questions that one asks about poetry any different from the questions that one asks about short stories and drama. Many of the questions asked are in fact the mere road work that lead to the real concerns that actually find their way into the paper that is written. The list of questions that follows may be asked about poems. Not all of the questions will apply to all poems; but like any comprehensive checklist, it enables the writer to consider the major ingredients. From these questions more germane points will offer themselves. Often the perfunctory analysis will lead to an original insight, and that insight will lead to the exhilaration of creativity and understanding. The experienced critic may overtly skip answering many of these elementary questions, but that does not mean that he does in fact skip them since like the experienced athelete he has incorporated the basic drills so that they are now smooth skills that produce results effortlessly. Much interesting and valuable literary criticism lies in paraphrase, analysis, and interpretation. Here follows a list of questions to ask about poems:

## PARAPHRASE:

1. Who is speaking?
2. To whom is he speaking?
3. What is the poem about?
4. What is the occasion?
5. What is the setting?
6. What is the mood?
7. Is there a dramatic situation?
8. What happens?
9. What kind of poem is it?
10. What is the literal meaning?

## METER AND STRUCTURE:

11. What is the pattern?
12. Does the poem follow one of the traditional patterns?
13. Are there stanzas?
14. What is the rime scheme?
15. What is the meter?
16. What other aspects of rhythm are present?
17. Are there metric innovations?
18. What transitional techniques and devices are used?

## DICTION AND STYLE:

19. What is the style?
20. What part does the diction play in the style?
21. What is the tone?
22. How is it obtained?
23. Does the poem have stylistic unity?
24. Are there problems with the denotation of words?
25. What special problems of connotation are present?
26. Is there deliberate ambiguity?
27. Do archaic words cause difficulty?
28. Are there other special problems with diction?

## IMAGERY AND FIGURATIVE LANGUAGE:

29. What are the allusions?
30. Is there symbolism? Explain it.
31. What imagery is present?
32. Identify and explain the figurative language.
33. What special rhetorical devices are used?
34. What other poetic devices are present?
35. Is there irony? Explain it.

## INTERPRETATION AND EVALUATION:

36. Is interpretation necessary for understanding?
37. Are there several interpretations possible?
38. Is there critical material to solve special problems of interpretation?
39. Are there details that do not fit interpretation?
40. Are there deliberate ambiguities?
41. How does this poem compare to other poems of this type? Time? Subject? Theme? Poet?

42. How does the evaluation of this poem emerge from all of the questions listed above?
43. What theory of criticism best aids in the evaluation of this poem?
44. Are there special problems of evaluation?
45. What aspects of evaluation seem most appropriate?
46. To what qualities does the poem appeal? Intellectual? Emotional? Academic? Popular?
47. Did you enjoy the poem?
48. Was the effort worth the result?
49. What does this poem contribute to poetry?
50. Are there broader benefits for the liberal arts and the humanities coming from this poem?

Once you have considered these questions and established which of them seem pertinent, pull together the diverse elements to obtain a unified point of view. A consistent or dominant critical approach may suggest itself and, hopefully, the total interpretation and evaluation may be a creative experience in itself. From understanding may arise an aesthetic appreciation. As good health may come from good nutrition and exercise, so appreciation may emerge from critical effort. A forced or directed appreciation does a disservice to good poetry. Thousands of high school students hate Shakespeare because they were directed to appreciate him. An understanding that leads to negative criticism is to be preferred to superficial or spurious understanding leading to equally superficial praise. One has to pay his dues to earn the right to criticize or to praise.

To write a paper on poetry one cannot utilize all of the possible questions. It is necessary to sharpen the focus of concern. It is not possible to write an effective paper on a vague or broad topic. A defendable thesis must be limited. Often the questions must be answered for one's own understanding, but it would be gauche to parade all the answers in the essay about a specific poem. It is necessary to concentrate on the crucial problems and include the other items as they become relevant.

What does one write about when he writes about a poem? One can paraphrase, analyze, interpret, explicate, and evaluate. It is possible to create a subject for a theme from almost all of the fifty items above. For example an entire essay may be written on the importance of the dominant figure of speech in the poem. A particularly difficult essay to write is one that tries to show a significant relationship between diverse ingredients of a complex poem. Often such key words as "show how," "discuss," "analyze," "explain," "how does," "evaluate," "compare," "contrast," "compare and contrast," and "comment" are used to force a writer into a set pattern of analysis. Most assigned essays on poetry are between 500 and 1500 words long. It is a truism that it is easier to write a long paper rather than a short one. Each length offers its own problems. For the purpose of this section only the topics that can serve as an assignment for a short paper will be considered. If you are given a specific poem to write about, the following is a list of assignments that may be chosen:

1. Write a paraphrase of _____.
2. Write an analysis of the imagery in _____.
3. Write an analysis of the figurative language in _____.
4. Analyze the structure of _____.
5. Analyze the prosody of _____.
6. Explicate the key passages of _____.
7. Show the relationship between sound and meaning in _____.
8. Demonstrate how the symbols determine the theme of _____.
9. Compare the various interpretations of _____.
10. Evaluate the effectiveness of the imagery in _____.
11. Discuss the dominant image in _____.
12. Compare _____ to another poem by the same poet.
13. Compare _____ to other poems having the same theme.
14. Discuss the tone of _____.
15. How does the figurative language contribute to the irony of _____?
16. How does the ambiguity of the language reflect the theme of _____?

17. Evaluate the originality of the symbols in _____.
18. How is _____ unified?
19. How do the poetic conventions contribute to the theme of _____?
20. Write a general critique of _____.
21. Evaluate _____ from two different critical perspectives.
22. Paraphrase, explicate, analyze, interpret, and evaluate _____.
23. Take two poems and write an essay in which you compare and contrast elements of mood, tone, diction, imagery, figurative language, and symbolism.
24. Compare and contrast the themes of two poems that have the same subject matter.
25. Take two poems from two different centuries and show how they differ in style and theme even though they are on the same subject.
26. Discuss the place of nature in poetry. Develop a thesis that encompasses several philosophies of nature and illustrate your analysis with specific illustrations from several poems.
27. Show what attitudes poets of different centuries have had about death. Illustrate their major themes with appropriate selections from their poems.
28. Take one major poet and illustrate his position on major issues like time, life, death, fate, war, love, and so forth. Indicate whether his position on these topics was unified or eclectic.

After all the analysis has been done, the topic chosen, the length determined, the focus sharpened, and the notes taken, the task of actually writing the essay remains. Again it should be pointed out that this essay will be the same as any other serious essay. It is a good idea to look at several of the essays in this book and from other sources as well to see how others get started. Writing is a very personal process and no two writers will approach it in exactly the same way. There is no magic formula for writing good essays. Endless and often mindless outlines do not help if the writer has no thought worthy of an outline. A myriad of transitions between intellectual lacunae do not improve the

nothingness. According to some psychologists a trial and error approach may lead to significant insights. Random behavior may be more productive than slavish conformity to some mediocre system of directions. There are many interviews with writers available for the student to study; one pattern emerges from them all: there are as many methods as there are writers. Albert Einstein in an answer to a question about his working habits said that he "groped."

One of the best statements about what writing involves is the excerpt from a letter written by Dr. James J. Lynch in answer to a plea by English teachers on how to prepare their students for college writing. Although he was talking about preparation for a hurdle test for English composition, his directions give a good summary of what effort a serious essay entails:

My only suggestion to pass on to teachers preparing students for the Subject A Examination is the one I act upon myself in advanced composition classes for prospective teachers of English (who in their turn will be preparing students for the Subject A Examination): concentrate on the slow, painstaking, often unrewarding, and never spectacular business of written composition. And I don't mean simply the assignment of papers and the reading and marking of them after they are turned in. I mean actual instruction in the various compositional steps: finding a suitable topic, narrowing it and determining its focus and point of view, marshaling the relevant data and/or opinion, classifying the data, making an outline, expressing the thesis or controlling idea, developing the various parts as sentences, paragraphs, groups of paragraphs, etc., supplying an appropriate introduction and conclusion, sharpening the focus, strengthening the transitions and other structural tissues, examining closely the expression and revising wherever flaws appear in the grammar, the logic, or the rhetoric, making the final draft in proper form. These are, of course, the obvious steps which have occurred to everyone who writes or teaches writing; but it is also true that many high school graduates seem not only never to have had any really systematic instruction in writing but also never to have had their attention called to the logical processes involved. Expository prose, in which ideas are developed logically, rather than narration or description, is the most suitable kind to prepare students for the Subject A Examination. The ability of the student to analyze and synthesize is of course the goal of the Examination, as it is also the goal of all education of an intellectual nature; and it is the hope that as the student acquires this ability he will acquire an ever greater power over and sense of responsibility to language.

An outline of Dr. Lynch's statement is a good checklist to follow for writing essays:

Find topic
Narrow topic
Determine focus and point of view
Get data and opinion
Classify data
Make outline
State thesis
Develop: Sentences
          Paragraphs
Supply: Introduction
         Conclusion
Sharpen focus
Supply: Transitions
        Rhetorical devices
Check: Diction
       Grammar
       Logic
       Rhetoric

Put diagrammatically the organization of a typical essay might look like this:

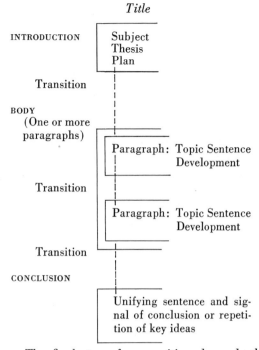

The final step of composition demands the act of rewriting to put the essay into final form to fit the assignment. The essays that follow offer a few examples that put in practice the elements noted in this section.

# SOUND AND SENSE: THE TEACHING OF PROSODY

*Jack E. Reese*

Apparently, instruction in prosody has all but disappeared from high school and college English classes, sharing the fate of the once-popular pastime of "parsing" sentences. I object. It is distressing that many college sophomores complete their required English courses with only the haziest notion of, say, the difference between an anapest and a handsaw, for their incompetence in the technical analysis of poetry will forever interfere with their realization of the total artistic triumph of any poem.

At the same time, this de-emphasis is in some ways an act of mercy; one recalls all too clearly his own painfully mechanical and wearying indoctrination in iambs and trimeters and rime royal. I would be very reluctant to champion a resuscitation of classroom *drill* in the techniques and vocabulary of prosody. Insisting that a student master the technical features of verse is not likely to produce either competence in or enthusiasm for reading poetry, unless he also learns to speculate on the particular appropriateness of a certain stanzaic form or meter in a specific poem. If the instructor does not exercise his students in this "application" of knowledge, then the best he can hope for in class discussion is a bored and grudging recitation of the "facts" about a poem. This essay suggests a reasonably systematic (though certainly not novel or comprehensive) approach to the teaching of prosody based on the simple proposition that form and meaning in poetry must be examined simultaneously.

A good place to begin any study of poetry in an introductory course in literature is Pope's *Essay on Criticism*, particularly that section (Part II, lines 337-382) which provides illustrated advice to neophytic poets and critics. Only the most stubbornly unimaginative student will refuse to be convinced by Pope's examples that, in a line of poetry, "The sound must seem an echo to the sense." (Do the alliterating "s's" here create a faint echo?) It is useful to invite a class to speculate on just that correlation between *sound* and *meaning* in lines outside the *Essay on Criticism*. Two good examples are "Do not go gentle into that good night" (the opening of Dylan Thomas' moving remarks to his dying father) and "To strive, to seek, to find, and not to yield" (the concluding line of Tennyson's "Ulysses"). In the first example, the alveolar and dental stops make the line reasonably difficult to utter, and this labored effect is a perfect accompaniment to the anguish of the speaker as he pleads with his father to hang on stubbornly to the last remnants of life. The final utterance of Ulysses (an apotheosis of the poem and his career) emphasizes the strength, determination, and indomitable will of this hero, qualities which are echoed in the "sound" of the line. That is, the double-bar junctures (verbal equivalents of comma punctuation) and the sibilants, fricatives, and terminal stops demand a deliberate, forceful enunciation which is highly appropriate to a line celebrating rugged fortitude.

Having illustrated just this one principle of poetry, the instructor may easily extend the scope of the discussion by pointing out that certain rhythmical and verse patterns in English lend themselves to specific purposes. There are many obvious examples: blank verse, because it comes close to the basic intonation patterns in spoken English, is eminently suitable for dialogue or monologue ("Death of the Hired Man" and "Andrea del Sarto"); the ballad stanza encourages ellipsis, understatement, repetition, and a carefully-cultivated naiveté ("Rime of the Ancient Mariner" and any of the quasi-folk songs currently being written); the Spenserian stanza, with its traditional medieval flavor and its amenability to narrative poetry, was a natural choice for Keats's "The Eve of St. Agnes." I am embarrassed to continue (here, not in the classroom) with such well-known illustrations.

Less familiar forms and patterns, however, challenge the ingenuity of instructor and students. For example, I use two examples to illustrate "typical" use of the infrequently-employed trochaic meter. One is Herrick's charming little "Grace for a Child":

Here a little child I stand,
Heaving up my either hand;
Cold as paddock though they be,
Here I lift them up to Thee,
For a benison to fall
On our meat and on us all.

Most students will agree that this "sounds like" a child, and most of them, if prodded to explain why, will point to the short lines, the simple aabb rhyme, the preponderance of monosyllables, and what they call the "sing-song" nature of the trochaic rhythm, which calls to mind a child's rote recitation of a blessing. The best students may even go so far as to notice that the adolescent tone is further increased by the rhymes, which are more noticeable than those in other poems they have read. The

rhymes are stressed, of course, because they occur on the final "upbeat" of the short, incomplete trochaic lines.

Having thus established that trochaic is a fitting medium for children's verse (remember "London brídge ĭs falling down"), the instructor can drive home the point that versification patterns are highly versatile by confronting his students with an example of trochaic verse as different from Herrick's as an innocent child at prayer is unlike the dreadful witches who accost Macbeth on the heath near Forres:

Fillet of a fenny snake
In the cauldron boil and bake
Eye of newt and toe of frog,
Wool of bat and tongue of dog ...

The strange thing is that the verse form here seems just as appropriate as it did in Herrick's little poem. The short lines, the aabb rhyme scheme, and the trochaic meter are well suited to the incantatory recitation. Furthermore, Shakespeare (or a later interpolator, as some critics believe) was anxious to stress both the unnaturalness of the witches and the terrible perversion of human values which characterizes the Macbeth universe. (Early in the play, the witches announce that "fair is foul, and foul is fair.") Is it not fitting for the weird sisters, then, to chant in trochaic meter, which wrenches "normal" English out of its customary iambic kilter? Finally, it is interesting to note that these lines are only three and one-half feet long, each line ending on a strong beat. What would have been the effect if Shakespeare (or whoever) had put the lines into regular tetrameter; if he had written, for example, "Fillet of a fenny serpent,/In the cauldron boil and ferment. . . ."

This version is, of course, ludicrous: the disyllables are much weaker than the monosyllables; feminine rhymes are usually comic, but, most important, the alteration of the rhythm totally debilitates the lines. The strong beat at the end of each line in the "original" version adds to the rhythmical certainty of the verse, and the incomplete foot seems to invite the following line. And *perhaps* the incompleteness of the meter further stresses the unnatural quality of the speaker.

It is possible, I think, to define and illustrate

almost all the devices and forms of versification in the fashion I have been indicating, always stressing the particular appropriateness of a certain technique to the intent of the author. I do not mean to suggest that students should go uninstructed in such matters as imagery, speaker, dramatic situation, tone, connotative values, allusions, and the other elements of poetry; the meaningful reading of a poem demands a sensitivity to all the problems faced by the poet and the methods he employs to meet them. What I do suggest is that students need not be required to "memorize" the "facts" about prosody in rote fashion; they can master the same information and utilize it intelligently if the instructor convinces them that form and meaning are inseparable. This he must do by a thorough class examination of a number of poems which clearly illustrate what he is talking about. Some good examples to work with are:

1. "You, Andrew Marvell." MacLeish's poem is built around the figure of a man, presumably in the United States, picturing in his mind the relentless coming of night at various parts of the world and waiting for that darkness to engulf this hemisphere. The metaphorical application is obvious: just as the great civilizations at Ecbatan and Kermanshah and Palmyra decayed and fell, so also will Western Civilization (or perhaps, more particularly, the United States) one day crumble and fade into the annals of ancient history. The structure of the poem reinforces the theme very effectively. The simple, regular quatrains, rhymed abab, and the absence of end-stop punctuation suggest the metronome-like regularity of the fall of evening at various points around the world. Obviously then, the versification helps shape the ominous tone of the poem.

2. "The Lotos Eaters." Tennyson's poem begins very neatly. The first section (down to "choric Song") consists of five Spenserian stanzas, the regularity of which may be seen in the fifth stanza:

> Thĕy sát thĕm dówn ŭpón thĕ yéllŏw sánd,
> Bĕtwéen thĕ sún ănd móon ŭpón thĕ shóres;
> Ănd swéet ĭt wás tŏ dréam ŏf Fáthĕrlánd,
> Ŏf chíld, ănd wífe, ănd sláve; bŭt évĕrmŏre
> Mŏst wéarў seémĕd thĕ séa, wéarў thĕ óar,

> Wéarў thĕ wandĕríng fiélds ŏf bárrĕn fóam.
> Thĕn sŏme ŏne saíd, "Wĕ wíll rĕtúrn nŏ moré";
> Ănd áll ăt oncé thĕy saíd, "Oŭr islănd hŏme
> Iš far bĕyŏnd thĕ wávĕ; wĕ wíll ňo lóngĕr róam."

The iambic meter is occasionally disrupted here, apparently for specific reasons. The trochees in lines 5 and 6 emphasize the repetition of the word "weary" and thus contribute to the mood of overpowering fatigue and lassitude, an effect Tennyson began shaping in the opening stanza by means of what he called the "lazing" "no rhyme" of "land"-"land." The two other disruptions of the meter in the above scansion are debatable: "wandering" I have marked as a dactyl, though it would be easy to read it as a disyllable ("wan'dring"); and one could, by wrenching the normal intonational pattern somewhat, read in line 7, à la General MacArthur, "Wĕ wíll rĕtúrn." Still, all these probably represent some interruption of the basic iambic meter, and it is interesting to note that each calls further attention to the alliterating "w's" which weight these weary lines. But there is no question about the essential regularity of this and the other opening stanzas.

By the end of the poem, however, the verse simply will not scan: the first of the eight stanzas in the "Choric Song" concluding the poem reads:

> There is sweet music here that softer falls
> Than petals from blown roses on the grass,
> Or night-dews on still waters between walls
> Of shadowy granite, in a gleaming pass;
> Music that gentlier on the spirit lies,
> Than tired eyelids upon tired eyes;
> Music that brings sweet sleep down from the
> blissful skies.
> Here are cool mosses deep,
> And through the moss the ivies creep,
> And in the stream the long-leaved flowers weep,
> And from the craggy ledge the poppy hangs in
> sleep.

Prosodic chaos. I have not even attempted to indicate "weak" and "strong" syllables, because such marking would be arbitrary and inconclusive. The rhyming (ababcccdddd) is also irregular, occasionally consecutive. The remaining seven stanzas contain 13, 14, 15, 15, 19, 12, and 29 lines respectively. What has happened to the versification since the opening section? One need only remember what has happened to the characters in the poem. At the opening of the narrative Odysseus' mariners, after incredible hardships afloat and ashore, fall prey to the temptation of the marvelous lotos, which offers forgetfulness and peace and makes their duties and obligations seem terribly insignificant. The men sink gradually into an opium-like reverie or dream; in essence, they lose control over themselves; they sprawl out, mentally and physically. The poem does just that, too: it "sprawls out" gradually, moving further and further away from the tight regularity of the early Spenserian stanza to the formlessness of the choric songs. (Note that the consecutive rhymes and the initial grammatical repetition also produce a soporific effect.)

3. "On Wenlock Edge the Wood's In Trouble." The quatrian stanza of Housman's poem is directly appropriate to the content. The speaker, located in England on the site of an ancient Roman encampment, is watching the trees of the forest being tossed and bent by the wind. He speculates that centuries before, a Roman soldier stood on that same spot observing the same scene in nature. This soldier, moreover, was himself likely bowed by the same "gale of life" which howls most miserably through the modern observer. Only death calmed the Roman soldier; only death will hush the troublesome winds of life in the speaker, and, one presumes, only death will alleviate the sharp anguish of men a thousand years hence being lashed by the same never-diminishing gale of life. The simple quatriain is a splendid vehicle for such a cheerless statement: the poem describes an ominously unchanging pattern of life, and does not the monotonously regular iambic tetrameter-quatrain structure itself suggest this vision of life?

But, one may object, this is stretching a point: it implies that Housman conscientiously selected the quatrain stanza for just this work; whereas in reality he utilized this form in a majority of his poems. I do not think this fact detracts from the above analysis of "Wenlock Edge," but it does introduce an interesting corollary consideration: Why was Housman so attracted to this form? Partly, one suspects, be-cause of his classical background; this neat little stanzaic form has about it a certain Attic grace. But, also, what interests us in Housman's poetry is the remarkable combination of thorough-going cosmic pessimism and the sardonic shrug, the understatement, the persimmon-sweet humor. "Heigh, ho, it was all a lie," says the speaker in "Mithridates," waking with a hangover and finding the drunken dreams of the previous night dispelled. This "incongruity" is paralleled in Housman's trick of imposing on the uncomplicated, straightforward quatrain the heaviest notions. The combination surprises, but does not offend us, and it appeals to that same core of unconventionality which responds to the pessimistic subject matter.

4. Shakespeare's Sonnet 97. Shakespeare's sonnets consistently illustrate the inseparability of form and meaning; the restrictive scope demanded, among other things, lyric statement, close unification, and (to provide amplitude) highly suggestive imagery. What fascinates us about the poems is that they exhibit infinite variety within the rigid framework of the three quatrains and final couplet which form four units, distinct from each other, yet closely related and carefully arranged to keep the reader in at least mild suspense until the final "expository" couplet.

Sonnet 97 is a splendid example of how Shakespeare operated within this framework. The first quatrain establishes what appears to be the general theme of the poem, that separation from his friend makes the speaker's life dreary and barren:

> How like a winter hath my absence been
> From thee, the pleasure of the fleeting year!
> What freezings have I felt, what dark days seen!
> What old December's bareness every where!

In the second quatrain, we learn that the "freezings" which the speaker has felt have actually occurred during the glorious summer and autumn months:

> And yet this time removed was summer's time,
> The teeming autumn, big with rich increase,
> Bearing the wanton burthen of the prime,
> Like widow'd wombs after their lord's decease.

The relationship between these two sections is significant. On the one hand, the eight lines are closely related; "this time removed" in line

5 refers specifically to the period of separation described in the preceding section, and it becomes obvious that the poem is going to be constructed around the central image of the rotation of the seasons. On the other hand, the "and yet" marks a turning or shifting in the poem; the contrast between the two quatrains is equally obvious. The dreariness of winter pictured in the first section (achieved partly by the connotative values of such words as "absence," "fleeting," "freezings," "dark," "old," and "bareness") is succeeded by the richness and vitality of spring, summer, and autumn, as suggested by the startling sexual figure of an autumn made pregnant by spring ("prime") and words suggesting growth and sexuality: "teeming," "big," "rich," "increase," "wanton," "burthen," and "wombs." And it is perhaps significant that "time," an obvious motif in the poem, here rhymes with "prime"; whereas in the following quatrain "fruit," which echoes the springlike and sexual mood of the second quatrain, is pared with "mute," which at once cancels that mood:

> Yet this abundant issue seem'd to me
> But hope of orphans and unfather'd fruit;
> For summer and his pleasures wait on thee,
> And thou away, the very birds are mute. . . .

Again, this quatrain carries over much of the previous four lines, "this abundant issue" referring to the earlier "wanton burthen" and "widow'd wombs," and once more the "yet" marks another turn in the poem. The "joy child" of spring and autumn becomes a poor bastard, and the speaker, remembering, after a temporary glance at the greenness and goldness about him, that he is still separated from his friend, feels again the cold blasts of winter. The concluding two lines chill to the bone; the "birds" of line 12 are either silent, "Or, if they sing, 'tis with so dull a cheer/That leaves look pale, dreading the winter's near." (Aside: notice that the penultimate line is a perfect illustration of the "marriage" of sound and sense; its totally monosyllabic character supplies a dreary accompaniment to the cheerless mutterings of the birds.)

This simultaneous examination of structure and meaning in Sonnet 97 makes clear its full significance. The poem is not just another "blues" lament ("When you're alone,/There are no starry skies;/When you're alone,/The magic moonlight dies . . ."); it is a good deal more sophisticated and effective than that. Shakespeare, working within the highly restrictive four-unit framework, achieved a surprising degree of movement. In one sense, the poem is like a musical composition constructed on an A B A basis. That is, the first quatrain establishes the theme of "winter" (A); the second shifts to spring, summer and autumn (B), and the final section, including the third quatrain and the couplet, returns to the (A) theme. Thus there is a cyclical movement in the poem, strongly suggesting the passage of the seasons through a calendar year. Consequently, the phrase, "the fleeting year," in line 2 takes on added significance; the poem becomes, in addition to a traditional enough lament for a separated friend, a subtle reminder to that friend of other traditional themes: *tempis fugit, momento mori, carpe diem.* The effect is like that attained by Andrew Marvell in "To His Coy Mistress." Just as the speaker in that poem attempts to frighten his reluctant mistress into submission by calling her attention time and again to the inexorable passage of time, so the speaker in Sonnet 97 in reality is pleading with his friend "To love that well which thou must leave ere long" (Sonnet 73).

At this point, I ask my students to make their own way through such poems as Henry King's "Sic Vita," Whitman's "Crossing Brooklyn Ferry," and Hopkins' "Pied Beauty." The results are sometimes very worthwhile. Notice the hedging: I do not claim that the approach to the study of prosody described in this essay will (1) create enthusiasm for poetry in people who do not like poetry, (2) raise IQ's, or (3) spawn student explicators of the caliber of Cleanth Brooks. Furthermore, this approach will not work on many poems, and there is a real danger that it may encourage ingenious analyses which are long on ingenuity and short on analysis. Yet, this method teaches the principles of prosody, and it teaches them in such a way, I think, that the student who receives this kind of instruction can read poetry more intelligently and with greater enjoyment.

# NO. 14 OF DONNE'S *HOLY SONNETS*

*John E. Parish*

Batter my heart, three person'd God; for, you
As yet but knocke, breathe, shine, and seeke to
    mend;
That I may rise, and stand, o'erthrow mee, 'and
    bend
Your force, to breake, blowe, burn and make me
    new.
I, like an usurpt towne, to'another due,
Labour to'admit you, but Oh, to no end,
Reason your viceroy in mee, mee should defend,
But is captiv'd, and proves weake or untrue.
Yet dearly'I love you,'and would be loved faine,
But am betroth'd unto your enemie:
Divorce mee,'untie, or breake that knot againe,
Take mee to you, imprison mee, for I
Except you'enthrall mee, never shall be free,
Nor ever chast, except you ravish mee.

Within the last ten years four critics have published articles about No. 14 of Donne's *Holy Sonnets*. In the first (*Explicator,* March 1953), J. C. Levenson suggested that in the opening quatrian God is compared to a tinker and sinful man to a damaged pewter vessel. Later in the same year (*Explicator,* December 1953) George Herman expressed doubt that the image of a tinker is implied. More likely, he felt, the sonnet is unified by a single extended metaphor which (if it could be realized) would demonstrate the part each Person of the Trinity plays in saving the penitent, since (according to Herman) in the first quatrain God the Father is implored to *breake* rather than merely *knocke*, the Holy Ghost to *blowe* rather than simply *breathe*, and God the Son (Sun) to *burn* rather than gently *shine* on the sinner's heart, "which is also the town and a woman." In the words *make me new* Herman believed that all three Persons are beseeched to act on the heart-town-woman and that, as applied to the woman, *make me* is a plea (like that in the sestet) to be violated. "Clearly, *make* had the appropriate popular meaning in Donne's day that it has today, and it seems to me likely that Donne here consciously employed the pun."

After three years George Knox replied to Herman (*Explicator,* October 1956), whom he wished to spare "the strain of trying to imagine the poet in the role of woman." According to Knox, "the traditions of Christian mysticism allow such symbolism of ravishment as a kind of 'as if.'" (One must infer that in Knox's opinion such symbolism shares nothing with metaphor in its effect on the imagination). Describing the interpretations of both Levenson and Herman as "somewhat oblivious of the obvious," Knox claimed to see the unifying conceit that had eluded Herman: "It seems very clear to me that the very first line invites contemplation of the Trinity and that this concept determines the structure of the whole sonnet. . . . The first quatrain calls on God the Father's omnipotence to batter the heart. The second envisions the admission of God through the medium or agency of Rectified Reason, Reason rectified through love [the Son]. The third exemplifies the reborn understanding (*enlight*ened through the Son) conceiving the consubstantiality of man and God through imagery of interpenetration [the Holy Ghost].

Then in 1961 Arthur L. Clements (*Modern Language Notes*, June 1961)—by citing biblical passages associating each of the verbs *knocke, breathe* and *shine* with all three Persons of the Trinity—proved beyond doubt (in my opinion) that "the sonnet's structure cannot then be viewed as the development of three quatrains each separately assigned to each of the Three Persons." Contending that "the organizing principle of the poem . . . is the paradox of death and rebirth, the central paradox of Christianity," Clements pointed out further that to illustrate this paradox of destroying in order to revive or throwing down in order to raise Donne employs throughout the sonnet two kinds of figurative language: "one kind is warlike, military, destructive; the other is marital, sexual, or uniting." The two kinds of metaphor are fused in lines 11-14 and are "made to achieve between themselves what Donne wishes to achieve with God."

Like Clements, I must join those whom Knox considered "oblivious of the obvious," those who cannot preceive three divisions of the sonnet devoted respectively to the Father, the Son, and the Holy Ghost. I believe that the sinner's only reason for addressing God as "three person'd" is that he is imploring him to exert all his power, his triple power, to rescue him from Satan. I hope that my interpretation will show, even more clearly than Clements has shown, how the interlocking of the various metaphors and of the stanzaic divisions gives the sonnet its unity.

In the first quatrain, I believe, the repentant sinner compares his heart to a walled town, one of many over which God is the rightful King. Upon approaching, the King has found this particular town closed to him, a Usurper (Satan) having captured it. Now the King with his army is encamped outside the walls, knocking at the gates and asking to be re-admitted so that he can restore (*mend*) whatever has been demolished in the capture and whatever has deteriorated during the occupation. But, declares the sinner, such gentle overtures will not suffice. The King must burst open the gates with *a battering ram*. (On another level, God *is* the battering ram). Beyond all mending, the town must be completely destroyed, after which a new one will *rise* in its place, built by the King to *stand* forever.

The verbs *batter, breake,* and *burn* all suggest storming a citadel; and even *blowe* may be intended to suggest the use of gun-powder to blow up the fortress or blow it into smithereens. One is reminded of the violent scenes described by Aeneas in telling Dido about the fall of Troy and (faintly) of the fact that a new Troy is fated to rise. Even richer and more apt, however, are the allusions to the destruction of Jerusalem by Nebuchadnezzar, (God's unwitting agent) and to the many predictions by the Prophets of the New Jerusalem to rise when a chastened people come to deserve it. There are also echoes of "the name of the city of my God, which is new Jerusalem" and of "Behold, I stand at the door and knock: if any man hear my voice and open the door, I will come in to him" (Revelation iii:12, 20).

The sonnet as a whole is unified by a shifting viewpoint which produces the effect of God's boring from the outside into the very center of the human heart. In the first quatrain the perspective is mainly that of the King outside the walls, seeking admission. In the second, the reader is carried inside the usurped town and sees the lamentable state of affairs through the eyes of the populace, rightfully the subjects of the King and of the Princess whom he has appointed as his Viceroy (these subjects being all the forces of man that should be governed by reason, here identified with the soul). In the sestet the point of view is that of the captive Princess herself (Reason, or the Soul), who has entered into a shameful marriage with the Usurper and is held in solitary confinement deep within the citadel.

Still further to invigorate and unify the prayer, Donne personifies the fortified town of the first quatrain as a woman, a woman urging her suitor to take her by force rather than by courtship. (In the Psalms, fallen Jerusalem or Zion is often personified as a mourning woman). This plea of the personified city for violent attack anticipates the similar plea which the dishonored Princess makes in the sestet.[1]

The phrase *usurpt towne* is deliberately ambiguous and transitional, connecting the first and second quatrains. It refers back to the walled town, of course; but simultaneously it designates the wretched people within the town, just as one might have said in 1944 "Paris awaits her deliverers," meaning that the *people* of Paris were hoping soon to be liberated. The complaint of the populace in the second quatrain is that though they acknowledge their duty to the King and labor to admit him, without the guidance of the Princess their efforts are futile. (It is not clear to me how the non-spirtual forces in man, unaided by the reason-soul, can labor at all to admit God). Since the capture of the town, the Usurper has held the Princess incommunicado; and her unhappy people, while aware of her shameful marriage, are unable to pass fair judgment on it, not knowing whether it was forced on her or whether she has voluntarily shifted allegiance to the Usurper and is therefore guilty of treason (*untrue*).

After the prayers of the personified city and of the leaderless people, finally in the sestet the captive Princess is heard from her solitary confinement. In language of almost unendurable anguish, which gives the sonnet much of its tone of passionate sincerity, she beseeches the King to deliver her from shame, declaring paradoxically that she can never be free unless he enthralls her and can never be chaste again unless he ravishes her. Appropriately, since the subject of the sonnet is remorse,[2] Donne is alluding again to he third chapter of Revelation —this time to the nineteenth verse: "As many as I love, I rebuke and *chasten*: be zealous therefore, and repent," and he has in mind two meanings of the verb *chasten*: to castigate and to purify.

Readers like Knox, who find it a strain "to imagine the poet in the role of woman," should remember that with Donne (as with Shakespeare, Spenser and others) the soul is always feminine. For example, in No. 2 of the *Holy Sonnets*, in the first nine lines the penitent describes himself as (among other things) one of God's sons and then as a temple of God's spirit presently usurped by Satan; but in the last five lines the feminine soul urges God to rescue her from Satan, who has kidnaped and ravished her.

To represent man's body as a temple or a castle and his soul as the priestess or governess was conventional.[3] Alma within her beleaguered castle, in Book Two of *The Faerie Queene*, is the most celebrated example; but since Alma has managed to remain chaste, a passage from *The Rape of Lucrece* more closely resembles Donne's sonnet. Shakespeare attributes to Tarquin, after he has committed the crime, something indistinguishable from Christian remorse. He is "a heavy convertite"; both his body (a temple) and his soul (a princess now as dishonored as Lucrece herself) have been polluted by his lustful will. Shakespeare's choice of words is remarkably like Donne's:

> Besides his soules faire temple is defaced,
>> To whose weake ruines muster troopes of cares,

---

[1] This begging for violation is less shocking when the woman is a personified city than when she is the soul of the repentant sinner. Few readers will detect this imagery in the first quatrain until *after* discovering it in the sestet; but in a re-reading, awareness of its first employment will mollify the shock of the second.

[2] Here I disagree with Helen Gardner, who regards this sonnet (No. 10 in her arrangement) as one of three "on the love man owes to God and to his neighbour." (*The Divine Poems* [Oxford, 1952], p. xli). Donne's sonnet seems to me to be a sinner's plea that remorse enough be put into his heart to start him on the way to repentance. As such, it would serve admirably as the first of a sequence; but perhaps all the sonnets are what Grierson called them—"separate ejaculations."

[3] During Elizabeth's long reign, English poets must have found new value in the old conceit, since a flesh-and-blood Princess was God's viceroy over them and sole head (under God) of their church.

To aske the spotted Princesse how she fares.
Shee sayes her subjects with fowle insurrection,
Haue batterd downe her consecrated wall,
And by their mortall fault brought in subjection
Her immortalitie, and made her thrall,
To liuing death and payne perpetuall.
   Which in her prescience shee controlled still,
   But her foresight could not forestall their will.
     (719-728)

But if the exhausted metaphor of the castle-body and the princess-soul was anemic by the 1590's, until Donne wrote his *Holy Sonnets* no poet had thought of wedding it to the equally weary and thinblooded convention of comparing a cold mistress to a castle and her lover to the general of an army besieging it. Miraculously, this marriage of two ancient weaklings produced an abnormally vigorous offspring, a sonnet in which Donne, with his accustomed daring, requires the reader to see God wearing (with a difference) the rue of a Petrarchan lover.

# THE PRINCIPLE OF MEASURE IN "TO HIS COY MISTRESS"

*Joan Hartwig*

Marvell's curious phrase "vegetable love" in "To His Coy Mistress" has been pictured jokingly as a "monstrous and expanding cabbage,"[1] or, more aesthetically perhaps, as "sequoia trees and other giant forms of plant life."[2] Either image, or indeed any image likely to be associated with the phrase, will prove embarrassing unless the reader considers Marvell's lady to be the object of jest rather than of seduction. Few women, after all, choose even metaphoric cabbages for lovers.

A delightful jest undeniably enhances stanza one, but its humor depends upon philosphical knowledge rather than upon a comic picture of enlarging vegetables. As L. V. Cunningham points out: "*Vegetable* is no vegetable but an abstract and philosophical term, known as such to every educated man of Marvell's day. Its context is the doctrine of the three souls: the rational . . . the sensitive . . . and, finally, the lowest of the three, the vegetable soul. . . . It is an intellectual image, and hence no image at all

but a conceit. . . . It is a piece of wit."[3]

Although Marvell was probably familiar with Robert Burton's adaptation of the doctrine of the tripartite soul in *The Anatomy of Melancholy*,[4] the intellectual play of his syllogistic poem suggests a direct knowledge of Aristotle's presentation, which interweaves the doctrine of souls with ideas concerning potential and actual.

The "vegetable" whereof Marvell speaks is in Aristotle the least active of all the types of souls; its potential includes only the power to attain and retain existence by the process of nutrition (including reproduction), decay, and growth (*De Anima*, II.413a.24-25).[5] Potential for "being" increases, first, with the sensitive soul, which may perceive and move locally, and, finally, with the rational soul, which possesses the additional capacity for calculation and thought (*De Anima*, II.415a.1-11).

Just as Aristotle uses these divisions to define a relationship—between matter, existing poten-

[1] J. V. Cunningham, *Tradition and Poetic Structure* (1960), p. 45.
[2] Rufus Putney, "'Our Vegetable Love': Marvell and Burton," *Studies in Honor of T. W. Baldwin*, ed. Don Cameron Allen (1958), p. 220. Brooks, Purser, and Warren, in *An Approach to Literature*, 3rd edn., (1952), p. 393, quite seriously point out that vegetable is "simply some great plant, like a sequoia."
[3] *Tradition and Poetic Structure*, p. 45. Helen Gardner, *The Metaphysical Poets* (1959), p. 249, has also noted this to be a reference to "the 'vegetable soul' [which] had only two powers: growth and reproduction."
[4] See Putney, "Marvell and Burton," pp. 220-228.
[5] Citations from Aristotle and method of section reference in my text are from *The Works of Aristotle*, ed. W. D. Ross, 12 vols. (Oxford, 1908-52).

tially and soul matter's activator—so Marvell alludes to the philosophical divisions "vegetable," not in order to describe a "sequoia tree" or even a "cedar of Lebanon," but in order to distinguish between levels of potentiality.[6] The vegetable state has potential only to grow, decay, and feed itself; and when the vegetable soul activates these potentialities, the vegetable becomes actual, realizing to the fullest its capacities for being. Man, on the other hand, possesses the potentiality to grow, decay, feed himself, perceive through the senses, move himself, calculate, and think. To actualize only his lowest powers of being, as Marvell suggests in stanza one, is to reduce himself to a state of minimal existence. To activate all his powers, however, would be to achieve a state of almost complete actuality, and, in the Aristotelian scheme, actuality is ultimately synonymous with perfection.

One further point from Aristotle, intimately connected with the divisions of soul and the idea of potential and actual, and, not incidentally, with Marvell's poem, is the significance of motion. In *Physica*, Aristotle defines motion as "the fulfillment of what exists potentially" (III.201a.10), and further states that "not only do we measure the movement by the time, but also the time by the movement, because they define each other" (IV.220b.15). In "To His Coy Mistress" as well, motion is the fulfillment of potential, and time is the measurer and definer of such movement from potential to actual. Notice Marvell's use of motion (or lack of it) in stanza one:

We would *sit down*, and think which way
To *walk*, ..........................
My vegetable Love should *grow*
Vaster than Empires, and more *slow*. ...
Nor would I love at *lower rate*.[7]

Because the vegetable's potential is the least of the divisions of being, the motion of actualization is reduced in this stanza to its minimum. For man to actualize all of his potential at the minimum rate of vegetable motion, however, would require a maximum extension of space and time.

The equation between time and space and motion begins its determining operation with the opening lines of the poem: "Had we but World enough, and Time. . . ." The measure of vegetable motion, or "vegetable love," would be slower than the time which measures man's normal movement from potential to actual. In the first stanza, then, Marvell speculates upon a hypothetically extended time-space motion equation; in the second stanza, he views the realistic negation of such a state; in the third, he suggests a reversal of the equation: speeded motion hurries time and compresses space.

Upon such a philosophical, abstract frame, Marvell builds his effective argument for seduction. Examination of the frame's embodiments will reveal how effective an argument it is.

The space required for "vegetable love" to complete its movement from potential to actual is defined in stanza one as the distance between the "Indian Ganges" and the "tide of Humber" —indeed, all the world. The vegetable love would eventually cover this space, growing "vaster than Empires," but its growth would require a "long Loves Day": all of the time from "before the Flood . . . till the Conversion of the Jews," a conversion that was to occur just before the world dissolved.[8] As time expanded, "loves day" would lengthen, and the sun, which measures this duration, would slow its journey across the world until each minute equaled an age.

The vegetable process would thus spread from the beginning to the end of time and from one end of the world to the other, through the slow motion of the most passive state possible to man. The slowly-grown, carefully-nourished love would reach actualization only just at the end of the world, the end of space, motion, and

---

[6] Patrick G. Hogan, Jr., "Marvell's 'Vegetable Love,'" *Studies in Philology*, 60 (January 1963), 9, argues also that the phrase is the key to the poem and that with it, "Marvell is classifying, not describing a process," but Hogan disagrees that the Aristotelian analogy has further significance.
[7] *The Poems and Letters of Andrew Marvell*, ed. H. M. Margoliouth (Oxford, 1927), I, 26-27.

[8] Ruth Wallerstein, *Studies in Seventeenth-Century Poetic* (1950), p. 337. Joseph H. Summers, *Marvell* (1961), p. 153, n. 10, states that the conversion is "to occur just before the Last Judgment."

time. The consummation, the ultimate actuality, would then coincide with the dissolution of its constituents. What finer consummation could be wished? And this is the state the poet's lady deserves "Nor would I love at lower rate," he assures her. Yet, at the height of compliment the lover's hyperbole turns playfully upon itself: regardless of his will, he *could* not love at lower rate because the idealized vegetable state is the minimum state available to any type of soul.

"But," the poet says, no longer teasing, but voicing his realistic and proximate complaint, "at my back I alwaies hear/Times winged Charriot hurrying near," pushing us not to vegetable vastness but to the "desarts of vast Eternity." The image of time's chariot reiterates, with increased speed, the association between time and its instrument of measure, the sun. In the vastness of eternity to which time pushes the lovers, there will be no motion to measure, and no time; no one will see the lady's beauty, nor will it exist; the poet will not sing, nor could his song be heard; appetite in the form of lust will cease; no embrace will satisfy the sense of touch.[9] The powers of the sensitive soul will be reduced below the point of potential; in the grave only the worms may act.

This stanza, more sombre in tone than the first, has its level of jest as well; but like the first stanza, the humor includes, rather than excludes, the lady's perception of it. The grave would, indeed, make a fine lovers' bower, if the dead had being. But they do not, and, the poet says sternly, neither shall we. He forces her to recognize that they are caught in a vise: time's hurrying on one side, eternity's motionlessness on the other.

In a complexity of interrelated but unextended images, the final stanza ties together all of the lines of intellectual play hitherto suggested. The first four lines,

Now therefore, while the youthful hew
Sits on thy skin like morning dew,[10]

And while they willing Soul transpires
At every pore with instant Fires,

draw attention to the lady's plantlike affinities —dew and transpiration—at the same time they suggest her human capacities for being, showing in effect that the highest category of soul subsumes all the other powers of soul. The image also may allude to the theory of Democritus (described in Aristotle's *De Anima*, I.404a.1-4) that the soul is composed of particles, or atoms of fire, which the body inhales and exhales. Nor is Aristotle's principle of potential and actual to be forgotten at this point. The soul, he states at the beginning of his classification, is the primary actualizing agent of the body, which is potential. The lady's soul is "willing" to act. Thus, her soul can be the actualizing agent for the body's potentiality—of both her and her lover—just as the poet's body and soul can actualize her. Becoming like each other at the point of actualization or transformation, the lovers will be potential no longer. Their sexual consummation, an act of both body and soul, will be for them a perfect state of actuality.

Thus far, Marvell has presented the processes of increase, decrease, and respiration (motions of the vegetable and sensitive souls), suggesting as well the potentialities of the rational soul. At this point he moves into an intensely active image of the higher power of local motion, or self-movement:

Now let us sport us while we may;
And now, like am'rous birds of prey,
Rather at once our Time devour,
Than languish in his slow-chapt pow'r.
Let us roll all our Strength, and all
Our sweetness, up into one Ball:
And tear our Pleasures with rough strife,
Thorough the Iron gates of Life.

The activation of images, verbs, and rhythm is perhaps too obvious to specify, but the reversal of roles which the poet advises is worth noting. Rather than allow time to devour us in his

---

9 Cf. Putney, "Marvell and Burton," pp. 223-224.

10 Margoliouth suggests the dialectal word *lew*, meaning "warmth," as the correct reading here. "Dew" is a conjectural emendation adopted by most anthologists, including Miss Gardner, Summers, and Brooks, Pur-

ser, and Warren. The moisture of youth being burnt off by time's hurrying chariot, the progress of decay, as in Aristotle, from moisture to dryness, together with the suggested affinity to the vegetable state, are my reasons for adopting "dew" as the more likely reading.

slow-moving, but powerful jaws (a further suggestion of the vise presented in stanza two), we can devour him in an instant of activity—just as birds of prey attack their food. The "birds of prey" image may be meant to intensify action even further. According to a long-standing myth, eagles, or hawks, when they copulate, soar high into the air, unite into a ball, and plummet through the air, breaking apart before colliding with the earth.[11] The aesthetic connection between "am'rous birds of prey" and the lovers' rolling themselves into a ball thus would reinforce both images. In any case, the poet urges that, having little space at best, we can compress our space into one ball, and by compression, we can intensify. We shall actualize all our potential for local motion and "tear our Pleasures with rough strife"; we will wage intense and persistent sexual strife at the "Iron gates of Life," the limitations of the temporal realm. We will tear from our limits the most complete actuality possible to us.

Not only can we intensify locomotion, but we can also perfect motion itself by making it circular.[12] Our created and perfected motion will then become time's measurer, as well as time's measured.

> Thus, though we cannot make our Sun
> Stand still, yet we will make him run.

Complete actuality, or stasis, the all-perceiving moment of eternity, cannot be ours, but we can at least achieve analogical perfection by forcing our potential to its actuality.

Marvell's final triumph, then, is a replacement of the instrument of time's measure with the sun which the lovers form in their act of consummation ("our Sun").[13] No longer victims of time, but momentary masters, the poet and his mistress, if she concedes, will have won the greatest limitations of life. Whether the victory is enough, being limited by life, is now the lady's question. But the argument could hardly be more persuasive.

---

[11] I have been unable to verify this theory of the birds' copulation, but it seems to be a familiar concept to biologists as well as to Marvell's literary critics.

[12] The highest form of motion, Aristotle says (*Physica*, VIII.216a.18), is locomotion, acquired in the course of becoming perfected, and the most perfect, most actual locomotion is circular.

[13] Lawrence W. Hyman, "Marvell's 'Coy Mistress' and Desperate Lover," *MLN*, 75 (January 1960), 10, likewise sees an equation between the lovers' "Ball" and "our Sun."

# A READING OF "THE WINDHOVER"

*Daniel Stempel*

Let us begin with an article of faith: Hopkins was not an "obscure" poet. What he had to say was complex and difficult and his verse reflects this complexity. His ambiguity—when he is ambiguous—is deliberate, not a byproduct of confusion or diffuse intuitions. The signs are there: with care and attention it is possible to follow him through to the heart of the poem. Any reading of Hopkins' verse must be based on the assumption that every word, every mark of stress, every line-division was placed there for an exactly planned and calculated effect. There is no carelessness in Hopkins' writing, no nonchalant tossing off of lines with a courtly *sprezzatura*.

Each critic begins from his own vantage-point and enters the maze of the poem from the angle corresponding to his peculiar perspective. The theologian approaches it as a vehicle for the embodiment of doctrine; the stylist as an experiment in metrics; the amateur psychologist as a personal confession, and so on. To review every reading of "The Windhover" would be a major task of research. Instead, let us begin again, not with doctrine or language or psychology but with the referent, the actual event which Hopkins witnessed and from which he abstracted those elements which make up the image that dominates the poem and gives it its ti-

tle. What Hopkins saw may give us the clue to what he is saying.

The flight of the windhover or European kestrel has been described in Thomas P. Harrison's article on "The Birds of Gerard Manley Hopkins" (*SP*, July 1957) and in the writings of amateur and professional birdwatchers. There are two modes of flight utilized by the bird: first, the type of flight indicated by its name, "hovering" or remaining fixed over one point by delicate control of the wind currents and rapid wing-beats. It is not, as Harrison points out, a soaring bird which circles over an area. The second type of flight is a swift darting to another fixed position by a rapid change in flight direction or by a downwind glide.

The structure of the octave reflects the two modes of flight of the windhover and the contrast between these modes is the theme which is developed through the entire sonnet. From the first words to the end of the long adjectival sequence modifying "air," the poet is describing the hovering of the kestrel, "his riding/Of the rolling level underneath him steady air." The bird is relatively motionless, completely at ease in its element, simply maintaining its position in the supporting medium. Then comes the change in flight. The bird "strides" *into the wind*, bends one wing and uses it as a pivot to swing around. The bending of the wing in order to "bank," as a pilot might put it, creates a kind of pointed arch in the wing structure, like the arch of a nun's wimple (not a rippling of the surface!). Then, with the added lift gained by flying into the wind, the bird swings downwind with the full force of the wind supporting his rapid glide. This is what Hopkins means by "the hurl and gliding/Rebuffed the big wind." In contrast to his former static flight, the bird has flung himself directly against the wind and has used its power for his own advantage; it has hurled itself against opposition and has made that opposing force work for it. This—not the hovering over one spot—is the essence of "the achieve of, the mastery of the thing!"

"My heart in hiding" seems to be a clear contrast between the bird in action, out in the open sky, and the "caged skylark" of the poet's spirit, "This in drudgery, day-labouring-out life's age." He marvels at the complete freedom of the bird and his heart stirs in sympathy with that heroic conquest of the air; it is a freedom which he does not and cannot share.

The basic image is carried on into the first three lines of the sestet. The key word is not "Buckle," on which so much exegetical talent has been expended, but "here." "Here" is not a vague adverb—it refers to that point in the bird's arc of flight about which its wing pivots, the apogee of the curve (" a bow-bend") the point at which direction changes and the "hurl" becomes "gliding." Literally, it is the turning point. "Here," at this turning point, "Brute beauty and valour and act, oh, air, pride, plume . . ./Buckle!" Note the choice of "air"—the wind itself is a component of the act of flight. "Buckle" is not an imperative. It is in the indicative mood, part of the description of the bird. The change to direct address begins in the next sentence. The word is a crucial word in the fabric of the poem, not so much because of its meaning in itself but because of its reinforcement of the meaning "here." It is a deliberate ambiguity, a pun, or, as the Japanese say, a "pivot-word." The latter describes it best for it is placed in the poem at the exact point where the turning takes place. At that point where the curve of flight bends, "buckles," all the vectors

of flight meet (buckle): the push of the wind, the strength of the bird, the feathered oar of the wing about which the bird swings its body, "air, pride, plume," these come together "here." "Buckle" is designed to be read with both meanings.

This second mode of flight, the hurl and gliding which rebuff the big wind, brings out the total potentiality locked in the "brute beauty" of the bird, a potentiality which remains hidden in the first mode of flight, hovering. That is why Hopkins stresses the transition in "AND the fire that breaks from thee then," that is, when the bird breaks away from the hovering position and flies upwind, the beauty of animal energy in action becomes "a billion/Times told lovelier, more dangerous. . . ." Lovelier, because mere potency has now been released into actuality, more dangerous because the bird is no longer simply maintaining its position in the wind but has thrown itself against the current of the river of air. Static becomes dynamic; endurance becomes risk. The epithet in "O my chevalier" is exact and precise. Now the bird is not the kingdom of daylight's dauphin, serene and fixed above his inherited realm; he is a knight, a warrior who challenges the element in which he moves in order to master it.

The last three lines of the sestet consist of reflections on and of the theme embodied in the dominant image. It is no wonder that the bird should display this beauty in its conflict with the forces of the air, for the pressure of the soil in the furrow against the ploughshare makes the blade shine—and this is at the humble level of earth, of "sheer plod." And "blue-bleak embers," embers that have lost their "fire," in falling, break the covering ash, "gall themselves," and "gash gold-vermilion," revealing their hidden fire, their hidden beauty.

In all of this there is no word of Christ, not even in "O my chevalier," and yet the poem, in its entirety, is truly a poem dedicated "To Christ our Lord." The bird is not a "symbol" of Christ—it is a prefiguration of the passion of Christ, just as persons and events in the Old Testament, by traditional Christian exegesis, are prefigurations of the content of the New Testament. Hopkins does not confuse his levels.

This poem moves on the level of nature: there is nothing supernatural or miraculous in the flight of the kestrel. Yet the flight proves that natural law, operating mechanically in its own realm of being—to be specific, the laws of aerodynamics—can be subdured to the purpose of a living creature to reveal the spark of divinity that animates each individual being or thing in the created universe. In this sense, it is a prefiguration, on the natural level, of the struggle of Christ against opposition and the turning of that resistance into victory and achievement. The Crucifixion is the necessary prelude to the Atonement. Here too is a pivot, a turning point, from bitterness and blood, "gall" and "gold-vermillion," to use the words of Hopkins prefiguration, to the redemption of man.

One conclusion can be drawn from the method applied in this reading of the poem. It points up the defects of the strictly formal approach to analysis, an approach which is best exemplified by Archibald A. Hill's article, "An Analysis of *The Windhover:* An Experiment in Structural Method" (*PMLA,* December 1955). Professor Hill applies the methods of modern linguistics to the poem; that is, he proceeds on the assumption that form alone is enough to indicate the preferred reading of the poem. Semantic considerations, problems of meaning, are removed from the range of investigation. This is essentially the approach of structural linguistics in language analysis, and it suffers from the weaknesses which accompany the rigid use of linguistic formalism. In this instance, it is necessary to known what the poet is saying *before* you can determine the exact form of the poem.

If you do not know what he means to emphasize and what is secondary to that emphasis, you cannot supply the proper stresses and junctures. Surely one would not argue that the written text is a complete corpus, to use the technical jargon, which provides the basis for an unequivocal phonetic reading. To get a transcription of this sort we should have to listen to Gerard Manley Hopkins reading "The Windhover." Unfortunately, that is no longer possible.

The printed form is a very poor guide to the reading of the poem; that reading depends on the reconstruction of meaning and we must shape the form of our reading so that it mirrors the meaning. For example, stress, as Dwight L. Bolinger has suggested (*Word,* August-December 1958), may be more than just loudness. Bolinger argues convincingly that it is actually a matter of tonality, pitch prominence. If "Buckle" is to be read as an indicative verb, a statement of fact, and not an imperative, the pitch contour will be radically altered: Here BUCKLE (imperative) becomes (in my reading) HERE buckle. Yet the printed text does not indicate this. There is a lesson to be learned from this, even for the structural linguist—if you don't have a complete understanding of what your informant is saying, with all of its nuances within the context of the language, an analysis based on external variations in form may be misleading and inaccurate. The methods of language analysis are still too crude, too gross, to handle the subtleties of literary discourse without some reliance on investigations of meanings. You can't catch sardines with a salmon net.

# THE MULTI-FACETED BLACKBIRD AND WALLACE STEVENS' POETIC VISION

*Peter L. McNamara*

Wallace Steven's shrewd insight into sensuous reality is granted by most competent critics of modern poetry. Even if one was unaware of the poet's preoccupation with painting, his concern with color, texture, and shading would give evidence of painting's influence on his poetry. Emilie Buchwald emphasizes that "the whole of Steven's work, to a greater degree than that of any other major poet of the first half of our century, atttempts to replace representational seeing and relating, to come to terms with the possibilities and the dilemmas which the impressionist painters and symbolist poets encountered."[1]

Stevens' work reflects an alternate dilating and narrowing of poetic vision. At one extreme (as in "Thirteen Ways of Looking at a Blackbird") is the world of open-air landscapes; at the other, in a work such as "The Emperor of Ice Cream," that of the painter's studio. Whichever view of reality may concern him in any given poem, the vision grows out of the poet's acute awareness of the constant mutations in the external world. It is this awareness of change, of the myriad facets of existential reality, which Stevens intends to convey through his poetry. The need for man to be attentive to each element of reality is the message of a poem such as "Thirteen Ways of Looking at a Blackbird."

Critics have limited themselves principally, in considerations of this poem, to the symbolic significance of the blackbird. M. L. Rosenthal has suggested that it symbolizes "the inseparability of life and death in nature."[2] This seems valid; his refinements on this observation are not. The poem certainly suggests more than "a terrified sense of death's inexorability." That man is to die is important for Stevens; but he is more concerned with stressing the need, while the individual continues to live, of his appreciating reality. Awareness of death is important, but only as a stimulus to man's exploration of the things of this life. Much closer to the heart of the matter, it seems to me, is George McFadden's comment that "In 'Thirteen Ways of Looking at a Blackbird' Stevens showed how consciousness, through the imagination, can dominate brute, unmeaning being (black) by recomposing it as 'reality'—thirteen imagined, fully conscious views, each ideally possible in the mind of the viewer, each charged with feel-

---

[1] Emilie Buchwald, "Wallace Stevens: The Delicatest Eye of the Mind," *A. Q.* 14 (Summer 1962), p. 186.

[2] M. L. Rosenthal, *The Modern Poets* (New York, 1960), p. 128.

ing. As blackbirds are part of a landscape, he tells us, so death is a part of life."[3]

The opening lines of the poem employ contrast to point up the vibrant life possessed by the bird, suggestive of the concept that death and life are one and that the potentiality of death exists in all living things. We are made immediately aware, however, of Steven's central concern; the poet pictures the blackness of the bird against the background of "twenty snowy mountains." The small, active eye of the bird, the "only moving thing," is played against the static majesty of inanimate nature. Already we have the key to the poem. Disturbed by man's self-satisfied neglect of nature, convinced that pleasure in it is the ultimate reward in a life that terminates in death, the poet emphasizes the importance of delving into life and seeing, understanding, and enjoying it fully. Contrasted here with the majestic mountains, the blackbird seems insignificant; knowledge of even the least significant aspect of nature is, however, the ideal to be realized.

Considering the blackbird in light of its representative symbolism, the poet is "of three minds." He concretizes these impressions in the image of "a tree/In which there are three blackbirds." Stevens' first thought is of the bird as it "whirled in the autumn winds." Here it is "a small part of the pantomime" of inanimate nature, which merely reflects, in dumb show, the order which becomes meaningful when intellectually appreciated and verbally communicated. His second meditation relates the blackbird more explicitly to its place in the realm of animate creatures. If it is valid to say that "A man and a woman/Are one," that together they form the natural unit of humanity, then it is true in a more comprehensive sense that all existent things ("A man and a woman and a blackbird") are one in the order of nature. This fact makes it additionally important for man to become aware of the creatures and things around him, for in knowing things re-

lated to him, he is able to know himself more fully.

Stevens next attempts to discern whether the blackbird's message to man, symbolized by its song, is valid and valuable only on a surface level, or whether the observer will find its ultimate significance in contemplation. Certainly the appreciation of the surface "beauty of inflections" is important. Without at least such observation, man does not fulfill the purpose of life. But shouldn't man also try to capture "the beauty of innuendoes," the implications of which may be derived from an analysis of external nature? Because he is convinced that there is no deeper significance to life than the appreciation of natural beauty, the poet does "not know which" of the two beauties "to prefer."

Stevens next contemplates the unsatisfactory vision achieved by observing "the shadow of the blackbird" through the "barbaric glass" which obscures the average man's preceptions. The image calls to mind St. Paul's comment (I *Corinthians* xiii. 12) that in this life "we see through a glass, darkly." Stevens' man, like St. Paul, sees the shadow of reality, but loses sight of the object which produces it. Having chosen the study of nature as the ultimate source of truth, Stevens, much in the manner of an Old Testament prophet, asks the "thin men of Haddam," those men who seek in "golden birds" a higher glory, why they ignore the discernible reality of "the blackbird [that]/Walks around the feet/Of the women about you." It is interesting, in connection with the poet's reference to the "thin men of Haddam," that the town of Haddam, Connecticut, was settled by the early Puritans. It is consistent with the poet's view of reality that he designates such men as "thin," in the sense that their vision of reality was distorted, their concerns being directed away from earthly reality.

Lest he be mistaken for a prosaic person, Stevens states that he knows "noble accents/And lucid, inescapable rhythms." He appreciates, in short, the appeal to the imagination which is made by the creative artist. Yet he is equally cognizant of the all-important fact "That the blackbird is involved/In what I know." If the

---

[3] George McFadden, "Probings for an Integration: Color Symbolism in Wallace Stevens," *MP*, 58 (1961), p. 187.

poetic imagination is important, how much more important the intelligence which illumines for man the beauties of nature!

Despite all the efforts which man may make to know physical life, human limitation will, of course, frustrate his full understanding of it. Symbolically, "When the blackbird flew out of sight,/It marked the edge/Of one of many circles." The circle, a traditional symbol of wholeness, represents the limits of the observer's view, the outer-most boundary of his perception of life. The poet knows that such limitation is in him, that the realities of spatial immensity can never be fully known; this should not, however, discourage the effort to know.

Stevens sums up his message by commenting that if each of us was able to experience "the sight of blackbirds/Flying in a green light," he could be satsified; even those of us who are "bawds of euphony," who seek truth in soporific visions, dreams or hopes of eternal life, would be jolted out of our misconceptions. Illumined reality, we note, appears "in a green light," suggestive to Stevens here as elsewhere of the vital force in nature which brings about harmony.

Instead of seeking understanding of this life, the average man will ride "over Connecticut/In a glass coach." Confident that technology has improved on nature in every way, he isolates himself from nature save when "a fear [pierces]

him," when his sham view of the world is momentarily shaken by a contrasting vision of blackbirds. Though he only momentarily mistakes "his equipage/For blackbirds," soon becoming smug and self-satisfied once again, "The river is moving." Time (symbolized here by motion, in the philosophical sense of constant flux or change of state in existential reality) is passing, and with it the life of the unheeding man. Searching for happiness, he has overlooked its source, an imaginative harmony with and understanding of the world.

Will man rectify this limitation in his vision of earthly reality? Stevens seems to doubt this. His final contemplation is one in which "it was evening all afternoon./ It was snowing/And it was going to snow." Man continues to ignore nature, or sees it imperfectly, as if it were viewed as dusk, or in a storm, when his vision was obscured by falling snow. "The blackbirds sat/In the cedar-limbs," but the populace was and is too busy and uninterested to notice them. That people are happy in their delusions disturbs Stevens. He makes the effort in many of his poems to shake his unfeeling fellow humans from their lethargy. His lack of confidence in the success of his efforts is reflected in the dignified but overwhelming sense of futility of the closing lines of "Thirteen Ways of Looking at a Blackbird," certainly a key composition for revealing the poetic vision of Wallace Stevens.

# THE POETRY OF DYLAN THOMAS

*David Daiches*

The sudden and premature death of Dylan Thomas produced elegies and appreciations in extraordinary numbers on both sides of the Atlantic. Thomas was the most poetical poet of our time. He talked and dressed and behaved and lived like a poet; he was reckless, flamboyant, irreverent, innocent, bawdy and bibulous. And his verse, too, had a romantic wildness about it that even the reader who could make nothing of it recognized as "poetic." In the February issue of the new *London Magazine* a 26-year-old British poet wrote a letter saying that Thomas represented the "archetypal picture of the Poet" for his generation, and that the death of this wild and generous character produced "something like a panic" in the world of letters. He was answered in the next issue of the magazine by a thirty-one-year-old poet who said that this was puerile nonsense and deplored what he called the "fulsome ballyhoo" which Thomas's death evoked on both England and America. There has perhaps been an element of ballyhoo in the recent spate of articles about Thomas; but sober critical judgment is difficult when one is writing of a brilliant young man who has died at the very height of his career (or at the very height of his promise: we shall never tell now). And surely the exaggeration of the sense of loss at the death of a poet is a sign of health in any culture. Now that the shock has in some degree worn off, however, we can turn more soberly to ask the question: What sort of poetry did Dylan Thomas write, and how good is it?

In a note to the collected edition of his poems, Thomas wrote: "These poems, with all their crudities, doubts, and confusions, are written for the love of Man and in praise of God. . . ." And in his prologue to the same volume he proclaimed his intention of celebrating the world and all that is in it:

> . . . as I hack
> This rumpus of shapes
> For you to know
> How I, a spinning man,
> Glory also this star, bird
> Roared, sea born, man torn, blood blest.
> Hark: I trumpet the place,
> From fish to jumping hill! Look:
> I build my bellowing ark
> To the best of my love
> As the flood begins,
> Out of the fountainhead
> Of fear, red, manalive, . . .

This prologue is a great hail to the natural world, and man as a part of it, and might be taken by the careless reader as an impressionist outpouring of celebratory exclamations:

> Huloo, my prowed dove with a flute!
> Ahoy, old, sea-legged fox,
> Tom tit and Dai mouse!

My ark sings in the sun
At God speeded summer's end
And the flood flowers now.

Yet in fact this spontaneous-seeming poem is a cunningly contrived work in two movements of fifty-one lines each, with the second section rhyming backwards with the first—the first line rhyming with the last, the second with the second last, and so on, the only pair of adjacent lines rhyming being the fifty-first and the fifty-second. Whether the ear catches this complicated cross rhyming or not, it is part of a cunning pattern of ebb and flow, of movement and counter-movement, which runs through the poem. This single piece of evidence is perhaps enough to prove that, for all the appearance of spontaneity and sometimes of free association that his poems present to some readers, Thomas was a remarkably conscientious craftsman for whom meaning was bound up with pattern and order. No modern poet in English has had a keener sense of form or has handled stanzas and verse paragraphs—whether traditional or original—with more deliberate cunning.

It is worth stressing this at the outset, because there are still some people who talk of Thomas as though he were a writer of an inspired mad rhetoric, of glorious, tumbling, swirling language, which fell from his pen in magnificent disorder. He has been held up by some as the antithesis of Eliot and his school, renouncing the cerebral orderliness of the 1920's and the 1930's in favour of a new romanticism, and engaging irresponsibility. And on the other hand there are those who discuss his poems as though they are merely texts for exposition, ignoring the rhyme scheme and the complicated verbal and visual patterning to concentrate solely on the intellectual implications of the images. The truth is that Thomas is neither a whirling romantic nor a metaphysical imagist, but a poet who uses pattern and metaphor in a complex craftsmanship in order to create a ritual of celebration. He sees life as a continuous process, sees the workings of biology as a magical transformation producing unity out of identity, identity out of unity, the generations linked with one another and man linked with nature. Again and again in his

early poems he seeks to find a poetic ritual for the celebration of this identity:

Before I knocked and flesh let enter,
With liquid hands tapped on the womb,
I who was shapeless as the water
That shaped the Jordan near my home
Was brother to Mnetha's daughter
And sister to the fathering worm.

Or again:

The force that through the green fuse drives the
    flower
Drives my green age; that blasts the roots of
    trees
Is my destroyer.

And most clearly of all:

This bread I break was once the oat,
This wine upon a foreign tree
Plunged in its fruit;
Man in the day or wind at night
Laid the crops low, broke the grape's joy....

This flesh you break, this blood you let
Make desolution in the vein,
Were oat and grape
Born of the sensual root and sap;
My wine you drink, my bread you snap.

Man is locked in a round of identities; the beginning of growth is also the first movement towards death, the beginning of love is the first move towards procreation which in turn moves toward new growth, and the only way out of time's squirrel-cage is to embrace the unity of man with nature, of the generations with each other, of the divine with the human, of life with death, to see the glory and the wonder of it. If we ignore the cosmic round to seize the moment when we think we have it, we are both deluded and doomed:

I see the boys of summer in their ruin
Lay the gold tithings barren,
Setting no store by harvest, freeze the soils;
There in their heat the winter floods
Of frozen loves they fetch their girls,
And drown the cargoed apples in their tides.

Those boys of light are curdlers in their folly,
Sour the boiling honey; ...

This is from an early poem; and several of these early poems strike this note—the note of doom in the midst of present pleasure, for concealed in each moment lie change and death. Thomas did not rush towards the celebration of unity in all life and all time which later became an important theme of comfort for him; he moved to it through disillusion and experiment. The force that drives the flower and the tree to full burgeoning and then to death, would destroy him also. Only later came the realisation that such destruction is no destruction, but a guarantee of immortality, of perpetual life in a cosmic eternity:

And death shall have no dominion.
Dead men naked they shall be one
With the man in the wind and the west moon;
When their bones are picked clean and the clean bones gone,
They shall have stars at elbow and foot;
Though they go mad they shall be sane,
Though they sink through the sea they shall rise again;
Though lovers be lost love shall not,
And death shall have no dominion.

It is this thought that sounds the note of triumph in "Ceremony after a Fire Raid" and which provides the comfort in "A Refusal to Mourn the Death, by Fire, of a Child in London."

"A Refusal to Mourn" is a poem worth pausing at, for it illustrates not only a characteristic theme of what might be called the middle Thomas, but also a characteristic way of handling the theme. The poem is ritualistic in tone; its dominant images are sacramental; and the cunningly contrived rise and fall of the cadence of each stanza adds to the note of formal ceremony. There are four stanzas, the first two and one line of the third containing a single sentence which swells out to a magnificent surge of meaning. Then, after a pause, the final stanza makes a concluding ritual statement, an antiphonal chant answering the first three stanzas. The paraphrasable meaning of the poem is simple enough: the poet is saying that never, until the end of the world and the final return of all things to their primal elements, will he distort the meaning of the child's death by mourning. One dies but once, and through that death becomes re-united with the timeless unity of things. But the paraphrasable meaning is not, of course, the meaning of the poem, which is expanded at each point through a deliberately sacramental imagery while at the same time the emotion is controlled and organized by the cadences of the stanza. The first stanza and a half describes the end of the world as a return from differentiated identity to elemental unity:

Never until the mankind making
Bird beast and flower
Fathering and all humbling darkness
Tells with silence the last light breaking
And the still hour
Is come of the sea tumbling in harness

And I must enter again the round
Zion of the water bead
And the synagogue of the ear of corn
Shall I let pray the shadow of a sound
Or sow my salt seed
In the least valley of sackcloth to mourn

The majesty and burning of the child's death. . . .

There is no obscurity here, to anybody who knows Thomas's idiom. We have only to recall "This bread I break was once the oat" to realise the significance of the first three lines of the second stanza. The water bead and the ear of corn are symbolic primal elements, to which all return at the end. But why *"Zion* of the water bead" and *"synagogue* of the ear of corn"? The answer is simply that these are sacramental images intended to give a sacramental meaning to the statement. It is a kind of imagery of which Thomas is very fond (one can find numerous other examples, among them such a phrase as "the parables of sun light" in "Poem in October" or his use of Adam and Christ in his earlier poems). One might still ask why he says "synagogue" and not "church." The answer, I think, is that he wants to shock the reader into attention to the sacramental meaning. A more everyday religious word might pass by as a conventional poetic image; but "synagogue" attracts our attention at once; it has no meaning other than its literal one, and therefore can be used freshly in a non-literal way. The third stanza continues:

I shall not murder
The mankind of her going with a grave truth
Nor blaspheme down the stations of her breath

With any further
Elegy of innocence and youth.

Here words like "mankind," "blaspheme," "stations of her breath" (recalling "station of the Cross") play an easily discernible part in the expansion of the meaning, while the pun in "grave truth" represents a device common enough in modern poetry. The concluding stanza gives the reason, the counterstatement:

Deep with the first dead lies London's daughter,
Robed in the long friends,
The grains beyond age, the dark veins of her
    mother,
Secret by the unmourning water
Of the riding Thames.
After the first death, there is no other.

This echoes, in its own way, the opening stanza; but its tone is new; it is that of liturgical proclamation. We need not wince at the suggestion that "long friends" means (among other things) worms; worms for Thomas were not disgusting, but profoundly symbolic: like maggots they are elements of corruption and thus of reunification, of eternity.

How much a poem of this kind owes to the imagery and to the cadence, as well as to the careful patterning, can be seen at once if one takes the perhaps extreme method of turning its paraphrasable content into conventional rhymed verse:

Not until doomsday's final call
And all the earth returns once more
To that primaeval home of all,
When on that insubstantial shore
The tumbling primal waters foam
And silence rules her lonely home,

And I return to whence I came,
The sacramental child of earth,
Joining with nature to proclaim
A death that is a second birth—
No, not until that final sleep
Will I for this dead infant weep.

She lies with her ancestral dead,
The child of London, home at last
To earth from whence all life is bred
And present mingles with the past.
The unmourning waters lap her feet:
She has no second death to meet.

This is doggerel, of course, but it contains, in however crude a form, the essential paraphrasable meaning of the Thomas poem—yet misses everything of any significance about it. The note of ritual, of sacrament, of celebration, achieved through his special use of imagery and by other devices, is central in Thomas's poetry.

I have not given a critical analysis of the poem, which space forbids, but merely suggested a way of looking at it. "A Refusal to Mourn" is a characteristic poem of one phase of Thomas's career, during which he was drawing together his impressions of the unity of all creation and all time to serve the purpose of a specific occasion. His earlier poems often fail by being too packed with metaphor suggestive of identity. Words like "Adam," "Christ," "ghost," "worm," "Womb," phrases like "the mouth of time," "death's feather," "beach of flesh," "hatching hair," "half-tracked thigh," abound, and though each has its orderly place in the poem the reader often feels dulled by the continuous impact of repeated words of this kind. The sonnet-sequence, "Altarwise by owl-light," contains some brilliant identifying imagery (suggesting the identity of man with Christ, of creation with death, of history with the present), but it is altogether too closely packed, too dense, to come across effectively. The opening is almost a self-parody:

Altarwise by owl-light in the half-way house
The gentleman lay graveward with his furies;
Abaddon in the hangnail cracked from Adam,
And, from his fork, a dog among the fairies,
The atlas-eater with a jaw for news,
Bit out the mandrake with to-morrow's
    scream. . . .

The careful explicator will be able to produce informative glosses on each of these phrases, but the fact remains that the poem is congested with its metaphors, and the reader is left with a feeling of oppression. A fair number of Thomas's earlier poems are obscure for this reason. It is not the obscurity of free association or of references to private reading, but an obscurity which results from an attempt to pack too much into a short space, to make every comma tell, as it were. With his continuous emphasis on birth, pre-natal life, the relation of parent to child, growth, the relation of body and spirit, of life to death, of human and animal to vegetable, and similar themes, and his constant search for devices to celebrate these and identify them with each other, he does not want one word to slip which may help in building up the total pattern of meaning. One of his poems shows how the making of continuous connections and identities can bewilder the reader:

> To-day, this insect, and the world I breathe,
> Now that by symbols have outelbowed space,
> Time at the city spectacles, and half
> The dear, daft time I take to nudge the sentence,
> In trust and tale have I divided sense,
> Slapped down the guillotine, the blood-red double
> Of head and tail made witnesses to this
> Murder of Eden and green genesis.

He is saying here, in his compact metaphorical way that expression in language (which means expression in time) breaks up and so distorts the original vision. In his desire to avoid that breaking up he sometimes piles up the images and metaphores until the reader simply cannot construe the lines (as in the sixth stanza of "When, like a Running Grace"). But is must be emphasised that this is not the fault of a bad romantic poetry, too loose and exclamatory, but comes from what can perhaps be called the classical vice of attempting to press too much into a little space.

Thomas progressed from those poems in which his techniques of identification are sometimes pressed too far, through a period of "occasional" verse in which he focussed his general notions on particular incidents and situations to give a grave and formal ceremonial poetry. ("A Refusal to Mourn," "Do not go gentle into that good night," "On the Marriage of a Virgin," etc.) to a period of more limpid, open-worked poetry in which, instead of endeavouring to leap outside time into a pantheistic cosmos beyond the dimensions, he accepts time and change and uses memory as an elegiac device ("Poem in October," "Fern Hill," "Over Sir John's Hill," "Poem on His Birthday"). But these divisions are not strictly chronological, nor do they take account of all the kinds of verse he was writing. There is, for example, "A Winter's Tale," a "middle" poem, which han-

dles a universal folk theme with a quiet beauty that results from perfect control of the imagery. It is far too long a poem to quote, and it needs to be read as a whole to be appreciated: it is one of Thomas's half dozen truly magnificent poems.

Another remarkable poem, which does not quite fit into my three-fold classification, is "Vision and Prayer," a finely wrought pattern-poem in two parts of six stanzas each. In no other poem has Thomas so successfully handled the theme of the identity of himself, everyman, and Christ. He imagines himself addressing the unborn Christ who, in his mother's womb, seems separated from himself by a "wall thin as a wren's bone." The infant in the next room replies, explaining that it is his destiny to storm out across the partition that separates man from God, and the poet identifies himself with the glory and suffering of Christ's redemptive career. The first part of the poem blazes to a conclusion with a vision of the triumph and pain of Christ's death. The second movement begins in a slow, hushed, almost muttering cadence: the poet prays that Christ remain in the womb, for men are indifferent and wanton and not worth redemption. Let the splendour of Christ's martyrdom remain unrevealed; "May the crimson/ Sun spin a grave grey/ And the colour of clay/ Stream upon his martyrdom." But as he ends this sad prayer the sun of God blazes forth and takes up the poet in its lightning. "The sun roars at the prayer's end." No summary or partial quotation can do justice to the force and brilliance of this most cunningly modulated poem. The stanzas of the first part are diamond-shaped, and those of the second part hour-glass shaped, and this visual device is not arbitrary, but reflects and answers the movement of the thought and emotion at each point.

Of the more limpid, open-worked poems of the third period, "Poem in October" (though written earlier than the others in this group) can stand as an excellent example. The poet, on his thirtieth birthday, is remembering his past and seeing himself in the familiar Welsh landscape as a boy with his mother:

> It was my thirtieth year to heaven

Woke to my hearing from harbour and neighbour
    wood
  And the mussel pooled and the heron
      Priested shore
    The morning beckon
With water praying and call of seagull and rook
And the knock of sailing boats on the net webbed
    wall
    Myself to set foot
      That second
In the still sleeping town and set forth.

Again we have the sacramentalising of nature ("heron priested shore") and we have also a sense of glory in the natural world which Thomas learned to render more and more effectively as his art matured. Again, one cannot see the quality of the poem from an extract; elegy is combined with remembrance and commemoration, and the emotion rises and falls in a fine movement.

Thomas's most recently published work is his radio play, "Under Milk Wood," which was broadcast by the B.B.C.'s Third Programme some months ago and won instant approval among professional critics and laymen alike. In writing for the radio Thomas naturally avoided any too close packing of the imagery, and chose a style closer to that of "Poem in October" than to that of his earlier poems. In spite of an occasional touch of sentimentality, "Under Milk Wood" is a remarkable performance—one of the few examples in our time of spoken poetry[1] which is both good and popular. In estimating the loss to literature of Thomas's early death, I should be inclined to put the cutting short of his career as a poet for the radio as the most serious of all. Thomas was by instinct a popular poet—as he wrote:

---

[1] I call the language of "Under Milk Wood" poetry, though it is prose to the *eye*. When I wrote this, I had *heard* the play twice but I had not read it, and there is no doubt that to the ear it is poetry. The opposite is true of T. S. Eliot's later plays, where the language is verse to the eye but prose to the ear.

Not for the proud man apart
From the raging moon I write
On these spendthrift pages
Nor for the towering dead
With their nightingales and psalms
But for the lovers, their arms
Round the griefs of the ages,
Who pay no praise or wages
Nor heed my craft or art.

He had no desire to be difficult or esoteric. He drew on the Bible and on universal folk themes rather than on obscure late classical writers or Jessie Weston's "From Ritual to Romance." In "Under Milk Wood" he put into simple yet powerful and cunning verse a day in the life of a Welsh village, with each character rendered in terms of some particular human weakness or folly. Unlike Eliot, Thomas accepted man as he was: he had a relish for humanity. By the end of his life he had learned to be both poetically honest and poetically simple—a difficult combination, especially in our time. And in choosing the spoken verse of the radio as a medium he was pointing the way towards a bridging of the appalling gap in our culture between professional critic and ordinary reader.

Was he a great poet? Against him it can be argued that his range was severely limited, that (in his earlier poems) he overdid a handful of images and phrases to the point almost of parodying himself, that many of his poems are clotted with an excess of parallel-seeking metaphors. I doubt if he wrote a dozen really first-rate poems (they would include, among those not hitherto mentioned here, "In the White Giant's Thigh" and "In Country Sleep"). In his favour it can be claimed that at his best he is magnificent, as well as original in tone and technique, and that he was growing in poetic stature to the last. Perhaps the question is, in the most literal sense, academic. It is enough that he wrote some poems that the world will not willingly let die.

# TOWARD NOTES FOR "STOPPING BY WOODS": SOME CLASSICAL ANALOGS

*Edward H. Rosenberry*

Fifteen years ago Robert Frost was quoted as saying that "Stopping by Woods on a Snowy Evening" contained all he ever knew and that he would like to print it with "forty pages of footnotes."[1] Yet as recently as 1960 John F. Lynen could write of this poem that there are "no literary parallels or signposts to guide us, much less a clear statement on the poet's part indicating the direction of his thought."[2] Even allowing for Frost's characteristic whimsy, there is a tantalizing discrepancy between the author's evident sense of the poem's opulence and the critic's sense of its stubbornly enigmatic reserve. Into this vacuum a generation of admirers has poured a relentless stream of commentary which has at once expanded the critical controversy and aggravated the author's native reticence to the point of withdrawal. "It means enough without its being pressed," he said at one time, and then added his own précis: "It's all very nice but I must be getting along, getting home."[3] The death-wish or return-to-the-womb school of readers gets even

shorter shrift: "No, all that means is to get the hell out of there."[4]

A new approach (short of leaving him alone) might be to take Frost at his word, exactly as far as it goes, and to try to place the poem in a literary frame of reference which supports the author's suggested reading in a way that structural and symbolic criticism are unable to do. This amounts to taking Lynen's observation as a challenge to show that there *are* literary parallels or signposts to guide us, and that the poet's remarks constitute in that light a perfectly clear statement of the direction of his thought.

The obvious reason for all the discussion of "Stopping by Woods" is that it is generally considered a major work of art, perhaps "one of the master lyrics of the English language."[5] As an important human document, for all its aesthetic singularity, it tends to occupy a crowded eminence. Great art is not less but more likely to say what has been said before, not because one work copies another but because they are equally concerned with the fundamental experience of humanity. The great ideas—a poet would say the great metaphors—persist; only

---

[1] Reginald L. Cook, "Robert Frost's Asides on His Poetry," *American Literature*, 19 (Jan. 1948), 357, 355.
[2] John F. Lynen, *The Pastoral Art of Robert Frost* (New Haven, 1960), p. 4.
[3] Reginald L. Cook, "Frost on Frost: the Making of Poems," *American Literature*, 28 (Mar. 1956), 64.

[4] Reginald L. Cook, *The Dimensions of Robert Frost* (New York, 1958), p. 33.
[5] John Ciardi, "The Way to the Poem," *Saturday Review*, 60 (Apr. 12, 1958), 13.

the images which embody them shift with changing cultures and various imaginations. The story of Faust, for instance, notwithstanding important differences in both theme and form, is in one of its dimensions precisely the story of Odysseus, the man with a god-given destiny whose salvation depends on his ability to keep moving toward his goal, to resist the blandishments of easy satisfaction in the here and now. Culturally and aesthetically it is a greater distance from Faust to a Yankee farmer than from Odysseus to Faust, yet this is the story of Frost's homeward-bound ponderer of woods, too. The man who turns reluctantly from the transitory perfections of Helen or decides against the static immortality of Calypso's embrace is at bottom the man who says,

> The woods are lovely, dark and deep,
> But I have promises to keep,
> And miles to go before I sleep.

He hears the song, but he is bound to the mast of his own resolve. He is a universal figure, whose archetypal foil a student of mine once recognized in *Heart of Darkness:* "Kurtz came to Circe's palace," she wrote, "and stayed."

These are analogs which any student or teacher, any reader, can find for himself, as no doubt many have done. Another, less likely to be encountered by the general reader, but closer to Frost's poem in concentration of image and development of theme, is a parable occurring toward the end of the Twenty-third Discourse of the Second Book of Epictetus. The heart of the metaphor, extracted from its didactic context, runs as follows in Matheson's translation:

> What then do we see men doing? They are like a man returning to his own country who, finding a good inn on his road, stays on there because it pleases him. Man, you are forgetting your purpose! You were not travelling *to* this, but *through* it.
> "Yes, but this is a fine inn."
> And how many other fine inns are there, and how many fine meadows? But they are merely a pass through; your purpose is yonder; to return to your country, to relieve your kinsmen of their fears, to fulfill your duties as a citizen, to marry, beget children, and hold office in due course. For you have not come into the world to choose your pick of fine places, but to live and move in the place where

you were born and appointed to be a citizen. . . . Some people are attracted . . . by some . . . seductive inn by the way; and there they stay on and moulder away, like those whom the Sirens entertain.[6]

Here, in yet another set of terms (but note the Homeric allusion), is the basic principle of moral life which Frost's poem dramatizes in his American setting and which he has felt impelled to explicate with such desperate clarity: "All that means is to get the hell out of there." The irony of the situation might well move a man to profanity: if the point of the parable is the importance of distinguishing between proximate and ultimate values, the author could only be exasperated by the earnest efforts of his readers to make the poem answer the merely proximate question of *what* ultimate values.

Even the context of Epictetus' parable is interesting in relation to Frost. The discourse in which it appears is entitled "On the Faculty of Expression," and it is, in effect, a sermon to poets not to confuse eloquence with substance, or the means of literature with its ends. Matthew Arnold, not surprisingly, seized on the image in this original context to underscore his case for the ethical value of Wordsworth's poetry.[7] It would hardly do to argue from such grounds that Frost, too, knew and consciously adapted Epictetus' metaphor in "Stopping by Woods"; yet the possibility of its having been as much a part of his professional equipment as Homer or Goethe is intriguingly great. Lawrance Thompson reminds us that Frost returned to college as a young man in order to "read more widely in the original texts of classical literature."

> His desultory reading in that field has continued and has been a vital stimulus to his own writing, although the effect is not at all obvious. Perhaps no American poet has ever brought to his own art such a wide acquaintance with classical literature with such a slight suggestion of it in details of direct reference or of slavish imitation.[8]

---

[6] *The Stoic and Epicurean Philosophers*, ed. Whitney J. Oates (New York, 1940), p. 337.
[7] *"Wordsworth," Essays in Criticism*, Second Series, 1888.
[8] Lawrance Thompson, *Fire and Ice* (New York, 1942), p. 151.

His keen interest in the classical philosophers, Thompson points out, has always been a poet's interest in their metaphors, in the analogies by which they have "sought to define spirit in terms of matter" (p. 191). The inn of Epictetus is memorable enough to have taken root in Frost's mind as it evidently did in Arnold's. A poet's knowledge, Frost has written, comes "cavalierly and as it happens in and out of books." Poets "let what will stick to them like burrs where they walk in the fields."[9]

Frost has professed himself a great believer in the role of the subconscious in poetic invention, and this could hardly have achieved freer play in his work than in the little lyric which came to him "in one stroke of the pen" at the end of an all-night session on "New Hampshire"—"the product," as he once called it, "of autointoxication coming from tiredness."[10] Somehow the ingredients of the poem boiled up and coalesced—image and theme, "stem end and blossom end"—and perhaps no one, including the poet, can ever be sure precisely what those ingredients were. All he knows, and all he needs to know, is that "he snatches a thing from some previous order in time and space into a new order with not so much as a ligature clinging to it of the old place where it was organic."[11] I think of Jean Starr Untermeyer's suggestion of an unconscious reminiscence in "Stopping by Woods" of Keats's line,

And I have many miles on foot to fare,[12]

and I find it the more plausible for the inadvertent echo of Keats that cropped up in my own preceding sentence and the unanticipated allusion to Frost in the sentence before that. ("How do I know what I think till I see what I say?") The process borders on the occult and threatens the scholar with an endemic vertigo. Just across the border lies the fact that Frost quoted Matthew Arnold three times in the last fifty lines of "New Hampshire" and called himself "a good Greek" within the last ten. I intend to let it lie.

What I wish to press for is not the establishment of an influence or a source, but the clarification of a method and a theme. In the first place, for the making of poems, doing and reading tend to produce inextricably mingled materials. The existence of analogs makes it just as likely that "Stopping by Woods" grew primarily out of Frost's reading as that it took its impulse from his having stopped by woods on a snowy evening or seen someone else do so. I believe that Lawrance Thompson should modify his opinion that this poem is prototypic of Frost's poems-from-experience, or poems in which image conceptually precedes theme.[13] Secondly, the analogs provide a thematic perspective which no work of art can have alone. The focus given to the poem's central concern with the antithesis of indolence and resolution, diversion and goal, blurs the distracting discussion over the exact limits of symbolic interpretation, and absolutely invalidates the partial view of Robert Frost as a "spiritual drifter."[14]

---

[9] "The Figure a Poem Makes," *Complete Poems of Robert Frost* (New York, 1949), p. viii.
[10] Elizabeth S. Sergeant, *Robert Frost, the Trial by Existence* (New York, 1960), p. 249; Cook, "Frost on Frost," p. 66. John Ciardi, too, reports having heard Frost say "time and again . . . that he just wrote it off, that it just came to him . . ." though he seems not to have heard what long poem Frost had been at work on through the night ("The Way to the Poem," p. 65).
[11] "The Figure a Poem Makes."

---

[12] From the sonnet, "Keen, fitful gusts." Quoted by Elizabeth Sergeant, *Robert Frost*, p. 251.
[13] *Fire and Ice*, p. 25.
[14] Yvor Winters, "Robert Frost: or, the Spiritual Drifter as Poet," *The Function of Criticism: Problems' and Exercises* (Denver, 1957), pp. 159-187.

# THE GHOST OF CHRISTMAS PAST: "STOPPING BY WOODS ON A SNOWY EVENING"[1]

*Herbert R. Coursen, Jr.*

Much ink has spilled on many pages in exegesis of this little poem. Actually, critical jottings have only obscured what has lain beneath critical noses all these years. To say that the poem means merely that a man stops one night to observe a snowfall, or that the poem contrasts the mundane desire for creature comfort with the sweep of aesthetic appreciation, or that it renders worldly responsibilities paramount, or that it reveals the speaker's latent death-wish is to miss the point rather badly. Lacking has been that mind simple enough to see what is *really* there.

The first line ("Whose woods these are I think I know") shows that the speaker has paused aside a woods of whose ownership he is fairly sure. So much for paraphrase. Uncertainty vanishes with the next two lines ("His house is in the village though;/He will not see me stopping here"). The speaker knows (a) where the owner's home is located, and (b) that the owner won't be out at the woods tonight. Two questions arise immediately: (a) what does the speaker know? and (b) how does the

speaker know? As will be made manifest, only one answer exists to each question.

The subsequent two quatrains force more questions to pop up. On auditing the first two lines of the second quatrain ("My little horse must think it queer/To stop without a farmhouse near"), we must ask, "Why does the little 'horse' think oddly of the proceedings?" We must ask also if this *is*, as the speaker claims, the "darkest evening of the year." The calendar date of this occurrence (or lack of occurrence) by an unspecified patch of trees is essential to an apprehension of the poem's true meaning. In the third quatrain, we hear "harness bells" shook. Is the auditory image really an allusion? Then there is the question of the "horse's" identity. Is this really Equus Caballus? This question links itself to that of the *driver's* identity and reiterates the problem of the animal's untoward attitude toward this evidently unscheduled stop.

The questions have piled up unanswered as we reach the final quatrain and approach the ultimate series of poetic mysteries to be resolved. Clearly, all of the questions asked thus far (save possibly the one about the "horse's" identity) are ones which any normal reader, granted the training in close analysis provided by a survey course in English Literature during his sophomore year in college, might ask. After

---

some extraneous imagery ("The woods are lovely, dark and deep" has either been established or is easily adduced from the dramatic situation), the final three lines hold out the key with which the poem's essence may be released. What, to ask two more questions, are the "promises" which the speaker must "keep," and why are the last two lines so redundant about the distance he must cover before he tumbles into bed? Obviously, the obligations are important, the distance great.

Now, if we swing back to one of the previous questions, the poem will begin to unravel. The "darkest evening of the year" in New England is December 21st, a date near that on which the western world celebrates Christmas. It may be that December 21st *is* the date of the poem, or (and with poets this seems more likely) that this is the closest the poet can come to Christmas without giving it all away. Who has "promises to keep" at or near this date, and who must traverse much territory to fulfill these promises? Yes, and who but St. Nick would know the location of *each* home? Only he would know who had "just settled down for a long winter's nap" (the poem's third line—"He will not see me stopping here"— is clearly a veiled allusion) and would not be out inspecting his acreage this night. The unusual phrase "fill up with snow," in the poem's fourth line, is a transfer of Santa's occupational preoccupation to the countryside; he is mulling the filling of countless stockings hung above countless fireplaces by countless careful children. "Harness bells," of course, allude to "Sleighing Song," a popular Christmas tune of the time the poem was written in which the refrain "Jingle Bells! Jingle Bells!" appears; thus again are we put on the Christmas track. The "little horse," like the date, is another attempt at poetic obfuscation. Although the "rein-reindeer" ambiguity has been eliminated from the poem's final version,[2] probably because too obvious, we may speculate that the animal is really a reindeer disguised as a horse by the poet's desire for obscurity, a desire which we must concede has been fulfilled up to now.

The animal is clearly concerned, like the faithful Rudolph—another possible allusion (post facto, hence unconscious)—lest his master fail to complete his mission. Seeing no farmhouse in the second quatrain, but pulling a load of presents, no wonder the little beast wonders! It takes him a full two quatrains to rouse his driver to remember all the empty stockings which hang ahead. And Santa does so reluctantly at that, poor soul, as he ponders the myriad farmhouses and villages which spread between him and his own "winter's nap." The modern St. Nick, lonely and overworked, tosses no "Happy Christmas to all and to all a good night!" into the precipitation. He merely shrugs his shoulders and resignedly plods away.

---

[2] The original draft contained the following line: "That bid me give the reins a shake" (Stageberg-Anderson, *Poetry as Experience* [New York, 1952], p. 457).

# ▶ ▶ ▶ MORE FROSTING ON THE WOODS

*Virginia Faulkner*

I have read with no little interest Mr. Coursen's admirable explication of Robert Frost's "Stopping by Woods on a Snowy Evening" in the December 1962 issue of *College English*. It does not seem too much to say (or I wouldn't say it) that he has something perilously close to a definitive interpretation of this hitherto enigmatic poem. Moreover, his exegesis will be welcomed by social scientists and students of current affairs for its fascinating sidelight on American politics. Although he modestly refrains from pointing it out, it is now plain why Robert Frost was asked to participate in the recent Inauguration Day ceremonies and why the Kennedy administration has consistently sought to identify itself with the poet. Projecting the image of Uncle Sam as Santa Claus is, of course, inherent in the Democratic party's political strategy.

Nonetheless, despite what is tantamount to the White House Seal of Approval, I foresee some possible objections to his reading. In regard to the crucial question of the horse's identity, for example, many scholars will find it difficult to accept that "the animal is really a reindeer disguised as a horse by the poet's desire for obscurity." This explanation, although logically unassailable, completely ignores the semeiotic and symbolic significance of the horse in primordial imagery (and in the folkloristic con-

text postulated by this reading, we can hardly avoid acknowledging that such imagery must, on some level, be operative) ; and it also fails to take into account that Robert Frost spent a good deal of time in England, and it was there, in fact, that he enjoyed his first critical recognition. When we remember that in primitive thought the horse is frequently equated with male sexual potency and that in England Santa Claus is known as *Father* Christmas (italics mine), it will be immediately apparent that collocation of these two archetypes, the one a residue of our archaic heritage, the other a sophistication of medieval legend, is no accident. If we add to the points already elucidated—*horse-male potency; Santa Claus-father;* praise and understanding in a foreign land-*warm reception* —that *bed* is implied by "downy" (line 12) and "I have promises to keep" (line 14) certainly suggests a *rendezvous*, it becomes hard to escape the conclusion that the poem is dealing with an amatory adventure.

Analysis of the horse and Santa Claus imagery not only confirms our suspicions as to the poem's erotic content but establishes conclusively, I believe, that the reading of "horse" for "horse" is central to the poet's strategy. In the juxtaposition of the horse and Santa Claus concepts—the former drawn from the collective unconscious, hence timeless and universal; the latter taken from the Christian calendar, hence parochial and dated—the poet creates a seeming paradox which actually is nothing more nor less than negative capability at work. For a careful reading discloses that what at first blush appear to be two opposing ideas are simply two halves of a phylogenetic and ontogenetic truth: the sexual drive (horse) is eternal and common to all mankind, but its fulfillment (Santa Claus) is personal and ephemeral. Thus to maintain that the horse is not a horse *as such*, but a reindeer does violence to the all-important submerged imagery. It damages the poetic structure below the waterline, so to speak, effectually "sinking" the poem and preventing the meaning from floating to the top.

If Coursen's reading is modified to accommodate the above line of reasoning, I believe his position will be almost unassailable. That there are superficial weaknesses—notably in connection with the symbolical significance of the horse-archetype—I hasten to admit. According to one authority (C. G. Jung), " 'horse' is the equivalent of 'mother,' " hence our equating of horse with male potency might seem to be on shaky ground. But the *sex* of the horse and its relationship to the poet is, after all, but a detail: if *mother* is, indeed, intended, it merely adds another, darker dimension to the poem without substantially altering its content.

There remains, however, one major barrier to critical acceptance of his reading of the poem which is not likely to be overcome in our time. His whole interpretation is based on the premise that the poet knew what he was doing—and where will Mr. Coursen ever find a critic who will go along with that?

# EXPLICATION OF "TO HIS COY MISTRESS"

*student paper*

In the poem "To His Coy Mistress," Andrew Marvell presents an argument in three parts. It is a fundamentally serious poem; the subject is one which disturbs and occupies the poet to a great extent. Yet as he argues his case he displays a sense of humor and retains an ironic, amused attitude, which deepens and grows in sincerity, directness, and urgency as he reaches the conclusion. The gradual change in tone and emotional intensity is accomplished through changes in form, in the choice of words, phrases, and analogies.

In the first twenty lines, the poet describes how he and his mistress could conduct themselves if the world were different, if time were of no importance. His thoughts on such a hypothetical situation are expressed in light and lyrical terms. His mistress "by the Indian Ganges' side should'st rubies find" while he "by the tide of the Humber would complain," content with expressing himself through love poems. He would love her platonically, with a "vegetable love," unceasingly "ten years before the Flood" and "till the conversion of the Jews," in other words, infinitely. If there were no time consideration, he would admire her as he says she deserves to be admired, giving "an age at least to every part." Thus he describes in dreamy, fanciful terms the ideal situation, how he wishes life were.

The following twelve lines describe the reality of the situation; there is not infinite time. The poet hears "Time's winged chariot" and sees "deserts of vast eternity." He realizes that time and its accomplice, death, will reduce everything, her chaste coyness, his passionate love, to bleak nothingness. It will turn "your quaint honor . . . to dust" and "into ashes all my lust." The couplet concluding this second stage of the poem, "The grave's a fine and private place,/But none I think do there embrace" is a concise summation of the poet's feelings toward the tragic effect of advancing time and inevitable death of love, especially physical love.

The final fourteen lines present the poet's conclusions on what must be done. His tone becomes stronger, deeper, more serious and more emotional. He once again praises his mistress' beauty and then states his plea, in forceful and even violent terms. The phrases ". . . let us sport us while we may;/And now, like am'rous birds of prey," and ". . . tear our pleasures with rough strife" reveal the poet's sense of urgency and growing desire. He ends, as he begins, by stressing the incontestable, unconquerable power of time and mortality. He concludes that they must act, must consummate their love now before it is too late.

Thus, Marvell presents his argument to his mistress. It is both powerful and skillful in that he begins by explaining, in eloquent terms, what he would like to do if time were unimportant, goes on to clearly describe reality, and reaches a peak of fervor and intensity as he pleads for the only possible alternative to passively accepting time's corrupting power, immediate action. Marvell achieves his purpose by not merely expressing his position and his demands, but by supporting them with a carefully constructed case built on fact and, of course, on flattery. The poem is constructed so that it plays a dual role; it is both a general statement on the familiar subject of mortality and a very personal statement to the poet's mistress.

# ►►► EXPLICATION OF "GOD'S GRANDEUR"

*student paper*

In "God's Grandeur," Gerard Manley Hopkins expresses his view that God is very much alive, very much involved in earthly occurrences, and very much in evidence to those who seek Him. Man, living in his narrow world of toil and petty problems, may ignore or fail to adhere to divine rule, but the divine presence remains. The poem is constructed so that it begins with a tone of hope and brightness, sinks in mood as it discusses the world as inhabited by mortal man, and returns to hope at the conclusion, in which the divine presence is reintroduced and reaffirmed. To achieve the change in tone, the images and diction used in the beginning and concluding sections contrast sharply with those found in the middle section, the former expressing the glorious and sublime, the latter stressing the dull and mundane.

Hopkins' opening statement, "The world is charged with the grandeur of God," establishes the poem's basic theme. The word "charged" is significant in its vagueness; it could simply mean that the world is filled or supplied with, or renewed by, God's grandeur, using the idea of an electrical charge. It may also imply a duty, responsibility, even a burden, which the earth bears in its relationship with the Divine. When "charged" is used in the latter sense, the poet may be suggesting that the earth, or its inhabitants, are not realizing and responding to this responsibility. This becomes more apparent in the middle section of the poem, when man and his ordinary world are described.

The poet then describes the nature of God's grandeur. It may ". . . flame out, like shining from shook foil," or be revealed with stunning swiftness, suggesting thunder or some sort of storm. But it also ". . . gathers to a greatness, like the ooze of oil/Crushed," or appears slowly and gradually. This image of oil collecting slowly and smoothly in a concentrated, glittery mass suggests any natural event which occurs almost imperceptibly, but which has great magnitude and impact.

The poet then turns to man to determine how he relates to divine grandeur. Why, he asks, does man not "reck his (God's) rod," realize divine authority or perhaps adhere to the spiritual to a greater extent? In answering this question, he depicts man's weary, rather desperate pattern of life on earth, "Generations have trod, have trod, have trod;/And all is seared with trade; bleared, smeared with toil." The words "seared," "bleared," and "smeared" used in the same sentence, the repetition of "trod," all contribute to a sense of dreariness, an image of tiresome, tedious activity. Man has allowed or resigned himself to sink into an existence of practical dullness, and the earth now too ". . . wears man's smudge and shares man's smell."

The poet's belief that both man and the part of the earth which he controls are reduced to a common, mundane, soulless state, in direct contrast to the lofty, magnificent, divine grandeur described previously, is best summed up in the phrase "the soil/Is bare now, nor can foot feel, being shod." The foot being "shod" suggests materialism, or at least a lack of contact with nature, a deviation from the natural state.

But despite all this, God, and His force, nature, still persist, and in returning to this idea, the poet changes his tone, lifts his mood. As he says, "There lives the dearest freshness deep down thing," one sees this transformation. In the nobility of nature, there is relief from and perhaps an alternative to the banal, boring condition of man. Sunset and sunrise provide an example: "And though the last lights off the black West went/Oh, morning, at the brown brink eastward, springs—" although light, perhaps hope, is extinguished, there is renewal, the promise of a fresh start. This occurs, of course, because the Divine ". . . over the bent/World broods with warm breast and with ah! bright wings." This phrase symbolizes the tenderness, warmth, and hope provided by God, all aspects of grandeur.

Thus, the poet returns to his original idea and to his original mood, one of joy and of reverance for the inspiring nature of God's grandeur, which, he believes, triumphs over the vapid emptiness of man's earthly existence and provides the world with continual renewal and hope.

# INSPIRATION, INSIGHT AND THE CREATIVE PROCESS IN POETRY

*Albert Rothenberg*

Psychiatric and psychological studies of literary creativity have been greeted with varying degrees of enthusiasm or antagonism in literary circles. The spectre of Beardsley and Wimsatt's attack on the "intentional fallacy" justifiably points to a serious limitation on the applicability of such studies to literary criticism. It is clear, however, that explication of the psychology of literary creativity has pertinence to teaching. The current enthusiasm for encouraging neophyte writers to "free-up," think about and express their inner thoughts, feelings and conflicts, cries out particularly for psychiatric intervention, not necessarily because of encroachment on the professional bailiwick but because knowledge about psychological processes in literary creation seems direly needed. Accordingly, I will present some preliminary findings from my own research (including numerous and intensive interviews with many prominent and novice writers) which pertain to the poetic creative process. As a scientist, I will refrain from any specific conclusions about the application of these findings to teaching or to criticism and I will present the essence of the material as I understand it.

The major aspect of poetic creation I will consider here is inspiration. Generally, it is assumed that the poetic creative process starts with an inspiration. Popular descriptions of the poet creating a poem usually conjure up an image of a brooding and silent figure whose face suddenly becomes transfigured and illuminated by a thought or idea which is quickly converted into scribbled notes, full blown poetic lines or even entire poems at one sitting. Although sophisticated persons can, on a moment's reflection, easily reject this image as a caricature, it is amazingly persistent as an implicit influence on the most learned analyses of the creative process. This influence is not simply the result of a specific type of romanticism; it has a time honored basis in the writings of some of the most serious and revered thinkers in western history. Plato was probably the earliest, or one of the earliest, philosophers to analyze the nature of poetic creation and he described a "divine madness" inspired by the muse.

Like Plato, Aristotle, Longinus, Diderot, and the modern philosophers Croce, Bergson, Maritain, and Alexander have emphasized inspiration. Nietzsche's notion of a Dionysian principle in the creation of poetry represents a specific elaboration of the platonic idea: the Dionysian infusion of demonic frenzy refers to an intense type of inspiratory phenomenon. Outside of philosophy, Ernest Kris, the most prominent and influential psychoanalytic theorist of the creative process, also seemed to devote most of his attention to the phenomenon of inspiration although he may not have meant to do so. His term "regression in the service of the ego" is meant to designate the psychological basis of the entire creative process but it applies most particularly to inspiration and, indeed, it is most clearly worked out in relation to this phenomenon.

Poets have done little to correct or disavow this emphasis. In fact, they have generally appeared hell-bent on perpetuating it and enlarging it, in public statements at any rate. Blake and Coleridge are prominent examples of poets who published accounts of poems written in altered inspired states. Blake asserted that an entire poem came to him word for word in a dream and Coleridge's account of a dramatic genesis of Kubla Khan is well known. Although few poets claim this degree of automatism, the published remarks of many tend to emphasize the crucial importance of inspiratory experiences. The list includes: Chapman, Herrick, Milton, Sir Philip Sidney, Keats, Shelley, Russell (A.E.), Spender, Shapiro, and Ginsberg. One of the few notable exceptions is E. A. Poe but he went to the opposite extreme: he described a highly rationalistic plodding approach to the creation of "The Raven." His description makes the poem seem so contrived and uninspired that most serious critics and poets doubt its honesty. Some poets have begun to take a middle position about inspiration, indicating that it occurs but they de-emphasize its importance. The impact of testimonials by earlier poet giants still exerts considerable influence, however.

There is good reason to believe, public testimonials to the contrary notwithstanding, that the emphasis on inspiration is fallacious. Inspiration is neither the invariant starting point of the poetic creative process nor is it necessarily the most critical aspect of poetic creation. It has become important to assert this, not only for scientific reasons, but because erroneous notions about inspiration have led to an almost dangerous situation in contemporary American life. Many young people today have resorted to ingestion of mind expanding drugs, LSD and marijuana among others, partly on the basis of a rationalization that such drugs enhance creativity. Published examples of poetry and art produced under the influence of these drugs and controlled studies of creative performance do not, it is generally agreed, support this notion. Nevertheless, the belief continues because it is based in part on a widespread tendency to equate inspiration with the entire creative process. Since drug-induced experiences seem to be similar in some ways to inspirations, it is assumed that drug experiences will produce creations.

In correcting the emphasis on inspiration in relation to creativity, I would like to make clear that the term inspiration refers to an intrinsically dramatic experience. It indicates more than the simple achievement of a good idea. As Kris and others have pointed out, the term refers etymologically to the act of breathing and the implication that what is inspired or taken in sustains or imbues life, is inextricably bound into its meaning. Suddenness, a sense of breakthrough, an impulse to action (usually writing something down but also running out of the bath shouting "Eureka, I found it") and an associated transient emotional relief (often associated with an actual physical sigh or explication of "Aha") are all, to some degree, invariant components of the experience. The term does not simply refer to the inception of a thought process although it is sometimes loosely used in this way. In other words, the popular image of the behavioral manifestations of an inspiratory experience is actually correct, but the popular as well as the scholarly conception of the *role* of inspiration in poetic creation is incorrect. My accomplished poet subjects report that they seldom, if ever, have an inspiratory experience at the inception of a poem and that very few such experiences occur during the course of the process of creation. These subjects represent many different styles of poetry including imagist, confessional, "beat," projectivist, and lyrical. Furthermore, an extensive study of poetic manuscripts and biographical material covering many centuries carried out by Phyllis Bartlett has turned up much evidence indicating that inspiratory experiences in poetry have been an exception rather than a rule. Statistically, it is probable that inspired ideas of all types are fairly common and that they have occurred rather frequently in the general population throughout the course of history. However, it has always been that true creators are those unique people who can work out ideas of any sort, inspired or uninspired. Careful study of poetic manuscripts, from first drafts to final poem, indicates that the free driving quality of good poems is arduously achieved, not born in one piece.

What is the actual role of inspiration in the poetic creative process? To answer this, let me briefly summarize what I have learned about psychological sequence in poetic creation. Generally, a poem begins with a mood, visual image, word, or phrase. The poet usually refers to the formulation of a word or phrase as the inception of a poem because moods or images which do not translate into words become diffused or changed. They are forgotten or else they do not remain associated with a specific poem. Occasionally, a poet reports that a poem began with a particular moral or intellectual statement in mind. Many poets are embarrassed to admit this because of their feeling that poems should not be constructed or contrived primarily to make a particular statement but that they should be spontaneous emotive outpourings.

The experience of beginning a poem differs from inspiration in that it is seldom accompanied by a sense of breakthrough, relief, or discovery. There is some degree of impulse to action or writing the poem which may operate in a range and variety of ways: actually interrupting a conversation or task to work on the poem until completed, jotting down some notes, or simply an active resolution in the mind to remember the word or words and work on the poem at some convenient later time. Rather than relief, however, the overriding feeling reported is that of tension. This tension is partly about getting down to work and writing. It is relieved by the process of writing and is only dissipated in large degree by the actual completion of the poem. It is also, however, a tension and an anxiety about *finding out what the poem is really about*. Over and over again, my subjects tell me that they seldom know what a poem is really "saying" until they are well into the writing, until they have actually finished it or, in some cases, until months or years later. When they do find out "what the poem is really saying," they experience a sense of illumination, discovery, and oftentimes, relief. The poet's allusion to "what the poem is really saying," the meaning of this phrase to him, is quite variable. Although most of my subjects are understandably reluctant to spell out a prosaic formulation of "what the poem is really saying," they may cite a particular line, phrase, or stanza in the poem itself as the embodiment of the idea. Often this line, phrase, or stanza is the final one in the poem, the punchline in a sense, but many other sections may also be cited. Generally, "what the poem is saying" is cited as an aesthetic statement such as, to cite one out of myriad possible examples, Wallace Stevens' last line of "Le Monocle de Mon Oncle": "but until now I never knew/That fluttering things have so distinct a shade." (Stevens has not been a subject of mine.) My more psychologically minded subjects may cite a particular line or set of lines and say, "it's talking about cannibalism" and my most psychologically minded subjects will cite the line also but will say, "it's about my own concerns about being cannibalistic." My point here is that the discovery has always seemed to me to be a personal discovery or insight of some sort (not induced by my presence) and that, even when cited as an aesthetic statement, the statement often seems to be a type of personal discovery. I base this conclusion both on what the most psychologically minded subjects have said and on my own knowledge of the less psychologically minded subjects' personalities and concerns.

Let me make it immediately clear that I do not mean that these later discoveries are true inspirations; quite the contrary. As I have said, true inspirations do occasionally occur before and during the course of writing but they are not discoveries of the meaning or purpose of the poem. These later discoveries are not particularly associated with an impulse to action but, depending on their strength and certainty, are often associated with a sense of completion, a signal that the poem is finished or virtually so. These discoveries function to reduce and resolve a good deal of the tension and anxiety which had been associated with starting and working on a poem (even when they occur several months later).

Although it is not immediately obvious, the true inspirations that occur during the creation of a poem are actually accompanied by a certain amount of anxiety. The sense of relief is so dramatic that anxiety is not apparent to the poet himself or to a possible observer. However, the other hallmark of true inspiration—feverish activity and working on the poem—indicates that anxiety requiring discharge is indeed present. Basically, I think this anxiety is similar to that accompanying the usually non-dramatic experience of starting the poem; *both anxieties are later reduced by the discovery of "what the poem is really saying."* The discovery, in other words, provides true relief because it contains elements of true psychological insight whereas both inspiration and the thoughts associated with the inception of a poem do not.

I am proposing a paradigm of the psychodynamics of the poetic creative process which de-emphasizes inspiration and differentiates inspiration from psychological insights. This latter distinction is quite important because inspiration appears, on the surface, to have many qualities in common with insight. The *sine qua non* of insight, for example, is considered to be a sense of illumination and breakthrough accompanied by relief (the vocalized or non-vocalized, breathing expletive, "Aha") and an impulse to further psychological exploration as action. Because this experience is behaviorally similar to the classical description of inspiration, it has been assumed that insight and inspiration are psychodynamically similar or equivalent, i.e., both involve overcoming repression and rendering unconsciousness and preconscious material into consciousness. Insight involves such a process, by definition, but inspiration, I believe, only appears to do so or only does so in part.

Psychodynamically, the inception of a poetic process and the inspirations that occur at the beginning or along the way are *metaphorical embodiments of the poet's unconscious or preconscious emotional conflicts.* The poet is not aware that the thought relates to a specific problem of his own but sees it primarily as an aesthetic issue. He may have some general feeling about its relationship to himself—psychologically sophisticated poets accept this as a matter of faith—and he senses its general psychological significance but he is not aware of the specific unconscious or preconscious issue involved at the time. In other words, the particular phrases, images, ideas, or poetic metaphors which constitute inspirations and inceptions of poems are themselves metaphors for personal conflicts. The personal importance of these phrases, etc. is felt, not conceived and, along with aesthetic considerations, leads the poet to use them in a poem.

I base these assertions on the following observations from my interview studies: 1) initial words and phrases reported to me often seem to denote a particular conflict. For example, a woman poet reported that a metaphor (which I cannot quote because of difficulty in obscuring the authorship) connecting an invaginated structure and the color green initiated a particular poem. This woman was, I had inferred from previous discussions, quite concerned about her feminine role, and had many specific anxieties about the vaginal bleeding represented by menstruation. The phrase, "green——," then, seemed to be a metaphorical or symbolic embodiment of her conflict between a wish to have a fecund growing sexual organ rather than a red bleeding one and a wish to have her vagina and remain female, in fact, exotically female. 2) initial words and phrases as well as inspirations are described as accompanied by the feeling of tension and anxiety I mentioned—psychodynamically, the anxiety is associated with an impending breakthrough of unconscious and preconscious material and an attempt to defend against it. The metaphorical and somewhat disguised quality of the thought is, in part, the defense. There is a certain amount of relief in arriving at initial ideas (more so in inspirations) but there is also a tension which is later resolved by finding out what the initial idea or the inspiration means, i.e., allowing the unconscious or preconscious issue into consciousness. For example, a poet thought of an image relating roses to blood. The idea inspired a poem—she felt relief, a sense of breakthrough and an impulse to write. However, she later described the poem itself as an attempt to find out what she felt about her own murderous impulses. 3) the reported discovery of "what a poem is saying" has always appeared similar to true insight or with some exploration it has become the basis of a true personal insight. This insight is often directly related to the conflict embodied in an original idea or inspiration. For example, a poet started a poem with an image about a man flying pigeons off his roof. He later discovered that the poem was about, "was saying," something negative about God and by extension, older people. With minimal exploration, he related these negative feelings to feelings about his father who never listened to him. Although we did not discuss the original lines about pigeons flying, my impression was that the image was a metaphor for the poet himself who let words fly off his roof (head). These words were not heard by his father and often, like pigeons, came back to plague him.

Initial ideas for poems and inspirations, then, seem to be metaphors for personal conflicts. They function as defenses against conscious recognition of the conflict although they may indirectly communicate the conflict to others. Furthermore, they contain the seeds that spur the poet to more conscious and specific recognition of the same conflict. It is interesting that anxiety laden and defense ridden initial ideas are courted by poets: they experience pleasure and excitement as well as tension when the idea occurs. Primarily, they are pleased that a poem (a highly valued achievement) is in the offing. Also, however, the defensive aspect of the idea is fairly successful at this stage; it serves to bind anxiety to a fair degree while enough tension is still experienced to stimulate discharge through the writing process. The fact that the defense is a way station toward later recognition of the source of anxiety may produce pleasureable anticipation of a deep form of gratification. Later discoveries are so pleasurable and so useful to poets that they may court the process of attaining them again and again.

Although inspirations and initial ideas both seem to be metaphors for personal conflict, inspirations are associated with a greater sense of relief. I suspect that this is so because inspirations represent conflicts and processes operating on deeper levels of consciousness and are associated with concomitantly stronger defenses.

This seems especially clear in those inspirations that occur late in the poetic process. Such inspirations are said to "solve" aesthetic problems and are experienced with relief and pleasure. At the same time, they occur at a point in the process when the poet has worked and reworked his material and has either brought unconscious material closer to awareness or succeeded in burying it deeper. Part of the sense of relief, therefore, may be due to unearthing emotional conflicts (albeit in disguised form) that come from deeper levels of consciousness than those at the beginning of the process.

The overall schema I am suggesting is as follows: the poet starts by unearthing or formulating problems, problems which are aesthetic and personal simultaneously. If the problem is particularly difficult and fraught with anxiety, he may experience an inspiration as he is working on it. This inspiration is dramatic because it often comes from a deep level of consciousness and because it is truly a breakthrough, a binding of diffuse anxiety. However, the inspiration itself contains many defensive and anxious aspects and it drives toward action—further writing and an attempt at gaining resolution and insight. When resolution and insight are achieved—during or after the process—the poet is no longer preoccupied with the poem.

In addition to the interview material I have already cited, some experimental data I have obtained from my poet subjects also tends to bear on these conclusions. Using special word association techniques during the course of an interview series, I have obtained preliminary results which indicate that poets work with psychological material in their poems that is increasingly more anxiety provoking to them as the writing process progresses. Space does not permit me to go into the particular techniques employed in this experiment or the similar results of another experiment carried out with creative high school students.

The acute psychological theorist will certainly, by this time, accuse me of having drawn a noxious analogy between initial ideas and inspirations and psychological symptoms as manifestations of psychiatric disease. Indeed, certain parallels do exist between the formation of symptoms and the formation of initial ideas and inspirations as I have described it. Symptoms represent a compromise formation between an impulse or conflict and the defenses against that impulse or conflict. I have said that initial ideas and inspirations are metaphors for conflicts and, although a metaphor is not, strictly speaking, a compromise but a combination or integration, there is an analogous concomitance of impulse or conflict and defense in the same process. Furthermore, the development of symptoms may be gratifying to a psychiatrically ill person as initial ideas are to a poet, in that symptom formation tends to bind and reduce anxiety. Symptoms also motivate the ill person to action, i.e., to seek help from a therapist in some way that is loosely analogous to the poet's drive to action after an initial idea or inspiration.

Many significant differences between the poetic process and the symptom process exist, however. Poems are communications in a sense that psychological symptoms never are or can achieve. Poetic metaphors are idiosyncratic and unique as well as communicative of universal truths and values. Psychological symptoms have some uniqueness but they reflect universal modes of dealing with anxiety. They may communicate meaning to the sensitive therapist but, in themselves, they adhere to some conventional pattern; e.g., performing rituals, having physical impairments or seeing visions. These patterns function primarily to conceal meaning both from the patient and those around him. The patient seeks help for these patterned symptoms because they don't adequately deal with his anxiety. On the other hand, poetic metaphors and other aspects of a poem stimulate both the poet and the reader to seek meaning. The poem may reduce anxiety to some extent for both the poet and the reader but also it stimulates the anxieties of both to a fair degree. Good poems touch on emotionally laden issues and deep meanings and they also are always anxiety provoking for all of us to some extent. Furthermore, poetic metaphors communicate intellectual content, a factor totally lacking in symptoms.

I do not mean to say that a poem is a manifestation of illness nor, even more emphatically, that the poetic process is a form of therapy. The poet chooses the conflict he prefers to work on and, more often than not, his metaphors only touch an aspect of the personal issue. He may achieve some insight and finish the poem but he seldom allows the full impact of the insight to affect him. This is seen in the fact that poets often return, again and again, to the same theme or image. Robert Frost, in answer to the perennial question, "why do you write poems?," has been quoted as saying, "to see if I can make them all different." By implication, Frost's whimsical reply is a criticism of the general poetic tendency to be hung up on a recurrent theme and points to his own attempts to overcome this tendency. This poetic hang-up, the need to return to the same conflict over and over again, is not an indication that poets are invariably sick: it simply means that poets, those great expressers and interpreters of our inner and outer world, the purveyors of such joy and understanding, are haunted.

# ▶▶▶ EXERCISES

## PARAPHRASE

### I

*Denotation and Connotation*

Explain the connative differences with each group:

Denotation = "dog"

  canine quadruped
  hound
  cur
  mutt
  working dog
  doggy
  man's best friend
  *Canis familiaris*
  bitch

Denotation = "house"

  home
  shack
  domicile
  castle
  mansion
  dwelling
  bugalow
  cottage
  boardinghouse
  homestead

### II

Give the literal equivalents of each of the following lines from Shakespeare:

1. My salad days,
   When I was green in judgement.
2. All the world's a stage,
   And all the men and women merely players:
   They have their exits and their entrances . . .
3. Men are April when they woo, December when they wed: maids are May when they are Maids, but the sky changes when they are wives.
4. It is meat and drink to me to see a clown.
5. Rubbing the poor itch of your opinion,
   Make yourself scabs.
6. He that sleeps feels not the toothache.
7. Use every man after his desert and who would 'scape whipping?
8. But thought's the slave of life, and life's time's fool;
   And time, that makes survery of all the world,
   Must have a stop.
9. Now is the winter of our discontent
   Made glorious summer by this sun of York . . .

10. We are such stuff
   As dreams are made on, and our little life
   Is rounded with a sleep.

## III

In a sentence for each, state the theme of five of the poems in this section.

   **Example:** "To His Coy Mistress"

   Time destroys youth; therefor one should
   love and seize pleasure without delay.

## IV

Write a prose paraphrase of one of the poems in this section.

## V

Choose one of the poems in this section that has a didactic theme. State the theme and show how the poet attempts to persuade the reader to accept it. Is the meaning explicit or implicit?

## VI

Discuss the dramatic situation in one of the poems in this section. Consider the following questions in your analysis:

1. Who is speaking?
2. To whom is he speaking?
3. What is the location?
4. How is time managed?
5. Is there action before the poem begins that is alluded to?
6. What is the dramatic conflict?
7. How is the conflict resolved?

## VII

Choose a poem in this section that can be read on two levels. Show the nature of the levels and evaluate the logic of the connection between them.

## VIII

Choose any two poems in this section that seem to have the same meaning or theme. Show the similarities and differences. Evaluate the poets' efforts.

# METRICS

## I

Mark each of the words listed below by putting ∕ over the stressed syllables and ‿ over the unstressed syllables. Identify the type of foot used.

**Example:** yéstĕrdăy = dactyl

1. deceive =
2. heavy =
3. comprehend =
4. tantamount =
5. goodbye =
6. intervene =
7. daily =
8. today =
9. accept =
10. trochee =
11. heartbreak =
12. poverty =
13. beauty =
14. crimson =

## II

Identify each of the following excerpts as *iambic, trochaic, anapestic,* or *dactylic.*

_____ 1. Double double, toil and trouble;
   Fire burn, and cauldron bubble.

_____ 2. To sail beyond the sunset and the baths
   Of all the western stars until I die.

_____ 3. The Assyrian came down like the wolf on the fold

_____ 4. I am monarch of all I survey

_____ 5. A thing of beauty is a joy forever

_____ 6. This is the forest primeval. The murmuring pines and hemlocks

_____ 7. By the shores of Gitche Gumee

_____ 8. Let me set my mournful ditty

_____ 9. She danced along with vague regardless eyes.

_____10. In the core of one pearl all the
shade and the shine of the
sea

## III

Above each syllable put the appropriate sign to
indicate the stressed syllables in the following
lines by Samuel Taylor Coleridge:

**Example:** Táke hěr ŭp téndĕrlў

Trochee trips from long to short.
From long to long in solemn sort
Slow Spondee stalks; strong foot! Yet ill able
Ever to come up with Dactyl trisyllable.
Iambics march from short to long.
With a leap and a bound the swift Anapests
throng.

## IV

1. Explain the meter in each of the selections
below.
2. In which selection does the sound match the
sense? Why?

### Psalm 23

The Lord is my shepherd;
I shall not want.
He maketh me to lie down in green pastures;
He leadeth me beside the still waters;
He restoreth my soul.
He leadeth me in the paths of righteousness for
his name's sake.
Yea, though I walk through the valley of the
shadow of death,
I will fear no evil, for thou art with me.
Thy rod and thy staff they comfort me.
Thou preparest a table before me in the presence
of mine enemies;                                    10
Thou anointest my head with oil;
My cup runneth over.
Surely goodness and mercy shall follow me all
the days of my life,
And I will dwell in the house of the Lord for ever.
—*The Bible, King James Version*

### A Psalm of David

The Lord to me a shepherd is; want therefore
shall not I.
He in the folds of tender grass doth cause me
down to lie.

To waters calm me gently leads, restore my soul
doth he;
He doth in paths of righteousness for his name's
sake lead me.
Yea, though in valley of death's shade I walk,
none ill I'll fear
Because thou art with me; thy rod and staff my
comfort are.
For me a table thou hast spread in presence of
my foes;
Thou dost anoint my head with oil; my cup it
overflows.
Goodness and mercy surely shall all my days
follow me,
And in the Lord's house I shall dwell so long as
days shall be.                                      10
—*The Whole Book of Psalms Faithfully Translated
into English Meter* (the "Bay Psalm-Book")

## V

Read and consider the five excerpts that follow.
Decide whether they are prose or poetry and be
prepared to justify your analysis and judgment.

1. I speak the pass-word primeval, I give the
sign of democracy, by God! I will accept
nothing which all cannot have their counter-
part of on the same terms. Through me many
long dumb voices, voices of the interminable
generations of prisoners and slaves, voices of
the diseased and despairing and of thieves
and dwarfs . . .
2. I believe in the flesh and the appetites, seeing, hearing, feeling, are miracles, and each
part and tag of me is a miracle. Divine am I
inside and out, and I make holy whatever I
touch or am touched from, the scent of these
arm-pits aroma finer than prayer, this head
more than churches, bibles, and all the
creeds.
3. No man is an island, entire of itself;
Every man is a piece of the continent, a part
of the main.
If a clod be washed away by the sea,
Europe is the less,
As well as if a promontory were,
As well as if a manor of thy friend's or of
thine own were;
Any man's death diminishes me,
Because I am involved in all mankind,
And therefore never send to know

For whom the bell tolls;
It tolls for thee.

4. The moon steeped all the earth
In its living and unearthly substance,
It had a thousand visages,
It painted continental space with ghostly
light;
And its light was proper to the nature
Of all the things it touched:
It came in with the sea,
It flowed with the rivers,
And it was still and living on clear spaces
In the forest where no men watched.

5. Thou on whose stream, mid the steep sky's
commotion, loose clouds like earth's decaying leaves are shed, shook from the tangled
boughs of Heaven and Ocean, angels of rain
and lightning: there are spread on the blue
surface of thine aery surge, like the bright
hair uplifted from the head of some fierce
Maenad, even from the dim verge of the horizon to the zenith's height, the locks of approaching storm.

# FIGURATIVE LANGUAGE

## I

Identify each of the figures of speech in the
excerpts.

_____ 1. Because I could not stop for
Death—
He kindly stopped for me—
—Dickinson

_____ 2. Was this the face that launched
a thousand ships
And burned the topless towers
of Ilium?
—Marlowe

_____ 3. Take me to you, imprison me,
for I
Except you enthrall me, never
shall be free,
Nor ever chaste, except you ravish me.
—Donne

_____ 4. O heavy lightness! Serious
vanity!

Mis-shapen chaos of well-seeming forms!
Feather of lead, bright smoke,
cold fire, sick health?
—Shakespeare

_____ 5. I will drink
Life to the lees.
—Tennyson

_____ 6. Stone walls do not a prison
make,
Nor Iron bars a cage . . .
—Lovelace

_____ 7. O, my love is like a red, red
rose . . .
—Burns

_____ 8. A little rule, a little sway,
A sun beam on a winter's day,
Is all the proud and mighty
have
Between the cradle and the
grave.
—Dyer

_____ 9. There is a garden in her face.
Where roses and white lilies
grow . . .
—Campion

## II

Identify the figures of speech in each example;
if the items is not figurative, label it "literal."

_____ 1. "a brow white as marble"
_____ 2. "a marble brow"
_____ 3. "I am unable," yonder beggar
cries,
"To stand or move!" If he says
true, he lies.
—Donne

_____ 4. I could not love thee, dear, so
much,
Loved I not honor more.
—Lovelace

_____ 5. Treason doth never prosper.
What's the reason?
For if it prosper, none dare call
it treason.
—Harrington

_____ 6. April is my mistress' face,

And July in her eyes hath place;
Within her bosom is September,
But in her heart a cold December.
                    —Anonymous
_____ 7. I spent the evening reading Shakespeare.
_____ 8. The crown has spoken.
_____ 9. There is a garden in her face.
                    —Champion
_____10. The grave's a fine and private place,
But none, I think, do there embrace.
                    —Marvell
_____11. Life, like a dome of many-coloured glass,
Stains the radiance of eternity . . .
                    —Shelley
_____12. A dog is like a *carnivore.*
_____13. When the hounds of spring are on winter's traces . . .
                    —Swineburne

### III

As is commonly known, Shakespeare's plays are mostly poetry; and most of the poetry is blank verse. All of the lines that follow have some figure of speech (trope) or figurative device in them. Sometimes there are several figures in a single line. Identify the most specific figure in each example; of course, a personification is a type of metaphor, but if it is a personification, label it such with the knowledge that it is also a metaphor.

1. Farewell, fair cruelty.
_____

2. Lawn as white as driven snow.
_____

3. Age, I do abhor thee, youth, I do adore thee.
_____

4. When forty winters shall besiege thy brow,
And dig deep trenches in thy beauty's field.
_____ _____

5. Like as the waves make towards the pebbled shore,

So do our minutes hasten to their end.
_____

6. For sweetest things turn sourest by their deeds;
Lilies that fester smell far worse than weeds.
_____

7. My mistress' eyes are nothing like the sun.
_____

8. If this be error, and upon me proved,
I never writ, nor no man ever loved.
_____

9. So shalt thou feed on Death, that feeds on men,
And Death once dead, there's no more dying then.
_____ _____ _____

10. I must be cruel only to be kind.
_____

### IV

1. Discuss the figurative language in the following excerpt from *Macbeth*:

To-morrow, and to-morrow, and to-morrow
Creeps in this petty pace from day to day
To the last syllable of recorded time;
And all our yesterdays have lighted fools
The way to dusty death. Out, out, brief candle!
Life's but a walking shadow, a poor player,
That struts and frets his hour upon the stage
And then is heard no more. It is a tale
Told by an idiot, full of sound and fury,
Signifying nothing.

2. Discuss the above passage as a source of allusions by contemporary authors.
3. Give a literal, prose paraphrase of the passage.

### V

Identify each of the following definitions:
A. Verbal irony
B. Understatement
C. Hyperbole
D. Paradox

_____ 1. The speaker's words mean the opposite of the literal statement.
_____ 2. A statement that is an apparent contradiction.

_____ 3. An irony developed by saying less than is meant.

_____ 4. An overstatement.

Identify each of the following illustrations by using one of the labels above.

_____ 5. The grave's a fine and private place,
But non, I think, do there embrace.

_____ 6. Go and catch a falling star.

_____ 7. Thus, though we cannot make our sun
Stand still, yet we will make him run.

_____ 8. We can die by it, if not live by love . . .

_____ 9. Our sincerest laughter
With some pain is fraught;

_____ 10. For whose sake henceforth all his vows be such
As what he loves may never like too much.

## VI

Make a list of allusions from the poems in this section. Explain the allusions.

**Example:** Poem:"God's Grandeur"
Allusion: Holy Ghost
Meaning: Part of the Holy Trinity
of Christian theology:
Father = God
Son = Jesus
Holy Ghost = Holy Spirit

Find five such allusions and prepare a similar analysis.

Poem:
Allusion:
Meaning:

## VII

Donne uses many conceits in his poetry. Choose one of his poems and show how his extended metaphors become conceits. Evaluate the originality, complexity, and appropriateness of the conceit to the subject of the poem.

## VIII

Some poems, especially of the metaphysical poets, are put in the form of an argument. Choose a poem of this type and outline the nature of the argument. Does the argument fit the topic? Does it convince?

## IX

_____ 1. A figure of speech in which a similarity between two objects is directly expressed with the indicator "like" or "as:"
a. simile
b. metaphor
c. assonance
d. synonymy

_____ 2. A quality of good style which demands that one select combinations of words which sound pleasant to the ear is called:
a. euphony
b. cacophony
c. assonance
d. alliteration

_____ 3. A figure of speech in which an indirect statement is substituted for a direct one in an effort to avoid bluntness; the substitution often has an ironic effect:
a. hyperbole
b. euphemism
c. jargon
d. cacophony

_____ 4. An ambiguity induced either by grammatical looseness or by the double meanings of words:
a. hyperbole
b. amphiboly
c. idiom
d. antithesis

_____ 5. The use of words whose sounds seem to express or reinforce their meaning is:
a. euphony
b. coordination

c. cacophony

d. anomatopoeia

_____ 6. An implied analogy which imaginatively identifies one object with another and ascribes to the first one or more of the qualities of the second:

a. allusion

b. image

c. metaphor

d. euphemism

_____ 7. The specific, exact meaning of a word, independent of its emotional coloration:

a. euphemism

b. denotation

c. hyperbole

d. connotation

_____ 8. A rhetorical term applied to that figure of speech making a casual reference to a famous historical or literary figure or event:

a. allusion

b. metaphor

c. image

d. simile

_____ 9. A figure of speech in which emphasis is achieved by deliberate exaggeration. It may be used to heighten the effect or it may produce comic effect:

a. gobbledegook

b. jargon

c. hyperbole

d. truism

_____10. The resemblance of sound between vowels or the repetition of similar vowel sounds:

a. assonance

b. alliteration

c. mimesis

d. onomatopoeia

_____11. A figure of speech which is characterized by the substitution of a term naming an object closely associated with the word in mind for the word itself:

a. synecdoche

b. litotes

c. inversion

d. metonymy

_____12. Emotional or dramatic overtones in certain words that are relatively similar in the minds of all speakers of the language.

a. denotation

b. idiom

c. jargon

d. connotation

_____13. A form of metaphor which in mentioning a part signifies the whole or the whole signifies the part:

a. litotes

b. simile

c. synecdoche

d. onomatopoeia

_____14. A rhetorical antithesis bringing together two contradictory terms. A brief paradox, expressed in two opposite terms that convey a total vivid concept:

a. inversion

b. oxymoron

c. analogy

d. exegesis

_____15. The literal and concrete representation of a sensory experience or of an object that can be one or more of the senses, a little picture:

a. cacophony

b. metaphor

c. connotation

d. image

_____16. An expression that is characteristic of a language but whose meaning comes from agreement and custom rather than from the exact meaning of the words:

a. idiom

b. asyndeton

c. figure of speech

d. analogy

_____17. Here's much to do with hate, but
more with love:
Why then, O brawling love! O loving
hate!
O any thing! of nothing first create.
A heavy lightness! serious vanity!
Mis-shapen chaps of well-seeming
forms!
Feather of lead, bright smoke, cold
fire, sick health!
Still-waking sleep, that is not what it
is!
This love feel I, that feel no love in
this!
Dost thou not laugh?
　　　　　　—Shakespeare

　a. similes
　b. oxymorons
　c. litotes
　d. tropes

_____18. The crown decided.

　a. hyperbole
　b. connotation
　c. metonymy
　d. understatement

_____19. The Rose was sick and, smiling, died:
　　　　　　—Herrick,

　a. simile
　b. personification
　c. oxymoron
　d. conceit

_____20. Extended metaphors that combine
dissimilar images and unexpected
relationships from difficult subject
areas often resulting in an outrageous
proposition:

　a. symbol
　b. allegory
　c. platitude
　d. conceit

# IMAGERY

I

Identify the items below with one of the labels:

　A. Visual image

　B. Auditory image
　C. Touch image
　D. Taste image
　E. Smell image
　F. Combination of above

_____ 1. small rain
_____ 2. far-heard clarionet
_____ 3. all the noise is gone
_____ 4. azure-lidded sleep
_____ 5. blanched linen
_____ 6. lucent syrops
_____ 7. a damp nook
_____ 8. purple petals
_____ 9. kiss of desire
_____10. clasps the crag
_____11. noiseless patient spider
_____12. sweet disorder in the dress
_____13. ribbands to flow confusedly
_____14. wind that chafes the flood
_____15. ruddy morn's approach
_____16. whirled her mop with dext'rous airs
_____17. small-coal man
_____18. the hapless soldier's sigh
_____19. down to a sunless sea
_____20. gardens bright with sinuous rills
_____21. woman wailing for her demon-lover
_____22. earth in fast thick pants were breath-
ing
_____23. mid this tumult Kubla heard
_____24. on honey-dew hath fed
_____25. bitter chill it was
_____26. silent was the flock in woolly fold
_____27. to think how they may ache in icy
hoods and mails
_____28. that ancient Beadsman heard the
prelude soft
_____29. upon the honeyed middle of the night
_____30. perchance speak, kneel, touch, kiss—
in sooth such things have been
_____31. let no buzzed whisper tell
_____32. and diamonded with panes of quaint
device
_____33. full on this casement shone the win-
try moon
_____34. to feel for ever its soft fall and swell
_____35. announced by all the trumpets of the
sky
_____36. the gray sea and the long black land

_____37. then a mile of warm sea-scented beach
_____38. and a voice less loud
_____39. than the two hearts beating each to each
_____40. now the black planet shadowed arctic snows

## II

All of the following images are taken from Robert Bridge's "London Snow." To what sense does each appeal? What effect do they have upon the total impact of the poem?

_____ 1. white flakes
_____ 2. city brown
_____ 3. loosely lying
_____ 4. hushing the latest traffic
_____ 5. drowsy town
_____ 6. deadening, muffling, stifling its murmurs failing
_____ 7. into angles and crevices softly drifting and sailing
_____ 8. frosty heaven
_____ 9. unaccustomed brightness
_____10. dazzling whiteness
_____11. and the busy morning cries came thin and spare
_____12. their tongues with tasting
_____13. a few carts creak and blunder
_____14. sparkling beams
_____15. tread long brown paths
_____16. at the sight of beauty

## III

Frost and Dickinson have emphasized imagery in their poems. Analyze a poem by either poet and illustrate the concern with the minutia of existence in the poem. How does the limited imagery make snug the limitless as Frost has said?

## IV

All of the images that follow are excerpts from Dylan Thomas' poems "Fern Hill" and "Poem in October." Identify the appeal of each; to what sense or combination of senses does each appeal?

_____ 1. happy as the grass was green . . .
_____ 2. Golden in the heydays of his eyes . . .
_____ 3. about the happy yard . . .
_____ 4. the calves/Sang to my horn, the foxes on the hills barked clear and cold . . .
_____ 5. the tunes from the chimneys . . .
_____ 6. it was air/And playing, lovely and watery . . .
_____ 7. As I rode to sleep the owls were bearing the farm away . . .
_____ 8. All the moon long I heard, blessed among stables, the nightjars/Flying with the ricks, and the horses/Flashing into the dark . . .
_____ 9. And then to awake, and the farm, like a wanderer white/With dew, come back . . .
_____10. And the sun grew round that very day . . .
_____11. Under the new made clouds and happy as the heart was long . . .
_____12. And nothing I cared, at my sky blue trades . . .
_____13. Before the children green and golden/Follow him out of grace . . .
_____14. I should hear him fly with high fields . . .
_____15. Time held me green and dying/Though I sang in my chains like the sea.
_____16. And the mussel pooled and the heron/ Priested shore . . .
_____17. And I rose/ In Rainy autumn/ And walked abroad in a shower of all my days . . .
_____18. I wandered and listened/ To the rain wringing/ Wind blow cold . . .
_____19. the blue altered sky/ Streamed again a wonder of summer/ With apples/ Pears and red

currants . . .
_____ 20. O may my heart's truth/ Still be sung/ On this high hill in a year's turning.

16. "A Fairly Sad Tale"

_____

17. "Dirge"

_____

18. "Divorced, Husband Demolishes House"

_____

19. "Still, Citizen Sparrow"

_____

20. "Some Foreign Letters"

_____

## TONE

### I

With an adjective or two describe the major tone or mood of the following poems found in this section.

**Example:** "On His Blindness"
resigned

1. "Since There's No Help, Come Let Us Kiss and Part"

_____

2. "The Flea"

_____

3. "To Lucasta, Going to the Wars"

_____

4. "Song" from *Marriage à la Mode*

_____

5. "The Solitary Reaper"

_____

6. "Composed Upon Westminster Bridge, September 3, 1802"

_____

7. "Don Juan"

_____

8. "My Life Closed Twice"

_____

9. "The Darkling Thrush"

_____

10. "Spring"

_____

11. "Invictus"

_____

12. "When I Was One-and-Twenty"

_____

13. "Miniver Cheevy"

_____

14. "Piano"

_____

15. "Anthem for Doomed Youth"

_____

### II

Irony is part of figurative language; however, irony also contributes to the tone of a poem. Identify the ironic passages in this poem and explain how these elements of irony determine the tone of the poem.

> I met a traveler from an antique land
> Who said: Two vast and trunkless legs of stone
> Stand in the desert. Near them, on the sand,
> Half sunk, a shattered visage lies, whose frown,
> And wrinkled lip, and sneer of cold command,
> Tell that its sculptor well those passions read
> Which yet survive, stamped on these lifeless things,
> The hand that mocked them and the heart that fed;
> And on the pedestal these words appear:
> "My name is Ozymandias, king of kings:   10
> "Look on my works, ye Mighty, and despair!"
> Nothing beside remains. Round the decay
> Of that colossal wreck, boundless and bare
> The lone and level sands stretch far away.
> —Shelley

### III

Choose one of the poems in this section and explain how figurative language, imagery, and diction lead to the total effect of tone. Further, illustrate how the tone contributes to the theme of the poem.

### IV

John Ciardi has said that understatement is one of the basic sources of power in English poetry. Choose one of the poems in this section and show how the understatement is achieved. What figures of speech are used?

## V

Overstatement or hyperbole contributes to the tone of a poem. Demonstrate and evidence of overstatements in one of the poems in this section and explain the role they play in the development of the tone.

## VI

Discuss the range of possible attitudes that may be expressed in poetry. Illustrate each attitude by an appropriate excerpt from a poem that reflects this tone. How is the tone achieved?

# SYMBOLISM AND ALLEGORY

## I

In everyday life we use many words that have become clichéd symbols for more general or abstract concepts. Explain what is meant by each of the following symbols:

1. beaten path
2. cradle to the grave
3. rocky road
4. between the devil and the deep blue sea
5. a bird in the hand
6. crossroads
7. a better mousetrap
8. golden years
9. sunset years
10. Mickey Mouse
11. black cat
12. blue blood
13. silver spoon
14. a wolf
15. a straw man
16. good as gold
17. silver lining
18. red-blooded American
19. mom and apple pie
20. a rolling stone

## II

In addition to the many clichéd symbols that we use in our language, there are other agreed upon symbols that have developed by custom, convention, and law. Explain each of the following symbols; tell what it stands for and how it got its meaning.

1. flag
2. crown
3. cross
4. red cross
5. virgin
6. hammer and sickle
7. Christmas tree
8. marriage ring
9. clenched fist salute
10. $

## III

There are also private symbols. Literature makes use of traditional symbols, conventional symbols, and private symbols. The private symbols are often difficult to interpret. The following symbols have been used in the poems in this section. Explain the possible meaning of each; the most accurate meaning would, of course, be the one that fits the context of the poem in which it is used; but the possible meanings illustrate the inherent ambiguity of symbols.

1. tiger
2. west wind
3. sea
4. loaded gun
5. falcon
6. swan
7. road
8. fire
9. ice
10. sleep
11. jar
12. ice-cream
13. yacht
14. snake
15. bear

16. wolves
17. lamb
18. Queen Victoria
19. toad
20. power mower

## IV

Explain the symbols in the following excerpt from Blake's *The Book of the Thel:*

Does the eagle know what is in the pit?
Or wilt thou go ask the mole?
Can wisdom be put in a silver rod?
Or Love in a golden bowl?

## V

Choose one of the poems in this section and discuss the symbols in it. Show the meaning of the symbols and explain their effect on the meaning of the poem.

## VI

What is the relationship between symbol and tone? Which of the two is more subtle? Choose a poem in this section and analyze the complicated relationship between symbol and tone.

## VII

An allegory is type of symbolism that is put into a narrative pattern and has a total system of symbolism. Specific characters and objects represent abstract concepts. Choose any poem in the text that has this type of symbolism and analyze the levels of meaning that you find. Start with a literal paraphrase and extend your analysis as far as you can.

# APPENDIX A: DEFINITIONS OF POETRY

It is difficult to define poetry. There have been attempts from Plato's time to the present to do so. The definitions that follow reflect a spectrum of positions and attitudes toward poetry and poets. In a way a definition is the first step to criticism; a definition presupposes a philosophical base or at least some standards from which ideas are judged. It is well to keep in mind the many types of definitions: formal, ostensive, lexical, stipulative, persuasive, figurative, and so forth. For each definition of poetry given, one should attempt to place it in the total attitude toward poetry implied. The definitions of poetry may lead to further analysis not only of the definitions themselves, but also of the literary and philosophical assumptions from which they sprang.

ANONYMOUS
Poetry is a language that tells us something which cannot be said.

Free verse: the triumph of mind over meter.

ARISTOTLE (384-322 B.C.):
Poetry is finer and more philosophical than history for poetry expresses the universal, and history the particular.

MATTHEW ARNOLD (1822-1888):
Poetry is at bottom a criticism of life.

[Poetry is . . .] a criticism of life under the conditions fixed for such a criticism by the laws of poetic truth and poetic beauty.

[Poetry is . . .] nothing less than the most perfect speech of man, that in which he comes nearest to being able to utter the truth.

Poetry is simply the most beautiful, impressive and widely effective mode of saying things, and hence its importance.

W. H. AUDEN (1907-    ):
A poet is, before anything else, a person who is passionately in love with language.

ISAAC BARROW (1630-1677):
[Poetry is . . .] a kind of ingenious nonsense.

FRANCIS BACON (1561-1626):
Histories make men wise; poets witty; the mathematics, subtle; natural philosophy, deep; moral, grave; logic and rhetoric, able to contend.

JEREMY BENTHAM (1748-1832):
The difference between prose and poetry is that in prose all lines in a paragraph except the last one go clear out to the margins.

WILLIAM BLAKE (1757-1827):
Poetry fettered fetters the human race.

MAXWELL BODENHEIM (1893-1954):
Poetry is the impish attempt to paint the color of the wind.

LOUISE BOGAN (1897-1970):
It's silly to suggest the writing of poetry as something ethereal, a sort of soul-crashing emotional experience that wrings you. I have no fancy ideas about poetry. It doesn't come at you on the wings of a dove. It's something you work hard at.

ROBERT BROWNING (1812-1889):
God is the perfect poet,
Who in his person acts his own creations.

ROBERT BURTON (1577-1640):
All poets are mad.

LORD GEORGE BYRON (1788-1824):
What is Poetry? The feeling of a former world and future.

JAMES BRANCH CABELL (1879-1958):
And poetry is man's rebellion against being what he is.

THOMAS CARLYLE (1795-1881):
We are all poets when we read a poem well.

GILBERT K. CHESTERTON (1874-1936):
All slang is metaphor, and all metaphor is poetry.

JOHN CIARDI (1916-    ):
You don't have to suffer to be a poet. Adolescence is enough suffering for anyone.

FRANK MOORE COLBY (1865-1925):
The only really difficult thing about a poem is the critic's explanation of it.

SAMUEL TAYLOR COLERIDGE (1772-1834):
I wish our clever young poets would remember my homely definitions of prose and poetry; that is, prose = words in their best order;— poetry = the *best* words in the best order. A poem is that species of composition, which is opposed to works of science, by proposing for

its *immediate* object pleasure, not truth; and from all other species—(having *this* object in common with it)—it is discriminated by proposing to itself such delight from the *whole*, as is compatible with a distinct gratification from each component part.

No man was ever yet a great poet, without being at the same time a profound philosopher.

EMILY DICKINSON (1830-1886):
If I read a book and it makes my whole body so cold no fire can ever warm me, I know that it is poetry. If I feel physically as if the top of my head were taken off, I know it is poetry. These are the only ways I know it. Is there any other way?

JOHN DRYDEN (1631-1700):
Delight is the chief if not the only end of poesy: instruction can be admitted but in the second place, for poetry only instructs as it delights.

T. S. ELIOT (1888-1965):
[Poetry is . . .] the intolerable wrestle with words and meanings.

The bad poet is usually unconscious where he ought to be conscious, and conscious where he ought to be unconscious.

RALPH WALDO EMERSON (1803-1882):
Language is fossil poetry.

Poetry is the only verity—the expression of a sound mind speaking after the ideal, not after the apparent.

PAUL ENGLE (1908-    ):
Poetry is ordinary language raised to the nth power. Poetry is boned with ideas, nerved and blooded with emotions, all held together by the delicate, tough skin of words.

GEORGE FACQHUAR (1678-1707):
Poetry's a mere drug, Sir.

ROBERT FROST (1874-1963):
Poetry is what evaporates from all translations.

Like a piece of ice on a hot stove the poem must ride on its own melting.

Writing free verse is like playing tennis with the net down.

Poetry is a way of taking life by the throat.

A poem . . . begins as a lump in the throat, a sense of wrong, a homesickness, a lovesickness.

Poetry provides the one permissible way of saying one thing and meaning another.

If left to its own tendencies, I believe poetry would exclude everything but love and the moon.

CHRISTOPHER FRY (1907-    ):
Poetry is the language in which man explores his own amazement.

JOHANN WOLFGANG VON GOETHE (1749-1832):
All my poems are "occasional" poems—occasioned by reality and grounded in it. Poems that come out of thin air are good for nothing.

WILLIAM HAZLITT (1778-1830):
Poetry is the language of the imagination and the passions . . . the universal language which the heart holds with nature and itself . . . an imitation of nature . . . the high-wrought enthusiasm of fancy and feeling.

HORACE (65-8 B.C.):
Poets were the first teachers of mankind.

"Painters and Poets" you say, "have always had an equal licence for bold invention!" We know this; we claim the liberty for ourselves and we give it to others.

A. E. HOUSMAN (1859-1936):
Experience has taught me, when I am shaving of a morning, to keep watch over my thoughts, because, if a line of poetry strays into my memory, my skin bristles so that the razor ceases to act.

EDGAR W. HOWE (1853-1937):
Poets are prophets whose prophesying never comes true.

A poem is no place for an idea.

ELBERT HUBBARD (1856-1915):
Poetry is the bill and coo of sex.

LEIGH HUNT (1784-1859):
Poetry is the utterance of a passion for truth, beauty, and power, embodying and illustrating its conceptions by imagination and fancy, and modulating its language on the principle of **variety and uniformity**. Its means are whatever the universe contains, and its ends pleasure and exaltation.

WASHINGTON IRVING (1783-1859):
Poetry is evidently a contagious complaint.

SAMUEL JOHNSON (1709-1784):
Poetry is the art of uniting pleasure with beauty by calling imagination to the help of reason.

Poetry cannot be translated; and therefore, it is the poets that preserve the languages.

To a poet nothing can be useless.

BEN JONSON (1573-1637):
For good poet's made as well as born.

JUVENAL (60-140 A.D.):
It is indignation that leads to the writing of poetry.

NIKOS KAZANTZAKIS (1885-1957):
[Poetry is . . .] no more than the analysis of a moan or joyous cry by musical language.

JOHN KEATS (1795-1821):
Poetry should surprise by a fine excess, and not by singularity; it should strike the reader as a wording of his own highest thoughts, and appears almost a remembrance.

The poetry of earth is never dead.

Poetry should be great and unobtrusive, a thing which enters into one's soul, and does not startle or amaze it with itself, but with its subject.

JOHN F. KENNEDY (1917-1963):
When power leads man toward arrogance, poetry reminds him of his limitations. When power narrows the area of man's concern, poetry reminds him of the richness and diversity of his existence. When power corrupts, poetry cleanses.

WALTER SAVAGE LANDOR (1775-1864):
Prose on certain occasion can bear a great deal of poetry: on the other hand, poetry sinks and swoons under a moderate weight of prose.

FRANCOIS DE LA ROCHEFOUCAULD (1613-1680):
If it were not for poetry, few men would ever fall in love.

THOMAS S. LILLARD (1928-    ):
Poetry is writing that does not go to the edge of the paper.

AMY LOWELL (1874-1925):
Finally, most of us [imagist poets] believe that concentration is the very essence of poetry.

THOMAS BABINGTON MACAULAY (1800-1859):
Perhaps no person can be a poet, or can even enjoy poetry, without a certain unsoundness of mind.

ARCHIBALD MACLEISH (1892-    ):
A poem should not mean but be.

If the poem can be improved by its author's explanations, it never should have been published.

DON MARQUIS (1878-1937):
Publishing a volume of verse is like dropping a rose petal down the Grand Canyon and waiting for the echo.

Poetry is what Milton saw when he went blind.

SOMERSET MAUGHAM (1874-1965):
I have always had a sneaking sympathy with George Crabbe who read the poems of Byron, Walter Scott, Keats and Shelley, and thought them all stuff and nonsense. After all, he might have been right.

The crown of literature is poetry. It is its end and aim. It is the sublimest activity of the human mind. It is the achievement of beauty and delicacy. The writer of prose can only step aside when the poet passes.

H. L. MENCKEN (1880-1956):
Poetry is a comforting piece of fiction set to more or less lascivious music.

*Vers libre:* A device for making poetry easier to write and harder to read.

Poetry has nothing to do with the intellect: it is, in fact, a violent and irreconcilable enemy to the intellect. Its purpose is not to establish facts, but evade and deny them.

A poet more than thirty years old is simply an overgrown child.

MONTAIGNE (1533-1592):
It is easier to write an indifferent poem than to understand a good one.

MARIANNE MOORE (1887-    ):
Poetry is a peerless proficiency of the imagination.

In a poem the words should be as pleasing to the ear as the meaning is to the mind.

OGDEN NASH (1902-    ):
I'd rather be a great bad poet than a bad good poet.

JOHN OLDHAM (1653-1683):
There's no second-rate in poetry.

BORIS PASTERNAK (1890-1960):
Poetry is a rich, full-bodied whistle, cracked ice crunching in pails, the night that numbs the leaf, the duel of two nightingales, the sweet pea that has run wild, Creation's tears in shoulder-blades.

WALTER PATER (1839-1894):
Let us understand by poetry all literary production which attains the power of giving pleasure by its form, as distinct from its matter.

PLATO (427-347 B.C.):
[Poets are . . .] those who "utter great and wise which they do not themselves understand."

Every man is a poet when he is in love.

EDGAR ALLAN POE (1809-1849):
I hold that a long poem does not exist. I maintain that the phrase, "a long poem" is simply a flat contradiction in terms.

SALVATORE QUASIMODO (1901-    ):
Poetry is the revelation of a feeling that the poet believes to be interior and personal [but] which the reader recognizes as his own.

JOHN CROWE RANSOM (1888-    ):
Poetry is still the supremely inclusive speech which escapes, as if unaware of them, the strictures and reductions of systematic logical understanding.

E. A. ROBINSON (1869-1935):
Poetry is a language that tells us, through a more or less emotional reaction, something that cannot be said.

JOSEPH ROUX (1834-1886):
Science is for those who learn: poetry, for those who know.

JOHN RUSKIN (1819-1900):
What is poetry? The suggestion, by the imagination, of noble grounds for the noble emotions.

ST. AUGUSTINE (354-430):
Poetry is devil's wine.

CHARLES SAINTE-BEUVE (1804-1865):
Poetry does not consist in saying everything, but in making one dream everything.

CARL SANDBERG (1878-1969):
[Poetry is . . .] a spot about half-way between where you listen and where you wonder what it was you heard.

Poetry is the opening and closing of a door, leaving those who look through to guess about what is seen during a moment.

Poetry is the achievement of the synthesis of hyacinths and biscuits.

GEORGE SANTAYANA (1863-1952):
The degree in which a poet's imagination dominates reality is, in the end, the exact measure of his importance and dignity.

WILLIAM SHAKESPEARE (1564-1616):
The lunatic, the lover, and the poet are of imagination all compact.

PERCY BYSSHE SHELLY (1792-1822):
A poem is the very image of life expressed in its eternal truth.

I consider poetry very subordinate to moral and political science.

Poetry is the record of the best and happiest moments of the happiest and best minds.

Poets are the unacknowledged legislators of the world.

PHILIP SIDNEY (1554-1586):
Poesy . . . is an art of imitation . . . a speaking, with this end,—to teach and delight.

EDITH SITWELL (1887-1964):
Poetry ennobles the heart and the eyes, and unveils the meaning of all things upon which the heart and the eyes dwell. It discovers the secret rays of the universe, and restores to us forgotten paradises.

OSBERT SITWELL (1892-    ):
Poetry is like fish: if it's fresh, it's good; if it's stale, it's bad; and if you're not certain, try it on the cat.

SOCRATES (470-399 B.C.):
It seems that God took away the minds of poets that they might better express His.

STEPHEN SPENDER (1909-    ):
Great poetry is always written by somebody straining to go beyond what he can do.

WALLACE STEVENS (1879-1955):
Ignorance is one of the sources of poetry.

DYLAN THOMAS (1914-1953):
I like to think of poetry as statements made on the way to the grave.

HENRY DAVID THOREAU (1817-1862):
Poetry is nothing but healthy speech.

My life has been the poem I would have writ, But I could not both live and utter it.

Poetry implies the whole truth, philosophy expresses a particle of it.

VOLTAIRE (1694-1778):
Verses which do not teach men new and moving truths do not deserve to be read.

HORACE WALPOLE (1717-1797):
Poets alone are permitted to tell the real truth.

ROBERT PENN WARREN (1905-    ):
The poem . . . is a little myth of man's capacity of making life meaningful. And in the end, the poem is not a thing we see—it is, rather, a light by which we may see—and what we see is life.

Poets are terribly sensitive people, and one of the things they are most sensitive about is cash.

E. B. WHITE (1899-    ):
My quarrel with poets is not the way they are unclear, but that they are too diligent.

WALT WHITMAN (1819-1892):
I sound my barbaric yawp over the roofs of the world.

OSCAR FINGAL O'FLAHERTIE WILLS WILDE (1854-1900):
Books of poetry by young writers are usually promissory notes that are never met.

One man's poetry is another man's poison.

A poet can survive everything but a misprint.

All bad poetry springs from genuine feeling.

WILLIAM CARLOS WILLIAMS (1883-1963):
I think all writing is a disease. You can't stop it.

WILLIAM WORDSWORTH (1770-1850):
Poetry is the breath and finer spirit of all knowledge; it is the impassioned expression which is in the countenance of all science.

I have said that poetry is the spontaneous overflow of powerful feelings; it takes its origins from emotions recollected in tranquility: the emotion is contemplated till, by a species of reaction, the tranquility gradually disappears, and an emotion, kindred to that which was before the subject of contemplation, is gradually produced, and does itself actually exist in the mind.

YEVGENY YEVTUSHENKO (1933-    ):
A poet's autobiography is his poetry. Anything else can be only a footnote.

# APPENDIX B: GLOSSARY OF TERMS

The glossary is meant to be a point of departure for further study. Many of the terms are more fully explained and exampled in the appropriate introductory essays. An important aspect of the glossary is to indicate terms that are of importance for the study of poetry. Some of the important terms will be understood only by further research and discussion.

**Abstract:** The concept that names qualities that may be shared by concrete things. These characteristics enable poets to use figures of speech in which the similarities between objects may be made by using the abstract qualities shared by things, people, events, or ideas: justice, virtue, goodness. Latin: *ab + trahere* = away + pull.

**Accent:** The emphasis given a syllable or word by loudness or stress. There may be a secondary as well as a primary accent: *yesterday*.
Latin: *accentus* = emphasis
Greek: *ad + cantus* = to + song or chant.

**Accentual verse:** Verse whose rhythm is developed by the number of accents in a line. Similar to sprung rhythm of Gerard Manley Hopkins.

**Aesthetic criticism:** A type of critical analysis that deals with writing from the beauty aspect. Also known as aestheticism.
Greek: *aisthētikos* = a sense of perception.

**Aesthetic distance:** The filter between the work of fiction and the reader. At the lowest level the reader knows that the poem is made of words. At the highest level the reader is moved to experience a state of understanding that may surpass an actual physical experience.

**Affective fallacy:** The critical theory that judges a work by its effect upon the reader's emotion.

**Agon:** Greek for struggle. Agony is an internal struggle or suffering. The protagonist is opposed by the antagonist in a conflict.

**Alexandrine:** A line of verse having twelve syllables. Used in a Spenserian stanza. Named after a 12th century romance about Alexander the Great.

**Allegory:** A narrative in which abstractions are presented by actual characters. Such abstractions as greed, love, hate, and evil are personified. It is a type of extended symbolism.
Greek: *allos + agorein* = other + to speak publicly.

**Alliteration:** The repetition of initial consonant sounds of adjoining words: wet, wild woods; wooly word.
Latin: *ad + littera* = to + letter.

**Allusion:** A reference to another event, person, thing, work, idea, or symbol.
Example: Pandora's Box
Latin: *alludere* = to refer to.

**Ambiguity:** The problem of meaning if a word, phrase, or sentence has more than one meaning. The ambiguity may be intentional or unintentional. In poetry it is usually intentional and becomes a device. A formal type of ambiguity is amphiboly. Empson's *Seven Types of Ambiguity* established ambiguity as a critical plus in poetry. Ambiguity is a useful concept in interpreting complicated and ironic poetry.
Latin: *ambi + agere* = both + to drive.

**Amphibrach:** A trisyllabic foot with a stressed syllable between two unstressed syllables: The old oak/en bucket
Greek: *amphi + brachys* = both + brief (short at both ends).

**Amphimacer:** A trisyllabic foot with an unstressed syllable between two stressed syllables: Lift that bale.
Greek: *amphi + makros* = both + long (long at both ends).

**Anachronism:** A term meaning something out of the logic of time or not chronological: Shakespeare's use of clocks in *Julius Caesar*.
Greek: *ana + chronos* = backwards + time.

**Anacoluthon:** A change from one grammatical construction to another in the same sentence: We must—aw, forget it.
Greek: *an + akolouthos* = not + following.

**Anacrusis:** The addition of one or more unaccented syllables at the beginning of a line that would normally begin with an accented syllable.
Greek: *ana + krouein* = back + to strike up (begin a song).

**Analogy:** A comparison between two items, events, or situations. Usually the comparison is made to extend an obvious comparison into extended proportions.
Greek: *analogos* = proportionate
*ana + logos* = reason

**Analysis:** The process of breaking a literary work into its components to subject it to literary criticism.
Greek: *ana + lyein* = back (again) + to loosen.

**Anapest:** A three-syllable foot in verse having two unstressed syllables followed by an accented syllable: When the blue/of the sky. . . .

Greek: *ana + paiein* = back + struck (struck back).

**Anaphora:** The literary device that repeats a word or phrase at the beginning of successive sentences: To everything there is a season . . . a time to kill and a time to heal. . . .

Greek: *Ana + pherein* = backward + to carry.

**Anastrophe:** An inversion of normal word order for effect.

Greek: *ana + strephein* = backward + to lean (turning back).

**Anatomy:** An analysis or literally a cutting up of a subject: Burton's *Anatomy of Melancholy*.

Greek: *anatomē* = dissection or cutting.
*ana + temnein* = to cut.

**Animism:** A concept that all physical things have souls or spirits.

Latin: *anima* = spirit.

**Anthem:** Originally a responsive chant; now a religious or patriotic song.

Greek: *anti + phōnē* = against + sound.

**Anthology:** A collection of literary works.

Greek: *anthos + logia* = flower + collecting.

**Anticlimax:** A drop from the important to the trivial to create an ironic or humorous effect.

Greek: *anti + klimax* = against + ladder.

**Antiphrasis:** A type of irony in which the intended meaning is the reverse of the stated meaning; a type of dramatic irony as when Othello calls Iago "honest."

Latin: *anti + phrasis* = against + diction.

**Antithesis:** A device that gives the opposites to a line, stanza, or poem, usually in parallel structure.

Greek: *anti + tithenai* = against + to set (do).

**Apostrophe:** A figure of speech in which someone who is absent is addressed or in which a non-human object is addressed as if it were human and present.

Greek: *apo + strophē* = away + turning.

**Approximate rime:** A rime that may not be accurate or perfect. May include alliteration, assonance, consonance, half-rime, and other sound devices.

**Archaism:** The use of old and obsolete words to create an antique effect.

Greek: *archaios* = ancient.

**Archetype:** A term from Jung's psychology meaning a basic pattern. In fiction a plot which repeats basic life patterns or characters that may be stereotyped or stock. The theory is that the universal and fundamental aspects of human nature are incorporated into the archetypal pattern.

Greek: *archein + typos* = beginning + type.

**Artificiality:** A term used in literary criticism to describe affected or unnatural styles. The use of highly ornate style based on the conventions, figures of speech, and rhetorical devices.

Latin: *ars + facere* = art + to make.

**Assonance:** A sound effect achieved by the repetition of similar vowel sounds within a line of verse. A type of rime of the accented vowels but not the consonants: mane/mare, fine/pike.

Latin: *ad + sonare* = to + sound.

**Asyndeton:** A rhetorical device that omits connectives: I came, I saw, I conquered.

Greek: *a + syndetos* = not + bound.

**Atmosphere:** The feeling of the environment or ambience that is obtained from the setting, scenery, costumes, imagery.

Greek: *atmos + sphaera* = vapor + sphere.

**Ballad:** A narrative poem meant to be sung. A form often used in folk songs. It usually has alternating iambic tetrameter and trimeter lines riming *abcb defe ghih*, etc.

Latin: *ballare* = a song sung while dancing.

**Ballade:** A conventional form in poetry consisting of the three eight-line stanzas and a four-line envoi. There is a refrain at the end of each stanza.

**Bardic:** Pertaining to poetry of ancient poets (bards) who sang of heros, death, love, and so forth.

Gaelic: *Bard* = poet.

**Bathos:** A ridiculous depth of emotion, a type of false pathos. Sentimentalism, maudlinism.

Greek: *bathys* = deep.

**Beast epic:** A story in which animals assume human roles to develop a type of allegory. Chaucer, Aesop, and Orwell used this genre.

**Blank verse:** Unrimed iambic pentameter. Most plays written in verse have used this form since Shakespeare's time.

**Blues:** A type of Black folk music that reflects the sadness that went with slavery, poverty, repression, and hopelessness.

**Bucolic:** Pastoral or rustic in nature. Alluding to herdsmen and pastoral scenes. Idyllic.

Greek: *boukolos* = cowherd.

**Burlesque:** A satire of themes, conventions, people, and ideas. Makes things ridiculous by a kind of verbal caricature.

Italian: *burlesco, burla* = joke.

**Cacophony:** Having harsh and discordant sounds. Opposite of euphony.

Greek: *kak* + *phonōs* = bad + sound.

**Cadence:** A rhythm obtained by a regular pattern of falling sounds.

Latin: *cadere* = to fall.

**Caesura:** A break in the middle of a line. A pause in a line of verse.

Latin: *caedere* = to cut.

**Canto:** A main division of a long poem analogous to a chapter in a book. Used by Dante, Spenser, Byron, and Pound.

Latin: *cantus* = song.

**Caricature:** A deliberate distortion or exaggeration for the purpose of ridicule and satire.

Italian: *caricatura* = a loading.

**Carpe Diem:** The theme in poetry that advocates a hedonistic approach in lyric poetry. Horace, Herrick, Marvel, and Fitzgerald reflected this lyric tradition.

Latin: *carpe diem* = seize the day.

**Catachresis:** A form of a mixed metaphor or malapropism. Milton's blind mouths.

Greek: *kata* + *chrēsthai* = against + to use (misuse).

**Cavalier poets:** English poets in the court of Charles I characterized by the emphasis upon love, hedonism, cynicism, polish, terseness, and haughty attitude.

**Cento:** Mosaic verse, a collection of quotations put together to make gramatical meaning and new sense.

Sanskrit: *kanthā* = patched garment.

**Chain verse:** The linking of stanzas by mechanical devices like repetition words or rime.

**Chiasmus:** An inversion of subject and predicate of the second of two clauses. "Some eat to live; others live to eat."

Greek: *chiasmos* = to mark with chi.

**Choriamb:** A metrical foot of four syllables, the first and last accented.

Greek: *choros* + *iambos* = chorus + iamb.

**Classicism:** An approach to literature that emphasizes form, reason, and conventions.

**Cliché:** A tired, trite expression or figure of speech.

**Closed couplet:** Two lines with end rime.

**Collation:** An examination and comparison of two or more manuscripts to establish authenticity and accuracy.

Latin: *com* + *latus* = together + bring (bringing together).

**Conceit:** An image or figure of speech that develops an extended comparison between two situations. John Donne's metaphysical conceits used all knowledge to make outlandish metaphors as

for example comparing the relationships between his love and him to a draughtsman's compass.

Middle English: *conceiven* = mental activity.

**Connotation:** The emotional slant of words. The connotation may be conventional or individual. It is a superstructure of meaning above the denotative or literal.

Latin: *com* + *notare* = together + to note.

**Consonance:** A type of rime which occurs when consonants sound alike: Pull/sell.

Latin: *consonare* = sound of consonants.

**Convention:** An agreed upon custom, usage, feature, method, or form. Some poetic conventions include: sonnet, epic, stanzas, refrains, and so forth.

Latin: *con* + *venire* = together + come.

**Couplet:** Two lines of rimed verse.

**Criticism:** The analysis, classification, and judgment of literature. The major schools of criticism include: impressionistic, subjective, relativistic, historical, textual, practical, theoretical, and others.

Greek: *krinein* = to judge.

**Dactyl:** A three syllable foot containing one accented syllable followed by two unaccented syllables.

Greek: *daktylos* = fingers.

**Dead metaphor:** A metaphor which has become so common that it no longer is considered to be figurative: "The face and hands of the clock."

**Decasyllable:** A ten-syllable line of verse as, for example, a line of iambic pentameter.

Greek: *deka* + *syllable* = ten + syllable.

**Defense:** An argument to justify or defend.

**Denotation:** The literal meaning of a word.

Latin: *de* + *notare* = from + to note.

**Diaeresis:** The separation of a diphthong into two sounds in order to meet metrical patterns.

Greek: *diairein* = to divide.

**Dialogue:** An exchange between two characters in a literary work.

Greek: *dialogos* = speaking between (to converse).

**Dibrach:** A foot of two unaccented syllables.

Greek: *di* + *brachys* = twice + short.

**Diction:** An element of style that emphasizes the choice of words a writer uses.

Latin: *dictio* = speaking.

**Didactic poetry:** Poetry that attempts to teach or preach a special doctrine.

Greek: *didaktikos* = to teach.

**Dimeter:** A two-foot line.

Greek: *di* + *metron* = two + measure.

**Dirge:** A poem of grief and sorrow.
Latin: *dirige* = to direct.

**Dissonance:** A discordant sound. Cacaphony.
Latin: *dis* + *sonare* = bad + sound.

**Distich:** Two lines of verse that are similar in structure but not exactly repeated. Once a fool/always a fool.
Greek: *di* + *stichos* = two + rows.

**Dithyramb:** A Greek song in honor of Dionysius. Any emotionally laden poem.
Greek: *dithyrambos* = chant.

**Ditty:** A short poem meant to be sung.
Latin: *dictare* = to compose.

**Doggerel:** Poor, shoddy, meretricious, inferior poetry.
Middle English: *doggerel* = mixed verse.

**Double entendre:** A deliberately ambiguous or ambivalent term, one of the meanings usually being suggestive or risqué.
French: *double entendre* = double meaning.

**Dramatic monologue:** A poem in which there is one character speaking and creating a dramatic situation.

**Dysphemism:** A harsh phrase applied to something; the antonym of euphemism.
Latin: *dys* + *phem* = bad + phrase.

**Echo word:** A word that is aurally imitative, used for creating a refrain effect.

**Eclectic:** Selected from many sources. Modern poets like Eliot and Pound wrote eclectic poems.
Greek: *eklektikos* = to gather.

**Eclogue:** A short passage of a longer poem.
Greek: *eklogē* = a selection.

**Elegiac meter:** Alternating dactylic hexameter and pentameter in Greek and Latin dirge poems.
Greek: *elegos* = a song of grief.

**Elegy:** A poem of grief for and praise of the dead. Milton's "Lycida."
Greek: *elegos* = a song of grief.

**Elision:** The omission or shortening of syllables to obtain smoother meter.
Latin: *elidere* = strike out, elide.

**Elizabethan:** The period of Elizabeth I (1558-1603) with its history, culture, and literature.

**Ellipsis:** The omission of words or phrases that are necessary for grammatical construction but are understood in context.
Greek: *elleipsis* = a defect.

**Empathy:** The quality of being able to assume the feelings of another.
Greek: *en* + *pathos* = in + suffering.

**Encomium:** An extended high praise of a great warrior. Any formal expression of praise.
Greek: *en* + *komos* = in + revel.

**End rime:** The repetition of similar or identical sounds at the end of lines of poetry.

**End-stopped line:** A line of verse that stops at the end of the line. Used especially in heroic couplets.

**English sonnet:** Also known as the Shakespearian sonnet. A fourteen-line poem in iambic pentameter having three quatrains and a couplet. The rime scheme is *abab cdcd efef gg.*

**Enjambment:** A type of run-on line.

**Enlightenment:** The age of reason or the eighteenth century that emphasized rationalism, skepticism, and deism.

**Envoy (envoi):** a dedication or postscript to a literary work.
French: *envoier* = to send.

**Epic:** A long, narrative poem written in high style about a hero representing the origins and traditions of a race or nation: *Iliad, Odyssey, Beowulf, Paradise Lost.*

**Epigram:** A terse, witty saying or poem. Originally a short poem carved upon a tomb.
Greek: *epi* + *graphein* = upon + to write.

**Epigraph:** A statement put at the beginning of a literary work to set a tone.
Greek: *epi* + *graphein* = upon + to write.

**Epilogue:** A concluding section of a literary work.
Greek: *epi* + *legein* = upon + to say.

**Epiphany:** A sudden revelation of inner meaning. It is the awareness of the underlying truth of a situation. Verges on a religious insight, a *satori.* James Joyce used this term in writing.

**Epitaph:** A short verse or prose piece honoring one who has died.
Greek: *epi* + *taphos* = upon + tomb.

**Epithalamium:** A nuptial song. Spenser's "Epithalamion."
Greek: *epi* + *thalamos* = upon + nuptial chamber.

**Epithet:** A phrase showing some characteristic quality of a person or thing. Homer: "Rosyfingered dawn."
Greek: *epi* + *tithenai* = upon + to place.

**Epitome:** A brief or essential portion of a longer work or concept.
Greek: *epi* + *temnein* = to cut.

**Epode:** A classical lyric in which a long line is followed by a short line.
Greek: *epoidos* = sung afterwards.

**Equivoque:** An ambiguous term having a double meaning, a type of pun.
French: *equivoque* = an equal call.

**Eulogy:** Praise for an individual in poetry, may be like a dirge, elegy, encoium, ode, or panegyric.
Greek: *eu + legein* = good + to speak.

**Euphemism:** An expression that is less offensive or more genteel than another. "Loved one" for "deceased."
Greek: *eu + phēmē* = good + speech.

**Euphony:** A pleasant sound.
Greek: *eu + phonos* = good + sound.

**Euphuism:** An artificial, ornate, affected style characterized by many figures of speech, conventions, and conceits. From Lyly's *Euphues: The Anatomy of Wit.*

**Euterpe:** The muse of lyric poetry in Greek mythology.

**Exegesis:** A close, careful analysis and interpretation of a passage.
Greek: *exegeisthai* = to explain.

**Explication:** A close reading and explanation of a passage to put emphasis upon text and meaning.
Latin: *ex + plicare* = un + fold.

**Explication de texte:** French for close analysis of text.

**Expressionism:** A literary theory that emphasizes the objectifying of concepts by means of imagery, distortion, and exaggeration to project inner reality.

**Extended metaphor:** A metaphor that compares many aspects of the elements being linked, a type of analogy.

**Eye-rime (sight rime):** Words whose endings are spelled alike but may now have different pronunciation. Rimes that are in some way imperfect in sound but perfect to the eye: Rain/again.

**Fancy:** A word used through the history of English literature as synonym for imagination and fantasy. Fancy was held to be a lesser type of imagination. Fantasy connotes a lesser degree of probability.

**Farce:** A ridiculous or absurd situation designed for humor.
Latin: *farcire* = to stuff.

**Feet:** The measure of poetic rhythm. The major feet are iamb, trochee, anapest, dactyl, and spondee.

**Feminine ending:** A line of verse in which the final syllable is unstressed.

**Feminine rime:** A rime of two or three syllables with the accent on the first syllable only: Doleful/soulful.

**Figurative language:** Language which is not meant to be taken literally. It is the use of figures of speech: simile, metaphor, personification, synecdoche, hyperbole, irony, metonymy, understatement, and others. Although poetry is the main user of figurative language, prose utilizes all of the figures in a more restrained way.

**Figures of speech:** The labels for the specific techniques of nonliteral language to make comparisons, exaggerations, understatements, differences, ironies, and so forth. *See:* simile, metaphor, personification, irony, hyperbole, synecdoche, metonymy, litotes, oxymoron, and so forth. Figures of thought are also known as tropes. Figures of speech or rhetorical figures are sometimes called devices and emphasize the rhetorical rather than the figurative aspects. The distinction is usually ignored and blurred by the more general term "figurative language."

**Flyting:** Type of sarcastic taunting indulged in by characters in an epic. The provocations before battle.
Angle-Saxon: *flitan* = to quarrel.

**Folklore:** The body of common culture of the people that accumulated before the written culture took over.
Anglo-Saxon: *folc + lar* = people + learning.

**Foot:** A unit of measure used in poetry. A foot is a set of syllables arranged in a definite pattern of accents. The main ones are:

| | |
|---|---|
| Iamb ⌣ ⁄ | Anapest ⌣ ⌣ ⁄ |
| Trocee ⁄ ⌣ | Spondee ⁄⁄ |
| Dactyl ⁄ ⌣ ⌣ | Pyrrhic ⌣ ⌣ |

**Free verse (vers libre):** Verse without any formal or conventional rhythm but which imitates the natural rhythmic patterns of prose. The lines may vary in length. Walt Whitman made the form respectable; however, early free verse was found in the Psalms and Song of Solomon. Goethe, Whitman, Heine, Dickinson, and Eliot also used free verse.

**Freudian criticism:** Criticism that emphasizes the psychological views of Freud in interpreting meaning. It attempts to analyze the poet's unconscious projections in the poem.

**Genre:** A literary term for a type of literature: essay, poetry, short story, drama, novel, and biography.

**Gloss:** An explanation inserted between lines in a text. The word glossary comes from this practice of *annotationa* and *marginalia.*

Latin: *glossa* = tongue.

**Gothic:** A type of romantic utilization of medieval and supernatural atmosphere to create a mood.

**Graveyard poetry:** Poetry of the eighteenth century after style of Blair's "The Grave" and Young's "Night Thoughts" to create a mournful, sentimental, and romantic mood.

**Haiku (hokku):** An unrimed Japanese poem form having 17 syllables in a tercet of 5, 7, 5 syllables per line.

**Half-rime:** Approximate, near, or slant rime.

**Helicon:** One of the nine muses of mythology that was supposed to inspire poets.

**Hellenism:** A term coined by Matthew Arnold to designate the essence of classical Greek culture. The emphasis of Hellenism was upon balance, intellect, beauty, form, and justice and was contrasted with the moral emphasis of Hebraism.

**Hemistich:** Half a line of poetry that is formed by a caesura in Old English poetry.
Greek: *hemi* + *stichos* = half + verse.

**Heptameter:** A seven-foot line of verse.
Greek: *hepta* + *metron* = seven + measure.

**Heroic couplet:** A rimed iambic pentameter couplet usually containing a complete rhetorical unit.

**Hexameter:** A six-foot line of verse.
Greek: *hexa* + *metron* = six + measure.

**Historical criticism:** Criticism that emphasizes the importance of the historical tradition in the analysis and evaluation of literature.

**Hovering accent:** An accent divided between two adjoining syllables.

**Hubris:** Excessive pride; an arrogance toward the gods in ancient Greece. The Christians consider it a serious to unpardonable sin.
Greek: *hybris* = out.

**Humanism:** The philosophical attitude that puts the emphasis of value upon man rather than the supernatural.

**Hymn:** A formal song to praise someone or something.
Greek: *hymnos* = song of gods.

**Hyperbole:** A figure of speech that is a type of exaggeration that goes beyond the literal to emphasize a point: "Get with child a mandrake root."
Greek: *hyper* + *ballein* = over + to cast.

**Hypermeter:** A line having one or more extra syllables than the given metric pattern uses.
Greek: *hyper* + *metron* = over + meter.

**Iamb:** A foot containing one unaccented syllable and one accepted syllable: Tŏdáy.
Greek: *iambos* = iamb.

**Iambic pentameter:** Unrimed verse having five feet per line with iambic meter is called blank verse.

**Idyll:** A short work of bucolic life. A little picture or image.
Greek: *eidyllion* = literary form.

**Image:** A mental impression called up by figurative language.
Latin: *imago* = imitation.

**Imagery:** The poetic aspect of language that creates word pictures by the use of figures of speech and rhetorical devices. Imagery attempts to recreate sense experiences particularly visual and auditory ones.

**Imagism:** An early twentieth-century poetic movement that used images and imagery to convey impressions rather than using abstractions and conventions.

**Imperfect rime:** Approximate, near, or slant rime.

**Implied metaphor:** The subject (tenor) of the metaphor is not stated but implied by the verbal context: "The bloom was wasted on the desert air." (The bloom stands for a person.)

**Impressionism:** A critical theory that emphasizes the changing nature of reality. The poet attempts to create his impressions of this changing reality. These impressions are conveyed by the heavy use of imagery, figurative language, and symbolism.

**Impressionistic criticism:** Criticism that emphasizes the subjective reactions to a work rather than the historical, traditional, and objective standards.

**Incremental repetition:** A device by which a stanza or refrain is repeated with variation. Often used in ballads.

**In medias res:** The epic convention of starting in the middle of the action.
Latin: *in medias res* = in the middle of things.

**Intentional fallacy:** The error of judging a work on the basis of the writer's intention for his work.

**Internal rime:** The riming of words within a line of verse: "They burned and spurned."

**Interpretation:** An attempt to establish the meaning of a literary work.
Latin: *interpretatio* = explanation.

**Inversion:** A reversal of the normal sentence order.
Latin: *in* + *vertere* = in + to turn.

**Invocation:** A calling upon the muse at the start of an epic to request inspiration.
Latin: *invocare* = to call upon.

**Irony:** A literary device that depends on the disparity between reality and the depiction of reality. There are many kinds of irony: dramatic irony, verbal irony, and irony of situation.
Greek: *eirōn* = dissembler.

**Italian sonnet:** A poem written in iambic pentameter having fourteen lines divided into two sections, an octave and a sestet. The rime scheme is *abba abba cdcdcd* or *abba abba cde cde*. It is also called a Petrarchan sonnet.

**Jacobean:** The period of James I of England (1603-1625).

**Kenning:** A compound word that is an Old English metaphor: "Whale road" for sea.
Old Norse: *kenna* = knowledge.

**Lake poets:** Poets who lived in and wrote of the Lake District in England: Wordsworth, Coleridge, and Southey.

**Lament:** A poem that grieves a loss. A type of dirge or elegy.
Latin: *lamentari* = to wail.

**Lampoon:** A satirical poem meant to ridicule by exaggerating elements of the object.
French: *lampons* = let us drink.

**Lay:** A short narrative poem originally meant to be sung.
Celtic: *loid* = song.

**Light verse:** Non-serious verse of a humorous, satirical, or nonsense type.

**Limerick:** A poem having five lines riming *aabba*. Lines one, two, and five have three accents; lines three and four have two.

**Litotes:** A figure of speech in which something is expressed by a negation of the contrary. It is a type of irony: "She was not ugly" for she was beautiful.
Greek: *litotēs* = simple.

**Lyric poem:** A poem that expresses feeling and emotion. Greek poems of this nature were accompanied by a string musical instrument called a lyre.
Greek: *lyra* = lyre.

**Marxist criticism:** Criticism that uses the theories of Karl Marx to interpret and evaluate literature.

**Masculine ending:** A line of verse in which the final syllable is stressed.

**Masculine rime:** Rime of one accented syllable. Fly/sky.

**Metaphor:** A figure of speech that makes a direct comparison: "All the world is a stage."
Greek: *meta + pherein* = above + bear.

**Metaphysical conceit:** An extended metaphor used by John Donne and the metaphysical poets that uses daring, outlandish, extended, and complicated comparisons. In "A Valediction: Forbidding Mourning," Donne compares two souls with the two legs of a compass.

**Metaphysical poets:** Poets of the early seventeenth century whose poetry was characterized by conceits, irony, ambiguity, and love.
Greek: *meta + physics* = beyond + nature.

**Meter:** The pattern of stressed and unstressed syllables in verse measured by feet per line.

| | |
|---|---|
| monometer: one foot | pentameter: five feet |
| dimeter: two feet | hexameter: six feet |
| trimeter: three feet | heptameter; seven feet |
| tetrameter: four feet | octameter: eight feet |

The four standard feet in English are:
1. Iambic (noun: iamb)
2. Anapestic (noun: anapest)
3. Tochaic (noun: trochee)
4. Dactylic (noun: dactyl)

Two other feet are:
5. Spondaic (noun: spondee)
6. Pyrrhic (noun: pyrrhic)

**Metonymy:** A figure of speech in which a part of a concept or a related idea stands for the total as: "He often read Shakespeare."
Greek: *meta + onyma* = above + name.

**Metrical accent:** The accent or emphasis given a syllable in verse. The pattern is usually indicated by the marks—or ＿ (accented) and ◡ (unaccented) placed above the syllables.

**Microcosm:** A portion of the totality (macrocosm) that gives insight into that total reality.
Greek: *micro + cosmos* = small + universe.

**Mixed metaphor:** A metaphor that doesn't keep a consistent comparison.

**Mock heroic:** A poem that treats a trivial character or event in a heroic fashion to imitate an epic form.

**Monometer:** A line of poetry having one foot.
Greek: *mono + metron* = one + measure.

**Mood:** The feeling that permeates a work. A combination of all the ingredients.

**Muse:** Any one of nine goddesses of Greek mythology. They provided inspiration to creative efforts in the arts: Calliope, Clio, Erato, Euterpe, Melpomene, Polyhymnia, Tersichore, Thalia, and Urania.

**Myth:** An attempt to explain events by calling upon created truths or beliefs ranging from the playfully fanciful to the religiously reverent. Myths are usually considered to be pre-scientific truths.

**Narrative:** The story-telling part of a novel, short story, epic, or poetry.

**Negative capability:** Keat's term to describe a writer's ability to escape his own personality to create another character; a kind of empathy.

**New criticism:** The criticism that puts emphasis upon a close analysis of poetry and tends to disregard biographical and historical elements.

**Nonameter:** A nine-foot line of verse.
Greek: *nona + metron* = nine + measure.

**Nonsense verse:** Light verse that obtains its effect from the sound rather than the sense.

**Objective correlative:** T. S. Eliot's term to describe the method by which a poet tries to project objectively by images, figures, and symbols the particular emotion he feels. The poet tries to find those symbols to represent reality so that the same reality may be perceived by the reader.

**Occasional poem:** A poem written for a special purpose, event, or celebration.

**Octameter:** An eight-foot line of verse.
Greek: *octa + metron* = eight + measure.

**Octave:** The first or eight line division of an Italian sonnet. An *ottava rima* is an eight line stanza.

**Octosyllabic:** A line having eight syllables.

**Ode:** A lyric poem that treats an exalted theme in a lofty manner.

**Off-rime:** An approximate rime in which the vowel sounds are not quite identical.

**Onomatopoeia:** The device which makes words imitate the sound: "click," "boom," and "snap."
Greek: *onyma + poiei* = name + to fashion.

**Ossian poetry:** Inflated, pompous poetry patterned after the pretended translations of a legendary Gaelic poet Ossian.

**Overstatement:** An exaggeration, saying more than is literally the case for rhetorical purposes. A hyperbole.

**Oxymoron:** A figure of speech which has two contradictory terms in juxtaposition. A miniature paradox: "dark-light," "fiery ice."
Greek: *oxys + moros* = sharp + foolish.

**Panegyric:** Poetry or prose of high praise for many attributes of its object.
Latin: *panegyricus* = popular assembly.

**Paradox:** A seeming contradiction that turns out to be true in some hidden fashion. The contradiction is usually solved by a close analysis of the language.
Greek: *para + doxa* = beside + doctrine.

**Paraphrase:** Putting a passage into words to shorten or to explicate the meaning. A type of abstract or summary.
Greek: *para + phrasis* = beside + diction.

**Parody:** A literary imitation of a work exaggerating an aspect of style or theme in order to satirize, ridicule, or entertain.
Greek: *para + aoide* = beside + song.

**Pastoral elegy:** An elegy that emulates the country conventions of shepherds, muses, nature used by Greek poets.

**Pathetic fallacy:** The error of attributing human qualities to animals and inanimate objects. A term coined by John Ruskin for this type of personification.

**Pathos:** An examination of feeling or suffering caused by fate. Excessive pathos becomes sentimentality. Bathos is to pathos as sentimentality is to sentiment.
Greek: *paschein* = to suffer.

**Pentameter:** Five-foot line in verse.
Greek: *penta + metron* = five + measure.

**Perfect rime:** If the rime is exact, it is called "true" or "pure."

**Periods of English literature:**
450-1066: Old English or Anglo-Saxon Period
1066-1500: Middle English Period
1500-1660: The Renaissance
  1558-1603: Elizabethan Age
  1603-1625: Jacobean Age
  1625-1649: Caroline Age
  1649-1660: Puritan Period
1660-1798: The Neoclassical Period
  1660-1700: The Restoration
  1700-1745: The Augustan Age
  1745-1798: Age of Reason and Sensibility
1798-1832: The Romantic Period
1832-1901: The Victorian Period
1901-1914: The Edwardian Period
1914-present: The Modern Age

**Personification:** A type of metaphor that attributes human qualities to inanimate, abstract, or animal objects.
Latin: *persona + ficare* = a mask + to make.

**Petrarchan sonnet:** The Italian sonnet after Petrarch.

**Poet Laureate:** The office in the English royal household whose function is to compose poetry for state occasions. Now a title bestowed upon a poet as an honor.

**Poetic justice:** Justice in fiction in which good is rewarded and evil punished.

**Poetic license:** The writer's prerogative to change facts for the sake of fiction.

**Poetry:** A term used to differentiate a type of writing from prose. There is no exact definition;

there are many stipulative ones. Poetry puts an emphasis upon meter, rhythm, figurative language, imagery, rime, emotion, compressed language, connotation, imagination, and so forth.
Greek: *poiein* = to make.

**Poetry forms:** The classifications that are arbitrary divisions of content and structure: lyric, narrative, dramatic, symbolism.

**Practical criticism:** The analysis of actual works for pragmatic reasons of reviews and commentary.

**Proem:** A short introduction to a poem.

**Prolepsis:** Anticipation of the future as if it were already operative. A type of foreshadowing.
Greek: *pro* + *lambanein* = before + to take.

**Prologue:** An introduction to a long poem.

**Prosody:** The study of meter, form, rime, sound, and patterns used in poetry.
Greek: *pros* + *aoide* = toward + song.

**Proverb:** A saying that encompasses a lofty truth: "A rolling stone gathers no moss."

**Psychical distance:** A type of aesthetic distance by which a poet attempts to disassociate his own emotions from the emotions within the work.

**Pun:** The humorous use of words that sound alike but have different meanings: "One man's Mede is another man's Persian."
Italian: *punctilio* = quibble.

**Pyrrhic:** A two-syllable foot that has two unstressed syllables often used as substitutes for other feet.

**Quatrain:** A four-line, rimed stanza. The rime scheme may be *abba* or *abab*.

**Refrain:** The repetition of entire units (words, phrases, lines) for sound effects.

**Rhetoric:** The study of using words effectively in speech and writing. The art of persuasion by means of figures of speech and rhetorical devices.
Greek: *thetor* = orator.

**Rhythm:** A regular patterning of accented and unaccented syllables into metrical units (feet). The rhythm of poetry depends on stress or accent.
Greek: *rhythmos* = measured flow.

**Rime (rhyme):** The matching of sounds, usually to main similarities involving vowel sounds. The classification of rime includes the following: Beginning, alliteration, internal, middle, end, single, masculine, double, feminine, triple, polysyllabic, perfect, identical, true, weak, slant, approximate, suspend, half-rime, apocopated, cutoff, strained, analyzed, mosaic, broken, synthetic, visual, eye, historical.

**Rime royal:** An iambic pentameter, several-line stanza with the rime scheme *ababbcc*. Often used in narrative poetry.

**Run-on line (enjambement):** Verse without a grammatical stop at the end of the line. Opposed to end-stopped line.

**Satire:** Ridicule, sarcasm, criticism, and irony in literary work. The emphasis is upon the vices, ignorances, and foibles of man.
Latin: *satura* = full dish.

**Scan:** To scan a passage of verse is to analyze the meter for accents, pauses, and feet.

**Scansion:** The formal analysis of rhythm in verse. The signs *x* and ⌣ are used to show unaccented syllables and ′ or — to show accented syllables.
Latin: *scandere* = to climb.

**Scop:** An Old English name for poet, minstrel, or bard.

**Sentimentalism:** A term used to describe situations in literature that show a degree of emotion not commensurate with the realistic motivation. The emphasis is upon feeling and sentiment for sentiment's sake.

**Septenary (heptameter):** A line having seven metrical units or feet.

**Sestet:** The last six lines of an Italian sonnet.

**Simile:** A figure of speech comparing two items using "like" or "as": "My love is like a red, red rose."
Latin: *similis* = similar.

**Slant rime:** Any imperfect rime. Also called half-rime and imperfect rime.

**Song:** A short lyric poem or ballad that can be sung.
Anglo-Saxon: *singan* = to sing.

**Sonnet:** A fourteen-line iambic pentameter poem with a set rime scheme depending on the type:
English Sonnet: *abab cdcd efef gg*
Italian Sonnet: *abba abba cddc cd*
Spenserian Sonnet: *ababbcbc cd cd ee*

**Spenserian stanza:** A nine-line stanza, eight iambic pentameter lines and one line of iambic hexameter having the rime scheme *ababbcbcbcc*.

**Spondaic:** Pertaining to spondee: a foot with two accented syllables.
Greek: *sponde* = libation.

**Sprung rhythm:** A meter using frequent stress accents without a strict pattern of unaccented syllables.

**Stanza:** The stanza is a division within a poem. The verses may number two or more and be arranged in any pattern.

**Strophe:** A unit in poetry almost synonymous with

a stanza, the term most usually used.

**Style:** A poet's pattern or mode of expression. It is the combination of diction, devices, rime, rhythm, and all the other ingredients of poetry.

**Symbol:** Any item, word, or action that stands for something more than itself. It may be a traditional, conventional, personal, or ambiguous symbol.

Greek: *symballien* = throw together.

**Synecdoche:** A figure of speech in which a part stands for the total: "Fifty winters passed."

Greek: *syn* + *ekdochē* = together + to receive.

**Synesthesia:** The mixing of sensory responses. A certain color may evoke a particular sound. A figure of speech may deliberately mix the senses as in a "cool sound" or a "loud color."

**Tenor and vehicle:** J. A. Richards introduced the terms "tenor" and "vehicle" to stand for the two elements in a metaphor. The "tenor" is the subject and the "vehicle" is the metaphoric word itself. "My love is a red, red rose": love is the tenor, and rose is the vehicle.

**Tercet:** A stanza of three lines usually with end rime.

**Terza rima:** A stanza of three lines that inter-locks the rime scheme with the stanza that follows: *aba bcb cdc ded efe.*

**Tetrameter:** A line with four feet.

**Threnody:** A funeral song.

Greek: *threnos* + *aoide* = lament + song.

**Tone:** The permeating mood or atmosphere of the poem. It is an element of style. It may be the poet's attitude toward some aspect of his poem.

**Tribrach:** A metrical foot of three short, unaccented syllables found in Greek and Latin poetry.

Greek: *tri* + *brachys* = three + short.

**Trimeter:** A three-foot line in verse.

**Trochee:** A foot containing one accented syllable and one unaccented syllable.

**Trope:** A figure of speech.

Greek: *tropas* = turn.

**Understatement:** Saying less than the actual for ironic effect.

**Verse:** Language which is poetically identifiable. Also used to designate a single line of poetry.

Latin: *versus* = furrow.

**Vers libre:** Free verse. Verse without any formal patterns of rhythm.

# INDEX OF AUTHORS AND TITLES